COMMAND PERFORMA S

R:BASE®
SYSTEM V
INCLUDING R:BASE 5000

215285

NICHOLAS M. BARAN

Microsoft®
PRESS

The Microsoft®
Reference Guide to All
Commands, Functions, and Features

PUBLISHED BY
Microsoft Press
A Division of Microsoft Corporation
16011 NE 36th Way, Box 97017
Redmond, Washington 98073-9717

Library of Congress Cataloging in Publication Data
Baran, Nicholas.
R:BASE System V.
(Command performance)
Includes index.
1. R:base 5000 (Computer program)   2. R:base System V (Computer program)
I. Title.
QA 76.9.D3B364   1987   005.36′9   87-7860
ISBN 1-55615-023-7

Printed and bound in the United States of America.

1 2 3 4 5 6 7 8 9 FGFG 8 9 0 9 8 7

Distributed to the book trade in the
United States by Harper & Row.

Distributed to the book trade in
Canada by General Publishing Company, Ltd.

Distributed to the book trade outside the
United States and Canada by Penguin Books Ltd.

Penguin Books Ltd., Harmondsworth, Middlesex, England
Penguin Books Australia Ltd., Ringwood, Victoria, Australia
Penguin Books N. Z. Ltd., 182-190 Wairau Road, Auckland 10, New Zealand

British Cataloging in Publication Data available

Project Editor: Gary Masters   **Technical Editor:** Jeff Hinsch

COMMAND PERFORMANCE SERIES

dBASE® IV

RELEASE 5000

For Esther

Acknowledgments

I would like to thank Mr. Jeff Hinsch of Microsoft Press for both his technical and moral support during the writing and production of this book. His competence and patience were greatly appreciated. I would also like to thank Ms. Claudette Moore of Microsoft Press for making this project possible, Mr. Eddie Adamis for originating the *Command Performance* series, and the technical support staff at Microrim for that toll-free phone number and their answers to all my questions.

Introduction

Command Performance R:BASE is a complete reference guide for users of R:BASE System V and R:BASE 5000. This book consolidates and clarifies the information provided in the R:BASE user manuals, and includes an appendix that covers R:BASE Graphics. Unless otherwise noted, references to R:BASE refer only to R:BASE System V. The information in this book is based on R:BASE System V, version 1.1, R:BASE 5000, version 1.1, and R:BASE Graphics, version 1.0.

The major emphasis in this book is on examples. Every R:BASE command and syntax structure is illustrated with at least one example. More complex commands are illustrated with several examples, ranging from simple one-line commands to complete command files. Whether you are just starting out with R:BASE or are an experienced programmer, you will find examples that relate to your level of experience.

The book is organized much like an encyclopedia or a dictionary. Each R:BASE command is listed alphabetically and discussed in a separate entry. In addition, the book also contains entries about general database topics such as "data types" or "variables." Refer to the comprehensive index at the back of the book for extensive cross-references to entries.

Related entries are also cross-referenced within individual entries. For example, if you start with the *Programming* entry, you will find several cross-references to related entries as you read the general discussion of R:BASE programming concepts.

Note that this book uses the syntax convention of the R:BASE User's Manual. We would like to thank Microrim, Inc. for generously giving permission to use their syntax convention. The basic principle of this convention is that required parts of a command are specified from left to right on the main command line, while optional parts of the command are specified below the line. When more than one choice exists for a required argument, the command line splits to indicate the available choices. Let's look at an example:

$$
\text{PROJECT } tblname2 \text{ FROM } \left\{ \begin{array}{c} tblname1 \\ viewname \end{array} \right\} \text{ USING } \left\{ \begin{array}{c} collist \\ \text{ALL} \end{array} \right\} \left[\text{SORTED BY } collist \right] \left[\text{WHERE } condlist \right]
$$

In this case, "PROJECT *tblname2* FROM" and "USING" are required. In addition, you must choose to supply either a table or a view name and either a list of columns (*collist*) or *ALL*. The *SORTED BY* and *WHERE* clauses are optional parts of the command.

Readers of this book should have a basic understanding of MS-DOS and should be able to install the R:BASE software on their computers. It is helpful, but not required, to have some familiarity with database applications and previous experience with a programming language. However, basic concepts of database design and programming are discussed in this book.

The examples in this book are based on my own experience as an R:BASE user and consultant. I hope that they help you take advantage of the many powerful and flexible features of R:BASE.

*(comment)

▪ Syntax

`*(comment)`

▪ Description

Use the *(comment) command to include a line of descriptive text in your command file.

It's good programming practice to begin a command file with a comment that identifies the name and purpose of the file. If the file includes many variables or extensive looping and conditional routines, include comments describing them. When you refer to a command file at some later date, it will be much easier to understand if it includes a comment.

▪ Procedure

Begin the comment with *(, then type the text of the comment, and end it with). You can put the comment on the same line as a command or on one or several lines by itself.

▪ Example

The following excerpt from a command file shows various ways to use the *(comment) command.

```
*(Example command file showing the use of comment lines)
OPEN dbname
IF dbcheck NE 0     *(IF statement checks if database exists)
   WRITE "Sorry, database not found, press any key to continue."
   PAUSE              *(Waits for user to press key)
   GOTO end           *(Skips to end of file and starts over)
ENDIF
*(This comment continues on to another line,
   as you can see)
*(You can also embed sets of parentheses (like this) inside comment lines)
LABEL end
```

Cautions:

☐ Commands placed within the comment parentheses will not execute.

☐ Always check that comments end with a closing parenthesis.

☐ In procedure command blocks, you cannot enter comments on the first or second line of the block.

☐ Although you should include enough comments to adequately describe the purpose and function of your command file, using too many (more than 10-15 lines) can actually slow down program performance.

See: *Command files, Procedure files, Programming,* and *Variables*

▪ R:BASE 5000 equivalent

*(comment)

1

ALL

- **Syntax**

  ... ALL ...

- **Description**

  The *ALL* command modifier allows a command to operate comprehensively within its parameters. Its specific functions depend on the command with which it is used. The following table lists these commands and *ALL*'s corresponding functions:

Command	Description
BACKUP ALL	Backs up both data and database structure.
BROWSE ALL	Allows you to browse all columns in a table.
COMPUTE ALL	Computes all eight arithmetic operations available with the COMPUTE command.
EDIT ALL	Edits all columns in a table.
LIST ALL	Lists all tables in a database along with their characteristics (such as the password status and the number of rows and columns).
SELECT ALL	Selects all columns in a table.
UNLOAD ALL	Unloads both data and database structure.

  When *ALL* follows a *USING* clause, it always means "all columns in the table." The following commands can include the *USING ALL* clause: BACKUP, PROJECT, and UNLOAD.

- **Procedure**

  For examples of the *ALL* command modifier, see entries for the commands listed in the above table.

  See: *BACKUP, BROWSE, COMPUTE, EDIT, LIST, PROJECT, SELECT,* and *UNLOAD*

- **R:BASE 5000 equivalent**

  ... ALL ...

APPEND

■ **Syntax**

```
APPEND tblname1 TO tblname2 ┌─────────────────┐
                            └ WHERE condlist ┘
```

■ **Description**

The APPEND command copies rows from one table to another table in the same database. Rows from the source table are appended to the destination table. Only columns that are common to both tables are used in the APPEND operation. Rows in the source table are unaffected by the APPEND command.

■ **Procedure**

To append rows that meet specific criteria, include a *WHERE* clause in the command. This is useful if you want to copy rows from a table of general information to a table that contains specific information.

■ **Example**

Suppose you have a table called *CLIENT* that contains the names and addresses of your firm's clients in various cities. New clients are always added to this general table.

You periodically update another table, *CLI-SF*, from the general *CLIENT* table. *CLI-SF* contains only clients in San Francisco. The APPEND command is the appropriate command for the following update procedure:

```
R>APPEND CLIENT TO CLI-SF WHERE CITY EQ "SAN FRANCISCO"
 Successful append operation, 2 rows added
R>SELECT ALL FROM CLI-SF
 CLINUM     CLINAME                    STREET                 CITY
 ---------- -------------------------- ---------------------- ----------------
        2 Cal Gas and Electric       1000 Main Street       San Francisco
        4 Stone Construction Co.     100 Oak Street         San Francisco
        5 Ohio Electric Power Co.    101 Birch Street       San Francisco
        1 Johnson and Anderson Co.   101 Howard Street      San Francisco
        3 Power Research Associates  205 Elmwood Avenue     San Francisco
R>
```

If you omit the *WHERE* clause, all rows from the *CLIENT* table are appended.

Caution: Do not confuse the functions of the APPEND and PROJECT commands. APPEND *adds* rows to an existing table. PROJECT *creates* a new table based on columns from an existing table.

■ **Comments**

The APPEND command works only with tables within a single database. To append data from other databases, see *BACKUP, INPUT, RESTORE,* and *UNLOAD.* To import data from other software or different file formats, see *LOAD* and *FileGateway.*

See: *PROJECT* and *WHERE*

■ **R:BASE 5000 equivalent**
APPEND

Application EXPRESS

■ **Syntax**
Select Application EXPRESS from the RBSYSTEM menu.

You also can execute EXPRESS at the R> prompt if you entered R:BASE from the RBSYSTEM menu.

EXPRESS $\lfloor_{exec}\rfloor$

If you entered R:BASE from the MS-DOS prompt, you must exit R:BASE. You can then execute EXPRESS from MS-DOS:

EXPRESS $\lfloor_{-R}\rfloor \lfloor_{-Fn}\rfloor \lfloor_{-Bn}\rfloor \lfloor_{-Mn}\rfloor \lfloor_{-Tn}\rfloor \lfloor_{exec}\rfloor$

The *-R* option suppresses display of the R logo. The *-F* and *-B* options modify the foreground and background colors if you are using a color monitor. *-M* and *-T* modify other monitor characteristics. See the R:BASE System V Installation Guide for further information on monitor options. The *exec* option lets you specify an *exec* file that runs when you start EXPRESS from MS-DOS (see *RECORD* and *PLAYBACK*).

■ **Description**
Application EXPRESS is a separate module within R:BASE System V for creating menu-driven applications. You can use a menu-driven application to perform all the operations and functions of your database, from entering data to printing reports. Menu-driven applications make it easier to use databases, particularly for people with no experience using database programs. In addition, applications can be designed to allow restricted access to a database containing sensitive data.

Application EXPRESS is a menu-driven system that guides you through a series of steps for specifying the menus and functions of your application. A menu system developed in Application EXPRESS can include as many as 15 menus in a total of three levels (the main menu and two levels of submenus). If necessary, these limitations can be exceeded by nesting applications, which is discussed later in this entry. Based on your menu selections, Application EXPRESS writes a command file in the R:BASE programming language that will execute your application. Because applications generated by Application EXPRESS are written in the R:BASE programming language, you can modify and enhance these applications as you would any other R:BASE program. You can also add your own command files to an application created in Application EXPRESS. See the discussion in this entry on external command files and programming considerations.

■ Procedure

Although Application EXPRESS is easy to use, some planning is required before you can effectively create a menu-driven application.

Planning an application: The first step is to be sure that you are satisfied with the database for which you intend to develop an application. A fancy menu system is useless if your database is poorly organized and does not produce the results you need.

It is generally a good idea to design forms and reports before working on the menu system. Although Application EXPRESS provides a basic data entry form and report that you can use for simple applications, we assume in this discussion that you intend to use forms and reports that you have created with Forms EXPRESS and Reports EXPRESS.

The second step is to design the menu system using pencil and paper. Start by listing the tables (or views), forms, and reports that the application will access. List the main operations that the application will perform. Typical database operations are data entry, data editing, printing reports, and querying the database.

The main operations of your application should all be selections on the main menu. Under these main operations, you might need additional submenus. For example, *Print Reports* might be a main menu selection that is followed by a submenu giving four reports from which you can choose. As mentioned earlier, two submenu levels can follow a main menu selection.

5

Finally, list any additional operations your application will perform. List any command files that will be accessed from the application. Each operation in your menu system should be connected to at least one of the following items:

table or view
form
report
command file or set of R:BASE commands
submenu
exit

Your list should now contain enough information to sketch the actual menu system you plan to implement with Application EXPRESS. Keep in mind that you can always modify or expand the application later.

Using Application EXPRESS: The main Application EXPRESS menu is shown in the following screen:

```
                    Application EXPRESS
    Copyright (C) 1983,1984,1985,1986 by Microrim, Inc. (Ver. 1.00 PC-DOS)

          ┌──────────────Application EXPRESS Main Menu═══════════════┐
          │  (1)  Define a new application                            │
          │  (2)  Modify an existing application                      │
          │  (3)  DOS functions                                       │
          │  (4)  Exit from Application EXPRESS                        │
          │                                                           │
          └───────────────────────────────────────────────────────────┘





    [ENTER] Choose    [F10] Help
```

Using Application EXPRESS involves, for the most part, the first option, *Define a new application*. Modifying an existing application involves the same basic procedures as developing a new one. The *DOS functions* option lets you perform MS-DOS file and disk operations.

Application EXPRESS key functions are described in the following table:

Keys	Description
PgDn/PgUp	Moves the cursor between the menu title and the menu options.
Tab	Moves the cursor to the next option (horizontally or vertically).
Shift-Tab	Moves the cursor to the previous option.
Home	Moves the cursor to the first menu option.
End	Moves the cursor to the first blank space for entering another option.
Left/right arrows	Move the cursor one character to the left or right.
Up/down arrows	Move the cursor up or down one row.
Ins	Inserts a blank space at the cursor.
Del	Deletes the character at the cursor.
Backspace	Deletes the character to the left of the cursor.
Ctrl-right arrow	Moves the cursor to the end of the text in a menu title or option.
Ctrl-left arrow	Moves the cursor to the beginning of the text in a menu title or option.
Enter	Saves a menu title or option text and moves the cursor to the next option.
ESC	Saves the menu text and ends menu editing. Also cancels a current action.
F1	Inserts a blank option above or to the left of the current option.
F2	Deletes the current option.
F3	Displays the menu tree.
F5	Discards all changes to the current menu title or option.
Ctrl-Break	Discards all work from the current session and returns to the Main menu.

Creating the Main menu: After selecting a database and naming your application (in eight characters or less), you are prompted for the name of the Main menu. Because this menu name does not actually appear in the application but is used in the programming code generated by Application EXPRESS, it is easiest to leave the default name, *Main*.

Next, pick a horizontal or vertical menu format for the Main menu. Horizontal menus can contain as many as twelve options and the descriptive text for each option cannot exceed 10 characters. Vertical menus can have as many as nine options with descriptive text of 60 characters maximum. You can create larger menus with the CHOOSE command.

You are now ready to design the Main menu. A typical menu is shown in the following screen:

```
┌─────────Consultant's Database Main Menu (Press F10 for Help)─────────┐
│                    (1)  Enter New Clients                            │
│                    (2)  Edit Client List                             │
│                    (3)  Enter New Proposals                          │
│                    (4)  Review Clients and Proposals                 │
│                    (5)  Prepare Invoices                             │
│                    (6)  Print Invoices                               │
│                    (7)  Run the Summary Program                      │
│                    (8)  Exit                                         │
│                                                                      │
└──────────────────────────────────────────────────────────────────────┘


Assign actions to menu option        1

┌──────────────────────────Choose an action───────────────────────────┐
│  Load  Edit  Delete  Modify  Select  Print  Custom  Macro  Template  │
│  Menu  Password  Exit                                                │
└──────────────────────────────────────────────────────────────────────┘




  [ESC] Done    [F3] Actions    [F10] Help
  Application consult  --- Database CONSULT --- Menu Main
```

Application EXPRESS centers the menu title and draws the double-line box around the menu. The text of the menu is up to you. In this example, the menu title prompts you to press the F10 key to get help, because the menu design includes an optional help screen. If you use this option, the F10 key is set as the help key; whenever you press F10, the help screen appears. A message to this effect should therefore be included in the menu.

You also are given the option to include the ESC key as a means of exiting the menu. If you don't choose the *ESC* option, you cannot exit the menu unless you provide the *Exit* action as one of the menu selections.

Performing the menu actions: The next step is to define the actions of each menu item. The actions you define for a menu item are the R:BASE operations that take place when that item is chosen. You can define multiple actions for one menu item. If multiple actions are defined, the actions are performed sequentially in the order that you defined them. When the last action is performed, control returns to the menu from which you made the selection.

The available actions are listed in the horizontal box in the lower portion of the screen. Here is a summary of each of these actions:

Load: The *Load* action enters data with forms and represents the R:BASE ENTER command. After selecting the appropriate table for data entry, select an existing form from the list on the screen or design a new form. If you choose to use a new form, you can either select the Application EXPRESS default data entry form or design a custom form using Forms EXPRESS. Any forms that you have already designed for the selected table appear in the list. (You cannot access Forms EXPRESS from within Application EXPRESS if you started Application EXPRESS from the MS-DOS prompt.)

The default data entry form is a simple form that can only serve one table. In most applications, you need a customized form. See *FORMS* and *ENTER* for more information on designing forms and entering data.

Edit: The *Edit* action is similar to *Load* except that the selected form is accessed in Edit mode. The *Edit* action represents the R:BASE EDIT USING command. As with *Load*, you can select an existing form or a new one— either the default form or a custom form designed with Forms EXPRESS.

After you have a form, you are given the options to specify a sorted order and conditions that must be met by the rows to be displayed for editing. These options represent the *SORTED BY* and *WHERE* clauses, which can be appended to the EDIT USING command.

If you specify a condition, the following message appears: *Do you want the user to enter a comparison value?* This means that you can either have the user supply the condition value or build the value into the application. Generally, it's best to let the user enter the condition criteria. If you choose this option, you supply a message that will appear on the screen, prompting the user to fill in the condition value. This interaction is shown in the following screen:

```
Assign actions to menu option        2
Edit Client List
The rows to edit may be selected by column values
```

	Column	Operator	Value/Prompt
	CLINUM	EQ	

```
Enter the prompt message: Please enter the client number to edit:
```

```
[ESC] Discard    [F3] Actions    [F10] Help
Application CONSULT  ---  Database CONSULT  ---  Menu Main
```

See *EDIT USING, SORTED BY,* and *WHERE* for more information on setting up sort and conditional criteria.

Delete: The *Delete* action deletes rows from the selected table. It corresponds to the R:BASE DELETE ROWS command. Because the DELETE ROWS command requires a *WHERE* clause, the delete action requires you to specify conditions that rows must meet before they are deleted.

Test the *Delete* action carefully with a sample database before you use it in a real application. Comparison values for satisfying the *Delete* condition can either be provided by the user or built into the application. Except in unusual circumstances, the user should always enter the comparison value. If the comparison value is built into the application, the rows that match the comparison value are deleted when the *Delete* action is selected.

See the next section, *Modify,* for an alternative method of deleting rows.

Modify: The *Modify* action lets you edit the data in a table using a full-screen editing format. The action represents the R:BASE EDIT command. For single-table editing, this is often a convenient method since you can scroll through the rows in a table. The major limitation is that only 10 columns can be used with the *Modify* action. This limitation can be bypassed by using the *Custom* or *Macro* actions and the EDIT command (see the discussion of these actions below).

As with *Edit* and *Delete*, you can specify sort and conditional criteria for the *Modify* action. *Modify* also lets you select displayed rows for deletion. This method is often preferable to using the *Delete* action since you can inspect the data before deleting it.

Select: The *Select* action corresponds to the R:BASE SELECT command and offers the same capabilities. You can display a table or view and specify sort and conditional criteria. However, *Select* does not display columns outside the 80-character screen area. For larger tables, you can use the *Custom* or *Macro* actions and the BROWSE command.

Print: The *Print* action prints reports and corresponds to the R:BASE PRINT command. Specify sort and conditional criteria as described above in the section on the *Edit* action. You can select existing reports or design new ones in Reports EXPRESS or use the Application EXPRESS default report for simple reports. If you loaded Application EXPRESS from the RBSYSTEM menu, you can access Reports EXPRESS directly. (It is usually more efficient to design your reports before developing the application.)

Custom: The *Custom* action lets you include blocks of R:BASE commands in your application. When you choose the *Custom* action, the text editor, RBEDIT, is loaded and you can type as many as 150 lines of commands. Before using the *Custom* action, you should familiarize yourself with RBEDIT.

Although you can type as many as 150 lines, *Custom* is intended for short, simple command files of just a few lines. For example, you might want to use the BROWSE command rather than the *Select* action. Choose *Custom* from the Actions menu and assign a name to the command block. Then, type the command as you would in R:BASE.

It's good practice to end your command block with the RETURN statement. This ensures that control passes to the menu from which the action was selected. Although it makes no difference with the BROWSE command, the RETURN statement is necessary in command blocks that include the RUN command (used for running external command files or another application). See the discussion of external command files later in this entry.

Macro: The *Macro* action merges an existing, external command file into your application. The command file must be in ASCII format rather than in binary format. The reason for this is that Application EXPRESS compiles the entire application, including merged command files, into binary format, as described later in this entry.

When you select *Macro*, you are prompted for the command filename. This can be any legitimate MS-DOS filename on any path or directory. Of course, you must specify a path if the file is not in the current directory.

The disadvantage of the *Macro* action is that modifications to the external command file have no effect on your application unless you go back into Application EXPRESS and reexecute the *Macro* action to merge the new version of the command file. This is a cumbersome procedure, particularly if you are still testing your application.

An alternative is to use the *Custom* action to issue a RUN command, which executes the external command file. In this way, you can modify the command file at any time without recompiling your application. See the discussion on external command files later in this entry.

Template: The *Template* action lets you include a special command file called a template. A template is a command block that accepts variable values before it is added to your application. This is best understood by looking at an example. Using RBEDIT (or any text editor), create a template to perform a UNION on two tables and print a report designed for the resulting table. Here are the contents of the template file, which is named *UNION.TPL*:

```
%1 Enter the first table in the union:
%2 Enter the second table:
%3 Enter the name of the table to be formed:
%4 Enter the name of the report to print:
%TEMPLATE
REMOVE %3        *(First remove old copy of unioned table, if it exists)
UNION %1 WITH %2 FORMING %3     *(Form a new unioned table)
OUTPUT SCREEN WITH PRINTER
PRINT %4
OUTPUT SCREEN
CLS
WRITE "Press any key to continue" at 15,15
PAUSE
```

The first four lines are prompts that appear when you fill in the template in Application EXPRESS. The *%TEMPLATE* line indicates that the lines following it are commands to be filled in with the values from the first four lines. You may define as many as nine variables (%1 to %9) in a template.

When you select *Template* and specify the file *UNION.TPL*, here is what happens:

```
Assign actions to menu option        6
Print Invoices


 Enter the first table in the union:
CLIENT
 Enter the second table:
INVOICE
 Enter the name of the table to be formed:
NEWONE
 Enter the name of the report to print:
NEWONE
```

```
[ESC] Discard    [F3] Actions    [F10] Help
Application CONSULT  --- Database CONSULT  --- Menu Main
```

When the application is executed, the template is executed as a command block using the table and report names defined in Application EXPRESS.

Templates are only used with Application EXPRESS and are helpful only if you use the same command block in several different applications, using different table names, column names, and so forth, but performing the same operations. Because you have to "hard code" the variable names into the application, however, in many cases it is easier to include the command block as a *Custom* action.

Menu: The *Menu* action lets you create a submenu. Again, you fill in a menu heading and the menu items, as you did for the Main menu. The difference is that you do not define actions for the submenu until you complete the action definition for the Main menu.

You can have a total of three menu levels and 15 menus in an application. See the discussion on external command files for a way to exceed this limitation.

Password: The present design of the *Password* action in Application EXPRESS does not actually provide password control when the application is run, but only requires that the designer of the application enter the correct password when building the application.

13

In other words, let's say you have an OWNER password and an MPW/RPW password defined for a table that you plan to access through a menu selection for editing data. You must enter this password as the first action involving the table. You then define the second action as the *Edit* or *Modify* action. Remember that a single menu item can perform multiple actions.

Now, when you run the application, you can edit or modify the table with the password since the password has been built into the application. The problem is that anybody who knows how to run your application can also edit or modify the table! Thus, *Password* prevents unauthorized persons from designing an application, not from using it. If you want the user to enter a password when running the application, include the USER command as a *Custom* action (see *USER*)

Exit: The *Exit* action exits the current menu. It must be the last action defined for a menu since it also indicates to Application EXPRESS that you have completed the menu definition.

The *Exit* action is not required if you allow the user to press ESC to exit. However, if you do not include the *Exit* action, it is a good idea to include a message in the menu title such as *Press ESC to exit.*

Completing the definition: After you define all the menu items and their actions, you are asked if you want to change the EXPRESS default settings. If you answer yes, the following menu appears:

```
┌──────────────Settings═══════════════════────┐
│              (1)  Set messages               │
│              (2)  Set error messages         │
│              (3)  Set colors                 │
│              (4)  Set bell                   │
│                                              │
└──────────────────────────────────────────────┘
```

```
[ESC] Done    [F3] Actions    [F10] Help
Application test34   --- Database CLIENTS   --- Menu Main
```

The default settings cancel diagnostic and error messages during the execution of your application. In most cases, these settings are desirable unless you are testing the operation of the application and want to see the messages. Keep in mind, however, that you have to recompile the application when you change back to the default settings later. For more information about error and diagnostic messages, see *Error messages.*

The default settings also include an option for specifying different foreground and background colors on a color monitor. See the R:BASE installation instructions for more information about setting colors.

Next, the application is compiled, or encoded, to use the terminology of R:BASE System V (see *CodeLock*). The lines of programming code scroll on the screen during this process. The details of the Application EXPRESS coding scheme are discussed later in this entry.

Finally, you are asked if you want the application to be an initial command file. If you respond with a yes, Application EXPRESS creates a file in the current directory called *RBASE.DAT*, which contains the commands to execute the application. If an *RBASE.DAT* file exists in the startup directory, the commands in it are executed when R:BASE is started. This setup might be desirable if you want to simplify access to the application.

Creating application files: After you complete the definition of the application, Application EXPRESS creates three files in the current directory:

> appname.APX
> appname.API
> appname.APP

where *appname* is the name of your application.

The *.APX* file is the compiled, or encoded, binary version of the application. This is the same type of file generated by CodeLock and cannot be modified. You can, of course, generate a new version of this file by modifying the application in Application EXPRESS.

The *.API* file is an internal file used by Application EXPRESS when you modify your application. You cannot directly alter the *.API* file either.

The *.APP* file is an ASCII version of the R:BASE programming code that makes up the application. You can view and edit this file with the TYPE command and RBEDIT, respectively. If you edit the file, you have to use CodeLock to compile it, and it can no longer be modified or worked with in Application EXPRESS. See the *Cautions* section below for a discussion of external command files and programming considerations.

Running the application: If you created an initial *RBASE.DAT* file, your application runs automatically when you start R:BASE. Otherwise, type the following command at the R> prompt:

```
RUN appname in appname.apx
```

where *appname* is the name of the application. This command tells R:BASE to execute the main command block called *appname* in the procedure file called *appname.apx*. Application EXPRESS has created *appname* and *appname.apx* simply from the application name that you defined. See *RUN* and *Procedure files* for more details.

If you accepted the default settings for messages and error messages, these settings remain in effect after you finish running the application and return to the R> prompt. Issue the commands SET ERR MESS ON and SET MESS ON to turn messages on again.

Modifying the application: You can change an application created with Application EXPRESS. You can change the menu text or structure, insert or delete actions for a menu item, and add or delete command files.

In modification mode, press ESC to skip to the next part of the application. For example, if you are only changing menu actions, you might not want to change the actual text of the menus. Press ESC when presented with an edit screen for changing the menus.

Applications generated by Application EXPRESS are written in the R:BASE programming language. Here is a listing from a typical application corresponding to the main menu example shown above. Note that not all menu items include actions. You can always add actions later.

```
$COMMAND
CONSULT
SET MESSAGE OFF
OPEN CONSULT
SET ERROR MESSAGE OFF
SET COLOR BACKGRND BLACK
SET COLOR FOREGRND GRAY
SET BELL OFF
SET VAR PICK1 INT
LABEL STARTAPP
  NEWPAGE
  CHOOSE PICK1 FROM Main IN CONSULT.APX
  IF PICK1 EQ -1 THEN
    NEWPAGE
    DISPLAY help IN CONSULT.APX
    WRITE "Press any key to continue"
    PAUSE
    GOTO STARTAPP
  ENDIF
  IF PICK1 EQ 0 THEN
    GOTO ENDAPP
  ENDIF
```

(continued)

```
        IF PICK1 EQ 1 THEN
          ENTER client
          GOTO STARTAPP
        ENDIF
        IF PICK1 EQ 2 THEN
          SET VARIABLE WHVAL1 TO INTEGER
          FILLIN WHVAL1 USING "Please enter client number to use"
          EDIT USING client +
            SORTED BY CLINUM = A +
            WHERE CLINUM EQ .WHVAL1
          CLEAR WHVAL1
          GOTO STARTAPP
        ENDIF
        IF PICK1 EQ 3 THEN
          ENTER PROPOSAL
          GOTO STARTAPP
        ENDIF
        IF PICK1 EQ 4 THEN
          RUN scroll IN CONSULT.APX
          EDIT +
            CLINUM CLINAME STREET CITY STATE ZIP +
            PHONE +
            FROM CLIENT +
            SORTED BY CLIENT = A
          GOTO PARTAPP
        ENDIF
        IF PICK1 EQ 5 THEN
          SELECT +
            ALL +
            FROM invform +
            SORTED BY clinum = A
          WRITE "Press any key to continue"
          PAUSE
          GOTO STARTAPP
        ENDIF
        IF PICK 1 EQ 6 THEN
          RUN prntinv IN CONSULT.APX
          GOTO STARTAPP
        ENDIF
        IF PICK1 EQ 7 THEN
          GOTO STARTAPP
        ENDIF
        IF PICK1 EQ 8 THEN
          GOTO STARTAPP
        ENDIF
        GOTO STARTAPP
  LABEL ENDAPP
  CLEAR PICK1
  RETURN
  $MENU
  Main
  COLUMN Consultant's Database Main Menu (Press F10 for help)
  Enter New Clients
  Edit Client List
  Enter New Proposals
  Review Clients and Proposals
  Prepare Invoices
  Print Invoices
  Run the Summary Program
  Exit
  $SCREEN
  help
  This is the consultant's database for reviewing clients and proposals.
  $COMMAND
  scroll
  browse all from client
  $COMMAND
  prntinv
  REMOVE NEWONE
  UNION CLIENT WITH INVOICE FORMING NEWONE
  PRINT NEWONE
  WRITE "Press any key to continue"
  PAUSE
```

If you study this listing carefully, you will identify various components from the examples given earlier in this entry. Note the two $COMMAND blocks at the end of the listing. These correspond to the BROWSE command entered with the *Custom* action and the template built in with the *Template* action (see discussion of these actions above). You might find the entries for *CHOOSE*, *DISPLAY*, *GOTO*, and *LABEL* helpful in understanding how the listing works.

See: *Procedure files* and *Programming*

Cautions: The code in the preceding listing was generated entirely by Application EXPRESS. When you add command files, templates, or custom command blocks, these commands become part of the program generated by Application EXPRESS. It is therefore necessary to be aware of certain guidelines when developing command files for use with Application EXPRESS.

The following variable names are reserved by Application EXPRESS:

LEVEL2
LEVEL3
PICK1
PICK2
PICK3
PRNTOPT
WHVAL1–WHVAL10

The menu name *PRT$$$* and the labels *STARTAPP* and *ENDAPP* are also reserved words. Do not use any of these reserved words for variables, menu names, or labels in your command files. Do not use the CLEAR ALL VARIABLES command in your command files. If you do, you will also clear the Application EXPRESS variables. Clear variables explicitly as described in *CLEAR*.

Always use RETURN to end a command block or command file rather than QUIT. QUIT terminates the application; RETURN passes control to the menu or file from which the command file was executed.

Unless you are confident that an external command file will not require modification, it is better to use the *Custom* action and the RUN command rather than the *Macro* action to incorporate external command files. Do not assign the same name to the *Custom* file as to the file named in the RUN command.

Nesting an application: Use the *Custom* action to run an application within an application. The primary purpose for this is to allow more than three menu levels, which is the limit for a single application.

If the second application contains two or more levels of menus, the *LEVEL* variables must be reset in the Custom command block that runs the second application. The following example, courtesy of Microrim, shows the command block for running a second application with three menu levels:

```
SET VAR save1 TO .PICK1
SET VAR save2 TO .PICK2
SET VAR save3 TO .PICK3
SET VAR save4 TO .LEVEL2
SET VAR save5 TO .LEVEL3
RUN app2 IN app2.apx
SET VAR PICK1 TO .save1
SET VAR PICK2 TO .save2
SET VAR PICK3 TO .save3
SET VAR LEVEL2 TO .save4
SET VAR LEVEL3 TO .save5
RETURN
```

The *PICK* and *LEVEL* variables from the first application are temporarily stored in the *save* variables. After the second application is run, the *PICK* and *LEVEL* variables are reset to their original values and stored in the *save* variables.

See: *Command files, FORMS, Procedure files, Programming, RBSYSTEM, REPORTS,* and *VIEW*

See also: *CHOOSE, CLEAR, EDIT, EDIT USING, ENTER, QUIT, RUN, TYPE,* and *UNION*

■ **R:BASE 5000 equivalent**
Application EXPRESS in R:BASE 5000 is similar to its System V counterpart except that it also includes System V's database definition function, Definition EXPRESS.

The R:BASE 5000 version of Application EXPRESS does not include options for external MS-DOS commands or the capability to design custom forms and reports within Application EXPRESS. The *Modify* action in System V is called *Browse* in R:BASE 5000. In addition, templates are not supported in R:BASE 5000.

Arithmetic and mathematical functions

■ **Description**
Arithmetic and mathematical functions allow you to perform statistical and arithmetic operations on numeric data values using predefined formulas.

The following functions are categorized as arithmetic and mathematical functions:

Function	Returned value
ABS(arg)	Absolute value of arg
DIM(arg1,arg2)	Positive difference between arg1 and arg2 (if the difference is negative, a value of 0 is returned)
EXP(arg)	e raised to the arg power ($e = 2.71828$)
LOG(arg)	Natural logarithm (base e) or arg (arg must be greater than 0)
LOG10(arg)	Base 10 logarithm of arg (arg must be greater than 0)
SQRT(arg)	Square root of arg (arg must be greater than 0)
AVE(list)	Average of the values in the list
MAX(list)	Maximum of the values in the list
MIN(list)	Minimum of the values in the list
MOD(arg1,arg2)	Modulus (remainder) of arg1 divided by arg2 (arg2 must not be 0)
SIGN(arg1,arg2)	Transfers the sign of arg2 to arg1

All the above functions accept DOUBLE, REAL, or INTEGER values. *AVE()*, *MAX()*, and *MIN()* also accept DATE, TIME, and CURRENCY values.

- **Procedure**

  You can use arithmetic and mathematical functions for a wide variety of statistical and numeric data analysis. For statistical analysis of a set of column values, you may find the COMPUTE command more efficient than the functions described here.

- **Database examples**

  In this example, the hypotenuse of a right triangle based on the values in the columns *SIDE1* and *SIDE2* is calculated, using the *SQRT()* function.

  ```
  EXPAND RT-TRI WITH HYPOT = (SQRT (('SIDE1')**2 + ('SIDE2')**2))
  ```

  In this case, the *RT-TRI* table is expanded with the additional column called *HYPOT*. You could, of course, include this expression in an original definition of the *HYPOT* column.

As a second example, suppose you want to change all the numbers in a column from negative to positive. Type:

```
CHANGE SIDE1 TO (ABS(SIDE1)) IN RT-TRI WHERE SIDE1 LT 0
```

Here, the *ABS()* function converts negative numbers to their absolute values.

■ **Program examples**

The following command file for processing experimental data illustrates the use of several mathematical functions. The calculations are arbitrary and do not represent any specific application.

The command file allows you to enter four sample values. These values are not stored directly in the table but are the input for several calculations, the results of which are stored in the table. The *SAMPLES* table looks like this:

```
Table: SAMPLES          No lock(s)
Read Password: No
Modify Password: No

Column definitions
# Name      Type       Length          Key   Expression
1 SAMPNUM   INTEGER
2 SAMPMAX   REAL
3 SAMPMIN   REAL
4 SAMPAVE   REAL
5 SAMPDEV   REAL
6 SMPRSULT  REAL
7 SAMPMOD   REAL
```

Now, let's look at the command file:

```
SET MESSAGES OFF
SET VAR vcount TO SAMPNUM IN SAMPLES WHERE COUNT EQ LAST
SET VAR vcount = .vcount + 1
SET VAR more TO y
WHILE more EQ y THEN
  CLEAR vsamp1, vsamp2, vsamp3, vsamp4
  CLS
  FILLIN vsamp1 USING "Enter first sample: "
  FILLIN vsamp2 USING "Enter second sample: "
  FILLIN vsamp3 USING "Enter third sample: "
  FILLIN vsamp4 USING "Enter fourth sample: "
*()
  SET VAR vsampmax TO MAX(.vsamp1,.vsamp2,.vsamp3,.vsamp4)
  SET VAR vsampmin TO MIN(.vsamp1,.vsamp2,.vsamp3,.vsamp4)
  SET VAR vsampave TO AVE(.vsamp1,.vsamp2,.vsamp3,.vsamp4)
  SET VAR vsampdev TO DIM(ABS(.vsampmax),ABS(.vsampmin))
  SET VAR vsampmod TO MOD(.vsampmax,.vsampmin)
  SET VAR vresult TO +
    SQRT((EXP(.vsampmax) + EXP(.vsampmin)) / (EXP(.vsampmax)))
*()
  LOAD SAMPLES; .vcount .vsampmax .vsampmin .vsampave +
    .vsampdev .vresult .vsampmod; end
  SET VAR vcount = .vcount + 1
  SELECT ALL FROM SAMPLES
  FILLIN more USING "More samples? (Y/N): "
ENDWHILE
CLEAR ALL VARIABLES
RETURN
```

21

In addition to illustrating the use of functions, this command file includes examples of some useful programming techniques. The variable *vcount* increments the column *SAMPNUM*. It is initialized to the value of the last sample number plus one. The four sample values are entered by means of the FILLIN commands. These values are then processed by the SET VAR commands.

The variables *vsampmax*, *vsampmin*, and *vsampsave* calculate the maximum, minimum, and average of the four sample values respectively. The variable *vsampdev* calculates the positive difference between the absolute values of *vsampmax* and *vsampmin*. *vsampmod* calculates the modulus (remainder) of *vsampmax* divided by *vsampmin*. Note that if the modulus is 0, then *vsampmax* is evenly divisible by *vsampmin*. Finally, *vresult* calculates the square root of the expression that involves the *EXP()* function (*e* raised to the power of *vsampmax* and *vsampmin*).

Use the LOAD command to load the *SAMPLES* table with the calculated variable values. Note that these must be loaded in the sequence of the defined columns (see *LOAD*). The *vcount* variable is the first one to be loaded and is therefore entered in the *SAMPNUM* column. The SELECT command is then used to display the current contents of the *SAMPLES* table.

Here is a sample session with this command file:

```
Enter first sample: 6
Enter second sample: 9
Enter third sample: 4
Enter fourth sample: 3
 SAMPNUM    SAMPMAX  SAMPMIN  SAMPAVE  SAMPDEV  SMPRSULT SAMPMOD
---------- -------- -------- -------- --------- -------- ---------
         1      23.       4.     11.1      19.        1.       3.
         2     100.       2.    39.95      98.        1.       0.
         3       8.       3.       6.        5. 1.003363       2.
         4       8.       3.       6.        5. 1.003363       2.
         5     12.4     3.87   7.8175     8.53 1.000099     0.79
         6       9.       3.       6.        6. 1.001239       0.
More samples? (Y/N):
```

You may enter both integers and real numbers, because the CLEAR VARIABLE command is at the beginning of the WHILE loop. Otherwise, you would get an error if you first entered a variable as an integer and then, the next time around, attempted to enter a real number.

Other arithmetic and mathematical functions: The three remaining functions are *LOG()*, *LOG10()*, and *SIGN()*. The *SIGN()* function transfers the sign of the second argument to the first argument. *LOG()* and *LOG10()* are the natural and base-10 logarithm functions, respectively. The following session shows the use of these functions:

```
R>SET VAR check REAL
R>SET VAR test = 100
R>SET VAR newtest TO -50
R>SET VAR check TO SIGN(.test, .newtest)
R>SHOW VAR check
    -100.
R>SET VAR check TO LOG(.test)
R>SHOW VAR check
  4.60517
R>SET VAR check TO LOG10(.test)
R>SHOW VAR check
      2.
R>
```

ASCII characters and files

■ **ASCII characters**

ASCII is the abbreviation for the American Standard Code for Information Interchange. ASCII (often called the ASCII code) is a numeric code that represents the character set on many computers, including the IBM PC and compatibles. The ASCII numbers 1 through 127 are standard among all computers that use the ASCII code. ASCII numbers from 128 through 255 represent an *extended character set*, which is available on some computers.

Note: Some mainframe computers and minicomputers use other numeric codes for their character sets. For example, most IBM mainframes use the EBCDIC code. To transfer R:BASE data to a mainframe that uses EBCDIC, you need to convert the R:BASE files from ASCII to EBCDIC.

The ASCII numbering scheme on the IBM PC can be categorized as follows:

ASCII value	Character
0–31	Control characters
32	Space character
33–47	Punctuation characters
48–57	Digits 0 through 9
58–64	Punctuation and special symbols

(continued)

ASCII value	Character
65–90	Uppercase letters A through Z
91–96	Punctuation and special symbols
97–122	Lowercase letters a through z
123–126	Special symbols
127	DEL, a control character
128–255	Extended character set (foreign language and math symbols, graphics characters)

Control characters are primarily used to send commands to peripheral devices such as printers and modems. In R:BASE reports, for example, you can embed printer control codes for boldfaced or condensed printing or other functions supported by your printer.

You can use the extended character set in R:BASE data entry forms and reports for drawing borders and boxes or including mathematical and technical symbols in equations or text. For further information on the use of graphics characters, see *FORMS*.

■ **ASCII files**

Files consisting of ASCII characters (excluding the extended character set) are called ASCII files. Because ASCII code is standard among most personal computers, the ASCII file format is the most common format for transferring data between different computers and different software. Almost all database and word-processing programs can translate their data or files into ASCII format. Spreadsheet programs generally use the DIF or SYLK formats.

Both R:BASE System V and R:BASE 5000 provide the LOAD and UNLOAD commands and the FileGateway program for transferring data to and from ASCII format. For files that exceed the size of a floppy disk, see *BACKUP* and *RESTORE*.

Attribute

■ **Description**

Attribute is a term used in R:BASE 4000 and is synonymous with column.

See: *Columns*

Backing up data

B

- **Description**

The importance of frequently backing up your data cannot be over-emphasized. Be sure that you have backup copies of command files and applications and that you know where they are. Assuming that you use a hard disk for storing your data, keep a complete copy of the data on floppy disks.

If you are entering large amounts of data, back up the database frequently. Nothing is more frustrating than entering several hours' worth of data and then losing it to a power or hardware failure.

- **Procedure**

The easiest way to back up your data is to use the COPY command to copy the database to a backup floppy disk. To do this, simply exit your data entry form and type the COPY command at the R> prompt. (You can also store the COPY command in a command file or keyboard macro so that you can execute it with just a few keystrokes. For more information, see *COPY*.)

The COPY command duplicates the source database. You cannot use the COPY command to add records to an existing database. To add records from another database, use the UNLOAD and INPUT commands. For example, to add the contents of a database to a larger, master database, use the UNLOAD command to copy the data to a temporary file and then the INPUT command to load the contents of the file into the master database.

- **Example**

For an example of the above procedure, see *UNLOAD*.

Cautions: Be sure that the files to be backed up will fit on a floppy disk. When backing up database files larger than the capacity of a floppy disk, use the BACKUP and RESTORE commands. These commands are similar to UNLOAD and INPUT, respectively, but are designed to back up large files to multiple floppies. They are not equivalent to the MS-DOS BACKUP and RESTORE commands.

Note that the values of computed columns are not stored in files created with the UNLOAD or BACKUP commands. The values are recalculated, however, when you reload the backed-up file (see *RESTORE*). To save computed column values in a backup file or for export to another software application, use FileGateway.

- **Comments**

  It's much faster and more convenient to back up a small database. If you are adding to a large database, it's generally best to enter the data into a smaller duplicate database and then add the data to the large database later, using the UNLOAD and INPUT commands.

  See: *BACKUP, Command files, COPY, FORMS, INPUT, Keys, RESTORE,* and *UNLOAD*

BACKUP

- **Syntax**

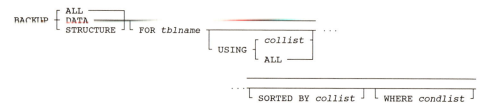

- **Description**

  The BACKUP command copies the database structure, the data, or both (ALL) on a hard disk or on one or more floppy disks. Files that have been backed up can be recovered by using the RESTORE command. The BACKUP command is similar to the UNLOAD command except that it can copy data on multiple floppy disks. Use BACKUP to back up database files that exceed the capacity of a single floppy. For files smaller than the capacity of one floppy, the BACKUP and UNLOAD commands perform the same function.

  The BACKUP command backs up your database in ASCII format. The database structure is backed up as a series of R:BASE commands that define your database. When you use the RESTORE command to recover a backed up database structure, the database is redefined. If the database that you are recovering already exists, the backup file commands produce a series of error messages when they attempt to redefine existing tables and columns, but the restore operation is still carried out. It is usually best to rename or delete an existing database before performing the restore.

  The data in your database is backed up in ASCII delimited format and, when restored, is loaded back into your database. If the database already exists, the backed up data is appended to the existing tables.

- **Procedure**

  You can back up a specific table by using the optional *FOR* clause, and you can back up specific columns in a table by using the optional *USING* clause. In addition, you can sort the data to be backed up by including a *SORTED BY* clause, or you can select specific rows by including a *WHERE* clause. You can use the *USING, SORTED BY,* and *WHERE* clauses only in conjunction with a *FOR* clause. If you omit the *FOR,* the entire database is backed up.

Before using the BACKUP command, you must specify the destination file for the backup by using the OUTPUT command.

■ Examples

To back up the *PROPOSAL* table in the *CONSULT* database to a file called *B:PROPOSAL.BK,* type the following commands:

```
OUTPUT B:PROPOSAL.BK
BACKUP DATA FOR PROPOSAL
OUTPUT SCREEN
```

The output of the BACKUP command is directed to *B:PROPOSAL.BK.* The second OUTPUT command redirects the output to the screen.

A listing of the *PROPOSAL.BK* file looks like this:

```
SET DELIMIT=NULL
SET DELIMIT=,
SET SEMI=NULL
SET SEMI=;
SET QUOTES=NULL
SET QUOTES="
SET PLUS=NULL
SET PLUS=+
USER  NONE
LOAD   PROPOSAL
1,"Building Analysis",30000.00,0.8,1
2,"Database Development",50000.00,0.4,2
4,"Stress Calculations",80000.00,0.9,3
5,"Seismic Eval. Report",150000.00,0.5,4
END
SET VAR YESNO = "E"
USER  NONE
SET DATE FORMAT "MM/DD/YY"
SET TIME FORMAT "HH:MM:SS"
SET DATE SEQUENCE MMDDYY
SET TIME SEQUENCE HHMMSS
```

Notice that the backup file is essentially a command file that can be used to restore the data in the *PROPOSAL* table. In addition, various special character and default settings are saved in the backup file. The BACKUP ALL command creates a similar, but more extensive, command file that contains all the data in the database, in addition to commands for defining the tables, the forms, and the reports.

An important feature of the output files generated by the BACKUP command is the ability to change the name of the database or table to which you want to restore files. For example, in the listing of *PROPOSAL.BK,* you can use the text editor RBEDIT to change the line *LOAD PROPOSAL* to *LOAD NEWTABLE.* Similarly, you can change the database name in an output file with the BACKUP STRUCTURE or BACKUP ALL commands. To do this, change *dbname* (the name of the database) in the line *DEFINE dbname*. In this way, you can copy data from one database to another. For further information on copying data from one database to another, see *UNLOAD*.

To back up the database structure for the *CONSULT* database, use the following commands:

```
OUTPUT B:CONSULT.STR
BACKUP STRUCTURE
OUTPUT SCREEN
```

As mentioned earlier, you can selectively back up data using a *WHERE* clause in the BACKUP command. To back up only those rows with a certain date in a table called *PURCHASE*, type:

```
BACKUP DATA FOR PURCHASE WHERE pdate EQ 01/05/87
```

■ **Comments**

In general, the best approach is to back up the database structure and the data separately. Unless you change the database structure, no purpose is served in repeatedly backing it up. On the other hand, the data in your database is constantly changing and should be backed up regularly. When the database is in regular use, you may wish to back up the structure and keep it on a separate floppy disk. Then, you only have to worry about backing up the data (see *Backing up data*).

If your database files exceed the size of a floppy disk, R:BASE prompts you to change disks when the disk becomes full. Number the disks sequentially as you change them.

Cautions: Be sure that the NULL value is set to "-0-" (the default value) before issuing the BACKUP command (see *SET characters and keywords* and *UNLOAD*).

Note that the BACKUP command does not store the values of computed columns in the backed-up file. The values are recalculated, however, when you reload the backed-up file (see *RESTORE*). To save computed column values in a backup file or for export to another software application, use FileGateway.

See: *OUTPUT, RESTORE, SORTED BY, UNLOAD,* and *WHERE*

See also: *ASCII characters and files, Command files, Database structure,* and *RBEDIT*

■ **R:BASE 5000 equivalent**

None

BEEP

■ **Syntax**

```
BEEP
```

■ **Description**

Use BEEP in command files to sound the computer bell. It operates independently of the SET BELL ON/OFF command.

■ **Procedure**

BEEP is useful for getting your attention either after an error has been made or at the completion of a process.

■ **Example**

In the following, the computer beeps if the database does not exist:

```
IF dbname EXISTS THEN
  OPEN .dbname
  IF dbcheck NE 0 THEN
    BEEP
    WRITE "Sorry, database doesn't exist, press any key to continue."
    PAUSE
    GOTO end
  ENDIF
ENDIF
LABEL end
```

■ **R:BASE 5000 equivalent**

None

BREAK

■ **Syntax**

```
BREAK
```

■ **Description**

Use the BREAK command within IF statements in WHILE...ENDWHILE loops to terminate the WHILE loop early. When the WHILE loop is terminated, the first command following the WHILE loop is executed. If the condition of the IF statement is not satisfied, then the BREAK command and all other commands within the IF statement are skipped.

29

■ **Procedure**

The following illustrates the use of the BREAK command:

```
SET VAR zipvar TO 0
WHILE zipvar EXISTS
  FILLIN zipvar USING "Enter the desired zip code or +
    <Enter> to exit:" AT 3,15
  IF zipvar FAILS
    SET MESSAGES ON
    SET ERROR MESSAGES ON
    BREAK
  ENDIF
  .
  .  *(Other commands in the WHILE loop)
  .
ENDWHILE
```

In the command file above, the variable is set to 0 and then the WHILE loop is executed. The FILLIN command requests a value for *zipvar*. If you enter a value, then *zipvar* exists and the IF statement is skipped. If you press Enter, the value for *zipvar* is null and *zipvar* fails. In this case, the IF condition is satisfied and the BREAK command is executed.

■ **Comment**

For more examples of the BREAK command, see *WHILE* and *Procedure files.*

■ **R:BASE 5000 equivalent**

BREAK

BROWSE

■ **Syntax**

```
          ┌ collist ┬──────┤           ┌ tblname ┐
BROWSE  ┤          └  =w  ├  FROM  ┤                      ├───────────────────────┤
          └ ALL ──────────┘           └ viewname ┘  └ SORTED BY collist ┘└ WHERE condlist ┘
```

■ **Description**

You use the BROWSE command to scroll through the data in a table. However, you cannot edit or modify the data. To scroll through data and edit it, use the EDIT ALL command.

■ **Procedure**

After typing the following BROWSE command,

```
BROWSE ALL FROM EMPLOYEE SORTED BY EMPID WHERE LIMIT EQ 8
```

the first 8 rows of a table called *EMPLOYEE* are displayed, sorted by the employee I.D. number:

```
                Press [ESC] to quit                                          More→
  EMPID     FRSTNAME         LASTNAME         DEPT      SALARY          HIREDATE LAS
  --------- ---------------- ---------------- --------- ---------------- -------- ---
  1         James            Wilson           Sls       $25,000.00 08/15/83 04/
          2 Marjorie         Lawrence         Sls       $25,000.00 01/26/82 07/
          3 Barbara          Graham           Admin     $18,000.00 07/15/85 04/
          4 Paula            Stanton          Oper      $32,000.00 08/03/81 02/
          5 Franklin         Johnson          Mktg      $37,500.00 05/15/82 06/
          6 Robert           Smith            Dev       $45,000.00 04/01/84 11/
          7 Karen            Howard           Sls       $45,000.00 04/01/84 11/
          8 Sebastian        Lancaster        Trn       $35,000.00 11/15/82 10/
```

The *LIMIT* condition in the *WHERE* clause specifies that only the first 10 rows are to be displayed. Notice that not all the data fits on the screen. You can use the Tab key to move horizontally through the data. If there is more data than can fit on the screen (indicated by *More* in the upper right corner of the screen), the columns shift position as you move the cursor to the right.

You can compress the column widths if you select individual columns to browse and append a width specifier. For example, to compress the data in the above example, type:

```
BROWSE EMPID=3 FRSTNAME=10 LASTNAME=10 DEPT SALARY=9 +
  HIREDATE LASTREV NEXTREV SEX FROM EMPLOYEE SORTED BY EMPID +
  WHERE LIMIT EQ 8
```

The following screen shows the result of the command:

```
                Press [ESC] to quit
  EMP FRSTNAME   LASTNAME   DEPT      SALARY     HIREDATE LASTREV  NEXTREV  SEX
  --- ---------- ---------- --------- ---------- -------- -------- -------- --------
  1   James      Wilson     Sls       25,000.00 08/15/83 04/03/86 05/04/86 M

    2 Marjorie   Lawrence   Sls       25,000.00 01/26/82 07/30/83 08/01/86 F

    3 Barbara    Graham     Admin     18,000.00 07/15/85 04/15/86 08/15/86 F

    4 Paula      Stanton    Oper      32,000.00 08/03/81 02/15/84 07/01/86 F

    5 Franklin   Johnson    Mktg      37,500.00 05/15/82 06/16/86 09/15/86 M

    6 Robert     Smith      Dev       45,000.00 04/01/84 11/30/85 08/15/86 M

    7 Karen      Howard     Sls       45,000.00 04/01/84 11/03/85 08/01/86 F

    8 Sebastian  Lancaster  Trn       35,000.00 11/15/82 10/15/83 07/15/86 M
```

The equal sign and number following a column name indicate that the column should be displayed with that specified width. The plus signs in the command line indicate continuation of the command on another line. This is a good example of a command to save using the *RECORD/PLAYBACK* option, since it is fairly tedious to type repeatedly.

■ **Comments**

The BROWSE command is useful in command files for situations where you do not want other users to be able to edit the data. In most other situations, it is better to use the EDIT ALL command.

See: *EDIT, PLAYBACK, RECORD,* and *WHERE*

■ **R:BASE 5000 equivalent**

EDIT ALL

BUILD KEY

■ **Syntax**

```
BUILD KEY FOR colname IN tblname
```

■ **Description**

The BUILD KEY command lets you modify an existing table to include column keys. Normally, you specify keys when you initially define the tables in the database. With BUILD KEY, however, you can specify keys after the database has been defined. You can specify any number of keys.

■ **Procedure**

To create a key for the *EMPID* column in the *EMPLOYEE* table, type:

```
BUILD KEY FOR EMPID IN EMPLOYEE
```

You can verify whether a column has a key or not by issuing the LIST command followed by the appropriate table name:

```
LIST EMPLOYEE
```

The following categories of information are displayed:

```
Table: EMPLOYEE        No lock(s)
Read Password: No
Modify Password: No

Column definitions
# Name      Type      Length        Key   Expression
1 EMPID     INTEGER                 yes
2 FRSTNAME  TEXT      15 characters
3 LASTNAME  TEXT      15 characters
4 DEPT      TEXT      5 characters
5 SALARY    CURRENCY
6 HIREDATE  DATE
7 LASTREV   DATE
8 NEXTREV   DATE
9 SEX       TEXT      1 characters
```

Columns with keys are identified by a *yes* in the key column.

■ **Comments**

Adding a key to a table that has several thousand rows takes a few minutes. It is, therefore, preferable to create keys when you initially define the table columns. For further discussion of when to use keys, see *Keys.*

You can delete keys using the DELETE KEY command.

See: *DEFINE, Keys,* and *LIST*

■ **R:BASE 5000 equivalent**
BUILD KEY

CHANGE

■ **Syntax**

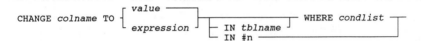

```
CHANGE colname TO ┌ value ─────┐                  ┌ WHERE condlist ┐
                  │            ├ IN tblname ┤
                  └ expression ┘ └ IN #n ──────────────
```

■ **Description**

Use the CHANGE command to alter the data values of a column. You can assign any valid value or expression to a column. If you specify *tblname* in the CHANGE command, the change affects only the column in the named table. If you leave out *tblname,* any changes affect the column in all tables of the database. You can also use a route number, *#n,* as specified by the SET POINTER command.

■ **Procedure**

A *WHERE* clause is required unless you are using the route number option (see the example below). Although this requirement is an inconvenience in some respects, it forces you to consider what rows you are changing. If the *WHERE* clause were not required, it would be easy to inadvertently change many rows in the database.

■ **Example**

The most straightforward application of the CHANGE command is to change a single column value in a single table. The following command changes the department to *ADMIN* for the employee whose ID number is 1:

```
CHANGE DEPT TO ADMIN IN EMPLOYEE WHERE EMPID EQ 1
```

To record an across-the-board salary increase of 10%, type:

```
CHANGE SALARY TO (110% SALARY) IN EMPLOYEE WHERE EMPID EXISTS
```

To increase everyone's salary, the *WHERE* clause specifies all rows in which an employee *ID* number exists.

Expressions used with the CHANGE command can include other column values and variables, as well as mathematical and string operators. The following changes a blank field called *ENTRDATE* to today's (the system) date:

```
CHANGE ENTRDATE TO .#DATE IN EMPLOYEE WHERE ENTRDATE FAILS
```

The above examples change rows using constant values or expressions such as the value of the *#DATE* variable and *110% SALARY*. Although the value of *110% SALARY* may change, the expression can be thought of as a constant because it does not contain variables. The CHANGE operation simply requires a one-line command in these cases.

In some cases, however, you may want to change the column value to the value of a variable that varies from row to row. For example, let's say you want to extract the first and last initials from each employee's name (*FRSTNAME* and *LASTNAME* columns) and put the initials in another column (*INITIALS*). You cannot make this change using a single value or expression. You need to use variables to extract the initials and then change the *INITIALS* column row by row to the new value. In other words, you need to use several commands that operate on each row.

You can change the *INITIALS* column by using a WHILE loop with the SET POINTER command and a route number. The *WHERE* clause is not required to use the CHANGE command with a route number.

Here is a command file that extracts the first and last initials from the *FRSTNAME* and *LASTNAME* columns of the *EMPLOYEE* table and inserts them in the *INITIALS* column:

```
SET VAR initvar TEXT
SET POINTER #1 p1 FOR EMPLOYEE
WHILE p1 = 0 THEN
  SET VAR initvar TO " . "
  SET VAR fname TO FRSTNAME IN #1
  SET VAR lname TO LASTNAME IN #1
  SET VAR initvar = (SMOVE(.fname,1,1,.initvar,1))
  SET VAR initvar = (SMOVE(.lname,1,1,.initvar,3))
  CHANGE INITIALS TO .initvar IN #1    *(change the INITIALS column)
  NEXT #1 p1
ENDWHILE
```

The following screen shows the affected columns from the first five rows of the EMPLOYEE table after running the command file:

```
R>SELECT FRSTNAME LASTNAME INITIALS FROM EMPLOYEE WHERE LIMIT EQ 5
   FRSTNAME        LASTNAME        INITIALS
   ---------------  ---------------  --------
   James           Wilson          J.W
   Marjorie        Lawrence        M.L
   Barbara         Graham          B.G
   Paula           Stanton         P.S
   Franklin        Johnson         F.J
R>
```

In this example, the variable *initvar* is initially set to a three character string with a period as the second character. The column values of *FRSTNAME* and *LASTNAME* are then stored in the variables *fname* and *lname*, respectively. The *SMOVE()* function moves the first letter from the *fname* and *lname* variables into the *initvar* variable. Finally, the CHANGE command changes the *INITIALS* column to the value in the *initvar* variable. The NEXT command moves the pointer to the next row, and the operation is repeated until all the rows have been changed.

■ **Comments**

In large tables, you can improve the performance of the CHANGE command by specifying a key column as the last column in the *WHERE* clause. Computed columns are often used in place of the CHANGE command because they are faster and more convenient.

See: *Columns, Command files, Expressions, Keys, NEXT, SET POINTER, String manipulation functions, Variables,* and *WHERE.*

■ **R:BASE 5000 equivalent**

The functions of the CHANGE command in R:BASE System V are split between two commands in R:BASE 5000: the CHANGE command and the ASSIGN command. In R:BASE 5000, the CHANGE command applies to values, and the ASSIGN command applies to expressions. The CHANGE DEPT example at the beginning of this entry would be identical in R:BASE 5000. In the CHANGE SALARY example, however, you would substitute ASSIGN for CHANGE in the command line.

CHDIR

■ **Syntax**

```
CHDIR d:pathname
```

■ **Description**

The CHDIR command lets you change the current directory without leaving R:BASE. CHDIR is almost identical to the MS-DOS CHDIR command. Unlike the MS-DOS version, however, a space is required between CHDIR and the leading backslash of a pathname.

■ **Procedure**

If you use CHDIR without specifying a drive or a pathname, the current directory is displayed. This is helpful if you want to know the name of the current directory.

■ **Example**

The following command changes the current directory on the default drive to
\RBFILES\DATA:

```
CHDIR \RBFILES\DATA
```

■ **Comments**

Changing to a directory on a drive other than the default drive does not make
it the current directory. For example, assume that the default drive is C and
the current directory is C:\RBFILES. If you issue the command,

```
CHDIR D:\DATA
```

the current directory will remain C:\RBFILES. If you want to work in the directory D:\DATA, you must also issue the command,

```
CHDRV D:
```

or simply,

```
D:
```

to change the default drive to D.

See: *CHDRV, DOS commands in R:BASE,* and *Filenames and structure*

■ **R:BASE 5000 equivalent**

CHDIR

CHDRV

■ **Syntax**

```
CHDRV d:
```

■ **Description**

The CHDRV command changes the default drive to the drive specified. If no
drive is specified, the present default drive is displayed.

■ **Procedure**

To change the default drive to drive C, for example, type:

```
CHDRV C:
```

or simply:

```
C:
```

as you would in MS-DOS.

■ **Comments**

Because you can type the drive specifier without the CHDRV command, the main reason to use CHDRV is to ascertain the current default drive. Also, CHDRV is more readable in command files.

See: *Command files*

■ **R:BASE 5000 equivalent**

CHDRV

CHECK/NOCHECK

■ **Syntax**

```
CHECK
NOCHECK
```

■ **Description**

The CHECK command turns rules-checking on. The NOCHECK command turns rules-checking off. CHECK and NOCHECK are used only in conjuction with the LOAD command.

■ **Procedure**

You can issue a CHECK or NOCHECK command only at an L> prompt.

When you issue the CHECK command, which is the default value, all data entered with the LOAD command is checked against existing rules. The NOCHECK command allows all data to be entered regardless of existing rules. In databases with password control, NOCHECK operates only after the appropriate OWNER password is entered.

■ **Comments**

Because the CHECK and NOCHECK commands are used only at the L> prompt, you will have few occasions to use them. The LOAD command is primarily used for loading data from external files—not keyboard data entry. To load external files, you must use the SET RULES command.

See: *LOAD, OWNER, PASSWORDS,* and *RULES*

■ **R:BASE 5000 equivalent**

CHECK/NOCHECK

CHKDSK

■ **Syntax**

```
CHKDSK d:
```

■ **Description**

The CHKDSK command displays the total number of bytes of disk space on the specified drive, how much space is available for use, and the total system memory size. The CHKDSK command is a limited version of the MS-DOS CHKDSK command, which also performs some error-correction functions and supplies more extensive information (such as the number of files on the disk and the number of bad sectors, if any)

■ **Procedure**

Typing:

```
CHKDSK C:
```

displays something like the following:

```
30203904 bytes total disk space
 9248768 bytes available on disk

  655360 bytes total memory
  132496 bytes free
```

Note that R:BASE System V occupies approximately 480,000 bytes of memory.

■ **R:BASE 5000 equivalent**

CHKDSK

CHOOSE

■ **Syntax**

```
CHOOSE varname FROM menuname ┬─ IN procfile ─┬ ┬─ AT scrnrow ─┬
```

■ **Description**

Use the CHOOSE command in command files to display a vertical or horizontal menu on the screen and to store the response in a specified variable.

■ **Procedure**

The text of the menu is stored in *menuname*, which can be either an ASCII text file or an R:BASE procedure file created by CodeLock. The response is stored in *varname*.

After executing the CHOOSE command, the command file normally evaluates the response with a series of IF statements to determine which menu choice to select.

It is generally easier and less time-consuming to use Application EXPRESS, because it automatically generates the CHOOSE commands and subsequent IF statements. If you prefer to do your own programming, however, the CHOOSE command provides a straightforward procedure for creating your own menus.

You can use the CHOOSE command in either ASCII command files or in binary procedure files created by CodeLock. When testing the operation of your menu, it is better to work with ASCII files. When the menu works properly, you can then convert the ASCII files to procedure files. This process is discussed in greater detail in the example below and in *Command files, Procedure files,* and *CodeLock.*

You can generate either vertical or horizontal menus with the CHOOSE command. A vertical menu lists the menu items in a vertical column and assigns each item a number (1, 2, 3, etc.). You can have as many as nine items. The text that describes each item may not exceed 65 characters. To select a menu item, type its number or move the cursor to the item and press Enter.

Horizontal menus display the menu items in a horizontal row. To select a menu item, use the cursor to highlight the item and then press Enter, or type the first letter of the desired item and then press Enter. Horizontal menus can contain as many as 81 items. However, the total number of characters in the menu cannot exceed 1134. When determining the total number of characters, add six characters to the length of each item's text to account for spacing. The text of a single item may not exceed 72 characters. These limits far exceed the practical requirements of most horizontal menus.

■ **Example**

In this example, a vertical menu is created that offers three choices: *Enter Data, Display Data,* or *Print Reports.* Use RBEDIT to create the menu file and the associated command file.

When you use the CHOOSE command in ASCII files, you must store the text of the menu in a separate file. Using RBEDIT, create a file called *MAINMENU.TXT* that will contain the text for the menu display:

```
Main Menu
COLUMN Main Menu (Esc to Exit)
Data Entry
Data Display
Print Reports
```

The first line is a description of the menu for documentation purposes and must be included. You can include any text you like in this first line. The word *COLUMN* in the second line indicates that this is a vertical menu. The remainder of the line contains the menu title (header). The next three lines list the choices that will appear in the menu.

Typing the following CHOOSE command:

```
CHOOSE choice FROM MAINMENU.TXT AT 5
```

displays the following screen:

```
                    ═══Main Menu (Esc to Exit)═══
                         (1)  Data Entry
                         (2)  Data Display
                         (3)  Print Reports
```

The *AT* clause specifies that the menu be displayed starting at row five. R:BASE formats the menu with the box and numbered menu items. The variable *choice* contains the response. Pressing ESC sets the variable *choice* to zero. Selecting item one sets the variable *choice* to one, and so on. If you do not press ESC or type a valid item number, R:BASE beeps and waits for a valid entry. You can verify the value of the variable *choice* by issuing the command SHOW VARIABLE CHOICE.

The following command sequence illustrates the typical procedure for evaluating a menu response:

```
SET ERROR MESSAGES OFF
SET MESSAGES OFF
CHOOSE choice FROM MAINMEN.TXT
IF choice EQ 0 THEN
   SET ERROR MESSAGES ON
   SET MESSAGES ON
   QUIT
ENDIF
IF choice EQ 1 THEN
   NEWPAGE
   ENTER USING MYFORM
ENDIF
IF choice EQ 2 THEN
   NEWPAGE
   EDIT ALL FROM CLIENT
ENDIF
IF choice EQ 3 THEN
   NEWPAGE
   PRINT CLI-LIST
ENDIF
```

Each IF statement corresponds to one of the four possible choices: *Exit (ESC), Enter Data, Display Data,* or *Print Reports.* If ESC is pressed, control returns to the R> prompt. The other choices perform simple R:BASE commands that enter, display, and print data. Clearly, more complicated command sequences are possible for a single menu selection. Always save the commands that operate with an ASCII menu file in a separate file.

You can display this menu as a horizontal menu by simply changing the second line of *MAINMEN.TXT* to include *ROW* instead of *COLUMN*. In that case, typing and entering:

```
CHOOSE choice1 FROM MAINMENU.TXT AT 5
```

produces a menu that looks like this:

```
=============================Main Menu (Esc to Exit)=============================
 Data Entry      Data Display    Print Reports
```

The variable *choice1* is now a text variable rather than a numeric variable. It is best to avoid using the same variable for both vertical and horizontal menus so that you will not have to keep resetting the data type.

With a horizontal menu, pressing ESC sets the variable *choice1* equal to *ESC*. Selecting the first item sets *choice1* to *Data Entry*. Therefore, you would have to modify the IF statements in the preceding command file to display a horizontal menu.

After you test your menu text file and its associated command file, it's best to convert these files into a procedure file. This is fully described in the entry *CodeLock*.

■ **Comments**

Application EXPRESS uses the CHOOSE command to generate menus. If you have an application generated by Application EXPRESS, you can display the application file (file extension *.APP*) by using the TYPE command or RBEDIT. Note that each menu in your application has a corresponding CHOOSE command and sequence of IF statements, similar to the example above.

Again, it is generally more convenient to use Application EXPRESS to generate menus rather than creating them from scratch with CHOOSE. You can, however, create larger horizontal menus with CHOOSE than you can with Application EXPRESS.

See: *Application EXPRESS, ASCII characters and files, CodeLock, Command files, Procedure files, RBEDIT,* and *Variables*

See also: *BEEP, Data types, DISPLAY, ENTER, PRINT, SHOW,* and *TYPE*

■ **R:BASE 5000 equivalent**

CHOOSE

The CHOOSE command operates identically as in R:BASE System V except that horizontal menus are limited to 40 menu items. This limit is adequate for most applications.

CLEAR

■ **Syntax**

```
CLEAR ⎡ varlist
      ⎣ ALL VARIABLES
```

■ **Description**

The CLEAR command deletes variables from memory. You can either delete a list of variables (*varlist*) or ALL VARIABLES. System variables, such as *#DATE*, are not affected by the CLEAR command.

■ **Procedure**

CLEAR is used primarily in command files to clear variables of their current values. This may be necessary if the variable is used repeatedly in a loop or if its data type changes. R:BASE sets variables to a specific data type when you assign an initial value. Programmers call this implicit data-typing. For example, if a variable is initially assigned a value of zero, it is implicitly set to the integer data type. If you later attempt to store a text value in that variable, R:BASE returns an error until you clear the variable. You also can use the SET VARIABLE command to change the data type explicitly.

It's good practice to clear the variables at the end of a completed procedure or application. Of course, exiting R:BASE clears all variables.

■ **Example**

If you add a CLEAR command to the command file from the example in the CHANGE entry:

```
SET VAR initvar TEXT
SET POINTER #1 p1 FOR EMPLOYEE
WHILE p1 = 0 THEN
  SET VAR initvar TO " . "
  SET VAR fname TO FRSTNAME IN #1
  SET VAR lname TO LASTNAME IN #1
  SET VAR initvar = (SMOVE(.fname,1,1,.initvar,1))
  SET VAR initvar = (SMOVE(.lname,1,1,.initvar,3))
  CHANGE INITIALS TO .initvar IN #1
  NEXT #1 p1
ENDWHILE
CLEAR initvar fname lname p1    *(clear variables)
```

the variables in the last line, *initvar, fname, lname,* and *p1,* are cleared.

Caution: Do not use the *ALL VARIABLES* option in Application EXPRESS macros or custom command files. This option also clears the variables used internally by Application EXPRESS. Instead, use a specific variable list.

■ **Comments**

See: *Application EXPRESS, CHANGE, CHOOSE, Command files, Data types, Procedure files, SET VARIABLE,* and *Variables*

■ **R:BASE 5000 equivalent**

CLEAR

In R:BASE 5000, you can specify only a single variable, not a list of variables. To clear a list of variables, you must issue a CLEAR command for each variable in the list. The *ALL VARIABLES* option is identical to its counterpart in R:BASE System V.

CLOSE

■ **Syntax**

```
CLOSE
```

■ **Description**

The CLOSE command saves any changes to the current database and then closes the database.

■ **Procedure**

Although the OPEN and EXIT commands also save changes and close the current database, and are used more often, the CLOSE command is useful if you want to continue using R:BASE without opening another database, if you plan to run an application or command file, or if you need to do some file maintenance. For example, you cannot delete an open database; you first issue the CLOSE command and then delete the database.

If you are using floppy disks to store your database, use the CLOSE command before you switch to a database on another disk.

■ **Comments**

See: *Application EXPRESS, Command files, DELETE, EXIT,* and *OPEN*

■ **R:BASE 5000 equivalent**

CLOSE

CLS

■ **Syntax**

CLS — FROM scrnrow — TO scrnrow

■ **Description**

The CLS command clears the screen.

■ **Procedure**

You can clear selective portions of the screen by specifying a range of screen rows (*FROM...TO...*). If you omit the range, the entire screen is cleared. If you omit the *TO* clause, the screen is cleared from the row specified in the *FROM* clause to the bottom row of the screen (row 25 on the IBM PC and compatibles).

■ **Comments**

CLS clears the screen regardless of any previous OUTPUT commands. This contrasts with the NEWPAGE command, which sends a form feed to the current output device (for example, the screen, printer, or disk output file).

See: *NEWPAGE* and *OUTPUT*

■ **R:BASE 5000 equivalent**

None

CodeLock

■ **Syntax**

Select CodeLock from the RBSYSTEM menu or, at the R> prompt, type:

CODELOCK — exec

You also can execute CodeLock from MS-DOS:

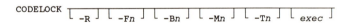

CODELOCK — -R — -Fn — -Bn — -Mn — -Tn — exec

The *-R* option suppresses the display of the R logo. The *-F* and *-B* options modify the foreground and background colors respectively (if you are using a color monitor). The *-M* and *-T* options modify other monitor characteristics. See the R:BASE System V Installation Guide for further information on the color and monitor options. The *exec* option lets you specify an *exec* file that will run when you start CodeLock (see *RECORD* and *PLAYBACK*).

■ Description

Note: Before you read this entry, we recommend that you read the entry *Procedure files.* If you want to develop applications using CodeLock, you should also read the section on Application EXPRESS. You might find that Application EXPRESS will meet your needs while saving you a great deal of time and effort.

CodeLock is a separate menu driven module in R:BASE System V that translates R:BASE command files and procedure files from ASCII to binary format. The following brief explanation of interpreted and compiled programs will help put CodeLock in the proper perspective.

When you execute an R:BASE command file generated by RBEDIT or another text editor, the commands are interpreted, meaning that the commands are analyzed and executed one at a time, each time you run the command file. Each time a command is executed, R:BASE translates the command into binary code that can be processed by the computer. The R:BASE programming language is therefore an interpreted programming language. Another example of an interpreted programming language is the version of BASIC that comes with the MS-DOS operating system.

A compiler, on the other hand, translates programming commands into a separate executable binary file. The translation takes place only once. Once the programming commands have been translated and compiled into an executable file, you can execute the file from the MS-DOS prompt. MS-DOS executable binary files have the file extensions *.EXE* or *.COM* (depending on how they are compiled).

Executable binary files are independent of the software that created them. This means that to execute an executable binary file, the original programming commands (source code) are not needed. Most commercial programs, such as R:BASE or Lotus 1-2-3, are distributed in compiled, binary format so that users have no access to the source code. In addition to providing program security, compiled programs execute much faster than interpreted ones.

CodeLock is not a true compiler, but it can be considered a hybrid of a compiler and an interpreter. Although CodeLock converts R:BASE commands into binary format, parts of the command file or procedure file still must be interpreted every time the file is executed. CodeLock does not generate an *.EXE* or *.COM* file that can be executed directly from MS-DOS. Although files translated by CodeLock might run somewhat faster than their ASCII counterparts, the performance difference does not compare with the performance difference between programs executed in interpreted and compiled BASIC, for example.

Although CodeLock is not a true compiler, it has some of the advantages of a compiler. CodeLock stores your procedures or command files in a format that cannot be edited or otherwise modified with a standard text editor, so files converted by CodeLock are secure from unauthorized tampering. Modifications to command files or procedure files must be made to the original ASCII command files, which then must be reconverted using CodeLock. You can maintain file security by using only the binary versions of your command files and storing the ASCII versions separately on floppy disks.

CodeLock also lets you consolidate command files, screen blocks, and menu blocks into a single binary procedure file that provides an organized and integrated approach to developing applications.

■ **Procedure**

The following screen shows the CodeLock Main menu:

```
                            CODELOCK
      Copyright (C) 1983,1984,1985,1986 by Microrim, Inc. (Ver. 1.00 PC-DOS)

      ╔══════════════════════════CODELOCK Main Menu══════════════════════╗
      ║ (1)  Convert an ASCII command file to a binary command file       ║
      ║ (2)  Add an ASCII command file to a procedure file                ║
      ║ (3)  Add an ASCII screen file to a procedure file                 ║
      ║ (4)  Add an ASCII menu file to a procedure file                   ║
      ║ (5)  Convert an ASCII application file to a binary application file║
      ║ (6)  Display directory                                            ║
      ║ (7)  Display the contents of an ASCII file                        ║
      ║ (8)  Exit                                                         ║
      ╚═══════════════════════════════════════════════════════════════════╝
```

The key to using CodeLock effectively is understanding the differences between the file types in the first five menu items. For a detailed description of these file types, see *Procedure files*.

Item *1* converts ASCII command files to binary format. These converted command files will operate as a stand-alone program and must not include screen, command, or menu procedure blocks.

Items *2, 3,* and *4* allow you to add command, screen, and menu blocks to an existing procedure. In each case, the files to be converted must follow certain conventions, as follows:

☐ Command blocks cannot include the $COMMAND keyword or the block name (normally the second line of the command block). You are prompted for the command block name when you select item *2*. CodeLock automatically adds it to the procedure.

☐ Screen blocks should include only the text that will appear on the screen. Do not include the $SCREEN keyword or the block name. You are prompted for the screen block name when you select item 3.

If the filename you originally used in the corresponding DISPLAY command does not coincide with the new screen name, you also must modify the DISPLAY command in the command block.

☐ Menu blocks cannot include the $MENU keyword, but they should include the menu name:

```
menu name
COLUMN Main Menu
Data Entry
Data Display
Print Reports
```

If the filename that you originally used in the corresponding CHOOSE command does not coincide with the new menu block name, you must modify the CHOOSE command used in conjunction with the menu block.

If a block name that you wish to add to the procedure file already exists, CodeLock asks you if you want to overwrite the existing block.

Item 5 converts complete procedure files from ASCII to binary format. For an example of a typical ASCII procedure file see *Procedure files*. This operation also can modify the ASCII versions of Application EXPRESS procedure files and can reconvert them. (An ASCII version always has the file extension *.APP*.) If you do this, however, you will no longer be able to modify the procedure from within Application EXPRESS.

■ Comments

It is generally easier to use Application EXPRESS to develop and convert your applications. Keep in mind that the *custom* and *macro* options in Application EXPRESS probably will let you include as much complexity as you require.

See: *Application EXPRESS, ASCII characters and files, CHOOSE, Command files, DISPLAY, Procedure files, RBEDIT,* and *RUN*

■ R:BASE 5000 equivalent

RCOMPILE is essentially identical to CodeLock. The only difference is that you cannot execute RCOMPILE from within R:BASE 5000. You must return to the R:BASE 5000 Main menu first.

Columns

■ **Description**

A database table consists of horizontal rows and vertical columns. Each column stores a specific item of information, such as a zip code, a last name, or a Social Security number. Columns often are referred to as fields in other database software. In R:BASE 4000, columns are called attributes.

You must assign each column a name of eight characters or less and a data type. The following are valid data types:

Data Type	Description
CURRENCY	Used for dollar or foreign currency amounts to a maximum of 23 digits. Each currency value uses eight bytes of storage space.
DATE	The default format is MM/DD/YY. Hyphens also can be used as delimiters. Date values use four bytes of storage.
DOUBLE	Double-precision real numbers are useful in situations requiring high degrees of numeric accuracy. However, double-precision values require twice the storage space (eight bytes) of single-precision numbers. See *REAL* below. The range of double-precision numbers is $\pm 10E^{\pm 307}$.
INTEGER	Whole numbers in the range of $\pm 999{,}999{,}999$. Each uses four bytes of storage.
NOTE	Note columns can contain as many as 4092 characters of text. Note columns require a storage space of four bytes plus the number of bytes of text.
REAL	Real numbers are in single-precision format in the range of $\pm 10E^{\pm 37}$. Single-precision numbers require four bytes of storage. Numbers with more than six digits are displayed in scientific notation (1.23456E-7, for example).
TEXT	Text columns can contain as many as 1500 characters of text. The default column width is eight characters, and the required storage space varies with the specified column width.
TIME	The default time format is HH:MM:SS. The time value uses four bytes of storage.

You can change the column width of text columns only. The other column types use default column widths. Columns may be specified as key columns and also as computed columns.

A computed column stores values resulting from the expression specified in the computed column definition. Computed columns may contain both constant values and values from other columns in the table. Computed column expressions may not include variables, however. Data cannot be entered directly into a computed column; it is calculated from the values in the column expression. An example of computed columns is given below.

Definition EXPRESS provides the easiest method for defining the columns in a database table. You can enter Definition EXPRESS from the RBSYSTEM menu or from within R:BASE with the RBDEFINE command.

It's also possible to define columns in R:BASE using the COLUMNS command in conjunction with the DEFINE and TABLES commands. However, there is no real advantage to using the DEFINE command instead of Definition EXPRESS. In fact, the DEFINE command is more difficult to use and much more susceptible to data entry errors. For the sake of completeness, the following command sequence shows how to use the COLUMNS command and gives an example of a computed column.

```
R>DEFINE CHARGES
 Begin R:BASE Database Definition
D>COLUMNS
D>CLI-NUM INTEGER KEY
D>ID-NUM INTEGER
D>HR-RATE CURRENCY
D>HOURS REAL
D>MULTIPLE REAL
D>CHARGE = ('HR-RATE' * HOURS * MULTIPLE)
D>COMMENT TEXT 30
D>TABLES
D>BILLING WITH CLI-NUM ID-NUM HR-RATE HOURS MULTIPLE CHARGE COMMENT
D>END
 End R:BASE Database Definition
R>
```

In this sequence, a database called *CHARGES* is defined and then the COLUMNS command is used to define the columns. Note that the COLUMNS command must be used in conjunction with the DEFINE command. When you are in DEFINE mode, the screen always displays a D> prompt rather than the R> prompt. Each line that follows the COLUMNS command is treated as a column definition until another valid command is encountered, in this case, the TABLES command. All columns must be associated with a table definition. Columns not specified in a table definition are lost when you exit the DEFINE mode with the END command. In this example, all columns are defined as part of the *BILLING* table.

The *CLI-NUM* column is defined as a key column. You also can use the BUILD KEY and DELETE KEY commands to alter the key status of columns after they have been defined.

The *CHARGE* column is a computed column that returns the product of the values of three other columns in the table. Because the computed column involves currency, its data type is set to CURRENCY. You can explicitly specify the computed column's data type; however, the data type must be compatible with the data types of columns used in the computed column expression. Of course, the columns within the column expression must also be compatible. For example, you cannot multiply date columns by integer columns or text columns by real numbers.

Note that because it contains a hyphen, the *HR-RATE* column must be enclosed in quotes in the computed column expression. The hyphen otherwise would be interpreted as a minus sign. Any column name that includes an arithmetic operator symbol must be enclosed in quotes. For valid arithmetic operators, see *Expressions* or *Operators*.

See: *Application EXPRESS, Data types, Database structure, Definition EXPRESS, Expressions,* and *Operators*

See also: *BUILD KEY, DELETE, EXPAND,* and *REMOVE*

■ **R:BASE 5000 equivalent**

R:BASE 5000 does not support computed columns or the double-precision and NOTE data types. The CURRENCY data type is called the DOLLAR data type and does not support international currency formats, although you can change the $ symbol to another character with the SET DOLLAR command.

Columns in R:BASE 5000 can be defined in the DEFINE mode, as described above, or with Application EXPRESS. As with Definition EXPRESS in R:BASE System V, Application EXPRESS in R:BASE 5000 provides an easy method for defining columns and is more convenient than the DEFINE mode.

Command files

■ **Description**

The command file is the basic file structure for programming in R:BASE. Although Application EXPRESS greatly simplifies the task of the programmer, specialized programs require custom command files.

A command file is a list of R:BASE commands that is created with RBEDIT or another text editor and is stored in a separate disk file. All R:BASE commands may be included in command files. The format for entering the commands is discussed in the *Command structure* entry. You execute the commands in a command file by issuing the RUN command followed by the name of the command file. Command files can be executed either in their original ASCII format or in the binary format that CodeLock creates.

■ **Example**

Any valid MS-DOS filename can be used to name a command file. It's good practice, however, to assign the file extension *.CMD* to command files to distinguish them from other types of files.

Although you can write complex command files, they also are useful for storing simple command sequences that you use often. For example, suppose you periodically create a text file that lists the first and last names of employees in alphabetical order and reports their hire date and last review date. You can store the commands to perform this operation in a command file, which we will call *UNLOAD.CMD*:

```
OPEN PERSONL
SET QUOTES = NULL
OUTPUT .%1
UNLOAD DATA FOR EMPLOYEE USING LASTNAME FRSTNAME HIREDATE +
   LASTREV SORTED BY LASTNAME FRSTNAME
OUTPUT SCREEN
```

The second line sets quotes to NULL so that the output names are not separated by quotes. The third line uses the variable *%1* to specify the output file named in the RUN command's *USING* clause. The + at the end of the fourth line indicates that the command continues on the next line. The following RUN command saves the unloaded data to B:TEST.OUT:

```
RUN UNLOAD.CMD USING B:TEXT.OUT
```

The RECORD/PLAYBACK feature is equally suitable for storing the above command sequence. Specify a variable output filename with a & character in place of the filename.

To execute a certain command file when R:BASE is started, name that file *RBASE.DAT*. R:BASE interprets a file with this name as an initial command file. Whenever R:BASE is started from a directory containing an *RBASE.DAT* file, it executes the commands in this file first. This feature is convenient if you are setting up an application to be operated by someone who will work only with this application or who should not have access to the other functions of R:BASE. For more information on the topic of initial command files, see *Application EXPRESS* and *RBASE*.

The ability to add custom command files to applications generated by Application EXPRESS is one of the most powerful programming features of R:BASE.

See: *Application EXPRESS, ASCII characters and files, Command structure, OUTPUT, PLAY-BACK, Procedure files, Programming, RBEDIT, RECORD,* and *RUN*

Command structure

■ **Description**

Command structure is the format and rules for entering commands in R:BASE System V. Although you can enter commands either directly from the R> prompt or indirectly from command files, the command structure is the same. (You can also use Prompt-By-Example to select commands from a list on the screen.)

R:BASE commands consist of the command itself, keywords, and arguments. A command is a word that tells R:BASE to carry out a specific operation. Keywords are words reserved by R:BASE for clauses that can accompany the command. An argument is information that you supply to limit the command.

■ **Example**

```
SELECT frstname lastname FROM employee [SORTED BY +
lastname] [WHERE city EQ "Oakland"]
```

SELECT is the command. *FROM, SORTED BY,* and *WHERE* are keywords that form clauses to restrict the scope of the command. The clauses in brackets are optional. The lowercase terms are arguments. You can enter R:BASE commands in either uppercase or lowercase. Do not use R:BASE reserved words as arguments. For example, you cannot use the word *rate* for a column or table name because this word is reserved in R:BASE for the *RATE* functions. See tables 1–8 and 1–9 in the R:BASE User's Manual.

Notice that the + sign continues the command on the next line. Commands longer than 75 characters must be continued on a second line. R:BASE System V inserts the + sign if you type more than the 75 character limit. In R:BASE 5000, however, you must enter the + sign manually.

All commands and keywords in R:BASE can be abbreviated to their first three or four letters. If two commands share the same first three letters, abbreviate to the first four letters. For example, abbreviate ENDIF and ENDWHILE to ENDI and ENDW, respectively. The command shown above could be entered as follows:

```
SEL frstname lastname FRO employee SOR BY lastname +
 WHE city EQ "Oakland"
```

You also can enter more than one command on a single line by separating the commands with a semicolon, as follows:

```
LIST EMPLOYEE; SELECT FRSTNAME LASTNAME FROM EMPLOYEE
```

When you enter commands from the R> prompt, several keyboard functions are available for editing and re-entering commands:

☐ The right arrow repeats the previously entered command, one character at a time.

☐ The Tab key repeats the previously entered command, 10 characters at a time.

☐ The Ctrl-right arrow combination or the End key repeats the previously entered command in its entirety.

You also can use the Ins and Del keys to edit a command line created with the above key functions. For more information on editing, see *RBEDIT*.

See: *Command files, Functions, Programming,* and *PROMPT*

COMPUTE

■ **Syntax**

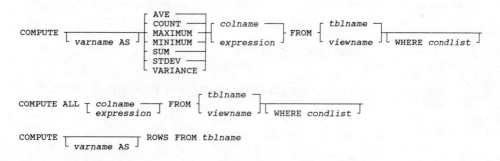

- **Description**

The COMPUTE command is used for performing arithmetic and statistical calculations on columns or expressions involving columns.

The COMPUTE command performs the following calculations:

Keyword	Function
AVE	Computes the average of numeric column values or of date and time values.
COUNT	Counts the number of entries in a specified column.
MAX	Computes the maximum numeric or alphabetic column value.
MIN	Computes the minimum numeric or alphabetic column value.
ROWS	Counts the number of rows in a specified table.
SUM	Computes the sum of numeric column values.
STD	Computes the standard deviation of numeric column values.
VAR	Computes the variance of numeric column values.
ALL	Computes all the above functions that apply to the column data type.

- **Procedure**

You can store the result of these calculations in a variable. If you omit a variable name, the result is displayed on the output device. For example, you can print the result or store it in a disk file by issuing the OUTPUT command before executing the COMPUTE command.

The following examples illustrate the use of the COMPUTE command:

☐ To compute the average salary of employees from a column named *SALARY* in the *EMPLOYEE* table, type:

```
R>COMPUTE AVE SALARY FROM EMPLOYEE
SALARY   Average =                 $35,608.97
```

☐ To compute the sum of employee salaries and store the result in the variable *sumvar*, type:

```
R>COMPUTE sumvar AS SUM SALARY FROM EMPLOYEE
R>SHOW VAR sumvar
          $1,388,750.00
```

□ To find the employee whose first name would appear last in an alphabetic list, type:

```
R>COMPUTE MAX FRSTNAME FROM EMPLOYEE
FRSTNAME Maximum =  Wayne
```

□ To find the employee whose first name would appear first in an alphabetic list, type:

```
R>COMPUTE MIN FRSTNAME FROM EMPLOYEE
FRSTNAME Minimum =  Adele
```

□ To count the number of rows in the *EMPLOYEE* table, type:

```
R>COMPUTE ROWS IN EMPLOYEE
        Rows =              39
```

□ To compute all statistics for employee salaries, type:

```
R>COMPUTE ALL SALARY FROM EMPLOYEE
SALARY   Count =            39
         Rows =             39
         Minimum =            $19,800.00
         Maximum =            $55,000.00
         Sum =             $1,388,750.00
         Average =            $35,608.97
         Std Dev =             $9,050.05
         Variance =       $81,903,316.90
```

□ To compute a proposed contribution of 5% of the total salary outlay and to store this result in a variable named *contrib*, type:

```
R>COMPUTE contrib AS SUM (0.05 * SALARY) FROM EMPLOYEE
R>SHOW VAR contrib
                $69,437.50
```

These are just a few of the possibilities available with the COMPUTE command.

■ **Comments**

If you perform a particular calculation frequently, you might find it easier to use a computed column rather than the COMPUTE command.

■ **R:BASE 5000 equivalent**

The COMPUTE command in R:BASE 5000 cannot use expressions with columns (as in the last example above), nor can it perform standard deviation (STD) or variance (VAR) functions. Otherwise, the syntax and operation of COMPUTE in R:BASE 5000 are identical to those in R:BASE System V.

CONFIG.SYS file

■ **Description**

The *CONFIG.SYS* file is a file that you create to modify MS-DOS system options. The file must reside in the root directory of your computer's startup or "boot" drive (usually drive C). When you start your computer, either with the power switch or the Ctrl-Alt-Del key combination, the operating system (MS-DOS) is loaded into memory. MS-DOS then looks for a *CONFIG.SYS* file. If one exists, MS-DOS executes the configuration commands contained in the file. Otherwise, MS-DOS uses its own default configuration settings.

■ **Procedure**

Normally you create a *CONFIG.SYS* file with a text editor such as EDLIN or with a word processor in ASCII file mode. When you install R:BASE, however, the Install program either creates a *CONFIG.SYS* file or edits the existing one to include the FILES configuration command. The FILES command specifies the maximum number of file handles that may be open at one time. R:BASE sets this number to 20. File handles allocate blocks of memory from which files may be accessed. If you ever get an *Out of File Handles* error message while in R:BASE, your *CONFIG.SYS* file has probably been deleted or altered.

The BUFFERS configuration command also can affect the performance of R:BASE. The BUFFERS command sets the number of memory buffers, which temporarily store data being read from or written to a disk. The default setting for BUFFERS is *two* for the IBM PC-XT and *three* for the IBM PC-AT (this value varies depending on the make and model of your computer and the version of MS-DOS you are using). For database applications, the MS-DOS user's manual recommends a BUFFERS setting between 10 and 20.

Note that R:BASE can operate with file handle values greater than 20. If you have another software product that requires a FILES value of 30, for example, R:BASE can operate at that setting without any problems. This also applies to the BUFFERS settings. However, with buffer values over 30, R:BASE might run more slowly.

Other available configuration command options are described in your MS-DOS user's manual.

Caution: If you are installing R:BASE System V on a local area network, be sure that you do not modify the existing configuration commands that the network requires.

Conversion functions

■ **Description**

Conversion functions change or temporarily convert the data type or modify the way the data value is displayed.

■ **Procedure**

The following conversion functions are available:

Function	Description
AINT (*real*)	Truncates a *real* number to its integer portion (the data type remains *real*).
ANINT (*real*)	Rounds a *real* number to the nearest integer (the data type remains *real*).
INT (*real*)	Truncates a *real* number to its integer portion and changes its data type to *integer*.
NINT (*real*)	Rounds a *real* number to the nearest integer and changes the data type to *integer*.
FLOAT (*integer*)	Changes the data type of a number from *integer* to *real*.
CTXT (*arg*)	Changes a nontext value to a character string.
ICHAR (*chr*)	Changes a character to its ASCII integer value.
CHAR (*integer*)	Changes an ASCII integer value to its corresponding character.

■ **Database example**

Many applications do not require precise numeric values. For example, suppose you wanted to calculate an employee bonus based on years of employment. You might want the number of years rounded to the nearest integer. Consider the following computed column:

```
YEARS = (NINT((.#DATE - HIREDATE)/365))
```

NINT() rounds the number of years of employment to the nearest integer and changes the data type of *YEARS* from real to integer.

The *ANINT()* function performs the same function as *NINT()* except that the resulting value remains a real number. Use this function to store the result in a variable or column that has been defined as real.

The *INT()* and *AINT()* functions are similar to the round-off functions *NINT()* and *ANINT()*, except that they simply truncate to the integer portion of the number. *INT()* and *AINT()* perform the same function but return integer and real values respectively. For example:

ANINT (1.7) = 2
AINT (1.7) = 1

Only a generous employer would use the *NINT()* or *ANINT()* function to round the years of employment because all employees who work more than six months would be counted as having worked a year. A more conservative employer would use the *INT()* or *AINT()* function, thus requiring all employees to have worked at least one year to become eligible for a bonus.

The *FLOAT()* function changes an integer data type to a real data type. Use this function if you want to store the result in a variable or column defined as a real data type.

■ Program example

A popular show-and-tell routine is a program that displays the extended ASCII character set. The following command file does this using the *CTXT()* and *CHAR()* conversion functions:

```
SET VAR vinc INTEGER
SET VAR vinc = 32
SET VAR vrow = 2
SET VAR vcol = 1
NEWPAGE
WRITE "ASCII CODE (IBM PC) from Decimal 33 to 255" AT 1,15
WHILE vinc GE 32 AND vinc LT 255 THEN
  SET VAR vrow = 2
    WHILE vrow LT 23 THEN
      SET VAR vrow = vrow + 1
      SET VAR vinc = .vinc + 1
      SET VAR vchar = (CHAR(.vinc))
      SET VAR vascnum = (CTXT(.vinc))
      SET VAR vchar = (.vascnum & .vchar)
      SHOW VAR vchar AT .vrow,.vcol
        IF vinc GE 255 THEN
          BREAK
          ENDIF
    ENDWHILE
  SET VAR vcol = .vcol + 7
ENDWHILE
WRITE "press any key to continue" AT 24,1
PAUSE
```

58

Before looking at the command file in detail, here is the result of executing it:

```
                  ASCII CODE (IBM PC) from Decimal 33 to 255

 33 !   54 6   75 K   96     117 u  138 è  159 ƒ  180 ┤   201 ╔   222 ▐   243 ≤
 34 "   55 7   76 L   97 a   118 v  139 ï  160 á  181 ╡   202 ╩   223 ▀   244 ⌠
 35 #   56 8   77 M   98 b   119 w  140 î  161 í  182 ╢   203 ╦   224 α   245 ⌡
 36 $   57 9   78 N   99 c   120 x  141 ì  162 ó  183 ╖   204 ╠   225 β   246 ÷
 37 %   58 :   79 O   100 d  121 y  142 Ä  163 ú  184 ╕   205 =   226 Γ   247 ≈
 38 &   59 ;   80 P   101 e  122 z  143 Å  164 ñ  185 ╣   206 ╬   227 π   248 °
 39 '   60 <   81 Q   102 f  123 {  144 É  165 Ñ  186 ║   207 ╧   228 Σ   249 ·
 40 (   61 =   82 R   103 g  124 |  145 æ  166 ª  187 ╗   208 ╨   229 σ   250 ·
 41 )   62 >   83 S   104 h  125 }  146 Æ  167 º  188 ╝   209 ╤   230 µ   251 √
 42 *   63 ?   84 T   105 i  126 ~  147 ô  168 ¿  189 ╜   210 ╥   231 τ   252 ⁿ
 43 +   64 @   85 U   106 j  127 ⌂  148 ö  169 ⌐  190 ╛   211 ╙   232 Φ   253 ²
 44 ,   65 A   86 V   107 k  128 Ç  149 ò  170 ¬  191 ┐   212 ╘   233 θ   254 ■
 45 -   66 B   87 W   108 l  129 ü  150 û  171 ½  192 └   213 ╒   234 Ω   255
 46 .   67 C   88 X   109 m  130 é  151 ù  172 ¼  193 ┴   214 ╓
 47 /   68 D   89 Y   110 n  131 â  152 ÿ  173 ¡  194 ┬   215 ╫
 48 0   69 E   90 Z   111 o  132 ä  153 Ö  174 «  195 ├   216 ╪
 49 1   70 F   91 [   112 p  133 à  154 Ü  175 »  196 ─   217 ┘
 50 2   71 G   92 \   113 q  134 å  155 ¢  176 ░  197 ┼   218 ┌
 51 3   72 H   93 ]   114 r  135 ç  156 £  177 ▒  198 ╞   219 █
 52 4   73 I   94 ^   115 s  136 ê  157 ¥  178 ▓  199 ╟   220 ▄
 53 5   74 J   95 _   116 t  137 ë  158 ₧  179 │  200 ╚   221 ▌   242 ≥
 press any key to continue
```

The *CHAR()* function changes the integer value of *vinc* to its corresponding ASCII character. The result is stored in the variable *vchar*. The *CTXT()* function changes *vinc* to a text value, *vascnum*, which is then linked with *vchar* to form a new value of *vchar*. The *vinc* integer value could be used in the table rather than *vascnum* except that it would generate trailing blanks and the entire set couldn't be displayed on one screen.

The final value of *vchar* contains both the text value of the integer and its corresponding character, which is displayed at the coordinates *vrow, vcol*. Each time *vrow* reaches 23, *vcol* is incremented and control passes to the main *WHILE* loop. *vrow* is then set back to 2 and the inside *WHILE* loop executes again. This continues until *vinc* reaches 255, at which point the program terminates.

ICHAR() performs the opposite function of *CHAR()*. For example,

```
ICHAR(A)
```

returns the ASCII integer value of the letter *A*: 65.

See: *Functions*

See also: *Arithmetic and mathematical functions, Date and time functions, Financial functions, Logical functions,* and *Trigonometric functions*

■ **R:BASE 5000 equivalent**
None

Converting from different R:BASE versions

Database files from R:BASE 4000, R:BASE 5000, and R:BASE System V are not completely compatible with each other. Files from one version of R:BASE must be converted in order to use them with another version.

Before you convert files from one version of R:BASE to use them with another version, be sure that none of your existing column, table, or variable names are *reserved words* in the other version of R:BASE. These words are reserved as part of the R:BASE command syntax. For example, the word *RATE* is a reserved word in R:BASE System V, but not in R:BASE 5000. If you have a column called RATE in the R:BASE 5000 database that you are converting to R:BASE System V, you must first change the column name to some other non-reserved word. See the list of R:BASE System V reserved words in tables 1-8 and 1-9 of the R:BASE System V User's Manual.

Caution· Before you convert your database, be sure to make a complete and up-to-date backup copy. The importance of this precaution cannot be overemphasized.

After you make the conversion (but before you delete the old database), be sure that the newly converted database operates as expected and that the data was properly transferred. You should pay particular attention to forms, reports, and rules.

Converting files from R:BASE 5000 to R:BASE System V: The CONVERT program provided with R:BASE System V provides the easiest method of converting databases. To use CONVERT, you need enough disk space to accommodate the newly converted copy of your database. If your hard disk does not have enough space for both the R:BASE 5000 database and the converted database, first copy the R:BASE 5000 database to a floppy disk and then delete it from your hard disk. Now the database on the floppy disk can be converted to an R:BASE System V version on the hard disk. (If your database is too large for a floppy disk, see the discussion below.)

The CONVERT program converts the specified R:BASE 5000 database to a R:BASE System V database in the *current directory.* Therefore, be sure that the current directory is the one in which you want to install the converted database. Copy the CONVERT program into the current directory, then issue the following command:

```
CONVERT d:\path\dbname
```

where *dbname* is the name of the R:BASE 5000 database. (The drive and path specifiers are necessary only if the R:BASE 5000 database is on a different drive or directory.) This command creates an R:BASE System V database with the same name in the current directory. Note that the *.RBS* extensions of R:BASE 5000 files are changed to the *.RBF* file extensions of R:BASE System V database files by the CONVERT program.

What if your R:BASE 5000 database is too large to fit on a floppy disk and you don't have enough room on the hard disk? The R:BASE System V documentation recommends using the UNLOAD command to perform the conversion process. An easier method is to make a copy of your R:BASE 5000 database that contains only the database structure, forms, reports, and rules. First, open the R:BASE 5000 database and use the UNLOAD DATA FOR *tablename* command to copy the data in each of the tables (excluding the forms, reports, and rules tables) onto floppy disks.

Next, delete all the rows in the tables (again, excluding the forms, reports, and rules tables). Use the DELETE command with an *EXISTS* operator in the *WHERE* clause. For example,

```
DELETE ROWS FROM EMPLOYEE WHERE ID-NUM EXISTS
```

deletes all the rows in the EMPLOYEE table in which an I.D. number exists. After you delete all the rows, pack the database (See *PACK*).

Now, use the CONVERT program to convert this database into a R:BASE System V database as described above. Finally, use the INPUT command to re-load the data into the new R:BASE System V database from the floppies you used with the UNLOAD command.

If, for some reason, you must convert from R:BASE System V to R:BASE 5000, use FileGateway to export the R:BASE System V data files into ASCII format and then use the R:BASE 5000 version of FileGateway to import the ASCII file. Note: You must create a compatible database structure in R:BASE 5000 before you begin the conversion.

Converting files from R:BASE 4000 to R:BASE System V: Use the CONVERT program as described above to convert your R:BASE 4000 database. Then delete the *RBSRULES* and *REPORTER* tables from the new database. R:BASE 4000 reports and rules tables cannot be used with R:BASE System V, so you will need to redefine them in the converted R:BASE System V database. You might also need to redesign your converted forms for R:BASE System V, but this varies depending on the form.

Converting files from R:BASE 4000 to R:BASE 5000: R:BASE 5000 provides a command file (*CONVERT.CMD*) to convert R:BASE 4000 databases. The conversion process converts the R:BASE 4000 *RBSRULES* and *REPORTER* tables to R:BASE

5000 *RULES* and *REPORTS* tables. After you complete the conversion, you can delete the *RBSRULES* and *REPORTER* tables. To execute the conversion command file, load R:BASE 5000 and type:

```
RUN CONVERT.CMD
```

Specify the correct path in the above command if you are executing *CONVERT.CMD* from a drive or directory that is not the default drive or current directory. *CONVERT.CMD* prompts you for the name of the database to convert. (Again, specify the correct path for the database if it is not on the current directory or default drive.)

After the conversion is complete, check the report variables in your new database. Type REPORTS, then the name of the report, and select *Define* from the Reports menu. This lists your report variables on the screen. If the expressions of any variables are listed as *ERRORS*, re-enter the variable expression.

■ **Comment**

See *R:BASE 5000 commands* for more information about command differences between R:BASE System V and R:BASE 5000.

COPY

■ **Syntax**

```
COPY filespec1 filespec2
```

■ **Description**

The COPY command is similar to the MS-DOS COPY command. Use it to copy files as you would in MS-DOS. The standard MS-DOS wildcard characters, *?* and ***, also can be used in the filename specifier.

■ **Procedure**

The COPY command is most commonly used to copy database files to a set of back-up files. For example, to copy a database called *CONSULT* to a disk in drive B, issue the following command:

```
COPY CONSULT?.RBF B:
```

This command copies the three files, *CONSULT1.RBF*, *CONSULT2.RBF*, and *CONSULT3.RBF* (see the example in *Filenames and structure*), to drive B using the same filenames.

The COPY command can also copy database files to another set of files with different names. For example, you might want to duplicate a database structure in another database, or you simply might want to test a command file in a temporary database. To copy the database files with one command that uses wildcard characters, the new (target) name must have the same number of characters as the original (source) name. For example, the following command:

```
COPY CONSULT?.RBF TEMPDTA?.RBF
```

creates three files: *TEMPDTA1.RBF*, *TEMPDTA2.RBF*, and *TEMPDTA3.RBF*. You can now open a new database called *TEMPDTA*. However, the command:

```
COPY CONSULT?.RBF TEMP?.RBF
```

will not work properly because the target name is smaller than the source name. You will end up with one useless file called *TEMPU.RBF*.

You can also specify drives and paths for both the source and target files, as you would in MS-DOS.

■ **Comment**
If you enter a large amount of data into a database, use the COPY command frequently (see *BACKUP*). It's often convenient to set up a one-line command file or keyboard macro (see *RECORD* and *PLAYBACK*) that contains the COPY command, the name of the database you are working on, and the destination drive. If you use a command file, simply give the file a one-letter name. For example, a command file named *B* might contain the following command: COPY MYDATA?.RBF B:. Then, to back up your database, you need only exit the data entry form and type:

```
RUN B
```

See: *Command files* and *OPEN*

■ **R:BASE 5000 equivalent**
COPY

COUNT

■ **Syntax**

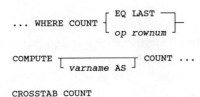

```
... WHERE COUNT ┌─ EQ LAST ─┐
               ┤           ├
               └─ op rownum ┘

COMPUTE ┌───────────┐ COUNT ...
        └ varname AS ┘

CROSSTAB COUNT
```

■ **Description**

The *COUNT* operator appears in *WHERE* clauses, in COMPUTE commands, and in CROSSTAB commands. In *WHERE* clauses, *COUNT* specifies the row numbers to be included in the *WHERE* condition. In the COMPUTE and CROSSTAB commands, the *COUNT* operator counts the number of entries or occurrences of the specified column item.

■ **Procedure**

In a *WHERE* clause, to specify that only row numbers greater than 100 should be included in an operation, type:

```
WHERE COUNT GT 100
```

To specify that only the last row should be included in an operation, type:

```
WHERE COUNT EQ LAST
```

Note that the math symbols =, <>, <, >, <=, >= can be substituted for the literal operands EQ, NE, LT, GT, LE, GE.

For detailed information on the use of *COUNT* with COMPUTE and CROSSTAB, see the entries for those commands.

■ **R:BASE 5000 equivalent**

COUNT

In *WHERE* clauses, *COUNT* serves the same function as it does in R:BASE System V, but it is limited to the *EQ rownum* or *EQ LAST* operations. Its function with the COMPUTE command is identical. R:BASE 5000 does not support the CROSSTAB command.

CROSSTAB

■ **Syntax**

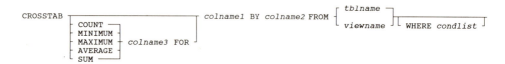

■ **Description**

The CROSSTAB command tabulates the occurrences of corresponding pairs of values from two columns in a table or view. CROSSTAB also computes a statistical result from a third column. This form of data inquiry is common in survey studies that tabulate the distribution of a certain quantity. Typically, one column represents the quantity (e.g., sex, age, race) and a second column represents the distribution criterion (e.g., city, state, department).

A familiar example of an application that uses cross-tabulation is the U.S. census. Among many other quantities, the U.S. census tabulates the ethnicity, age, sex, and economic distribution of the U.S. population according to city, county, and state. Using a command like CROSSTAB, this data can be represented in a chart.

You can use the following statistical functions with CROSSTAB:

Function	Description
AVE	Computes the average of numeric column values or of date and time values.
COUNT	Computes the number of entries in a column.
MAX	Computes the maximum numeric or alphabetic column value.
MIN	Computes the minimum numeric or alphabetic column value.
SUM	Computes the sum of numeric column values.

■ **Procedure**

A typical and simple application of the CROSSTAB command is an employment survey that displays the sex distribution in the office by department. This data inquiry involves two columns in the *EMPLOYEE* table: the *SEX* column and the *DEPT* column. In the syntax shown above, *colname1* would be *SEX* and *colname2* would be *DEPT*. Type:

```
CROSSTAB SEX BY DEPT FROM EMPLOYEE
```

to display the following:

```
DEPT    ¦ F        M        (Total)
--------¦--------  --------  --------
Admin   ¦    3         4          7
Dev     ¦    4         4          8
Mktg    ¦    3         3          6
Oper    ¦    2         3          5
Sls     ¦    8         2         10
Trn     ¦    1         2          3
--------¦--------  --------  --------
        ¦   21        18         39
R>
```

The numbers of males and females are displayed by department, as well as the totals for each department and for each sex.

You can also include a calculated statistic in a cross-tabulation. Suppose you want to determine the average salary according to sex in each department. Use the following command:

```
CROSSTAB AVERAGE SALARY FOR SEX BY DEPT FROM EMPLOYEE
```

to display the calculation:

```
DEPT    ┆ F                 M                 (Total)
------- ┆ ---------------   ---------------   ---------------
Admin   ┆    $24,200.00        $29,425.00        $27,185.71
Dev     ┆    $37,950.00        $38,500.00        $38,225.00
Mktg    ┆    $42,533.33        $36,483.33        $39,508.33
Oper    ┆    $35,750.00        $34,833.33        $35,200.00
Sls     ┆    $37,675.00        $36,850.00        $37,510.00
Trn     ┆    $33,000.00        $35,750.00        $34,833.33
------- ┆ ---------------   ---------------   ---------------
        ┆    $36,090.48        $35,047.22        $35,608.97
R>
```

Here, the *SALARY* column is arranged according to male and female employees, and the average value in each category is displayed. Note that the average totals are also displayed.

You can restrict the scope of the cross-tabulation by using a *WHERE* clause. For example, to compute the average salary for a specific age range in the last example, type:

```
CROSSTAB AVERAGE SALARY FOR SEX BY DEPT FROM /+
  EMPLOYEE WHERE BIRTH GT 12/31/42
```

This command computes the average salary according to sex and department, but only for employees born in 1943 or later.

■ **Comments**

The CROSSTAB command is one of the most powerful additions to the R:BASE command language and solves a major problem for database users: generating statistical results. In earlier versions of R:BASE and in most other popular database products for microcomputers, the cross-tabulation routines shown here require some fairly sophisticated programming.

Note that the TALLY command performs a similar function, but it is not the same as the CROSSTAB command. The TALLY command only counts unique occurrences in a single column.

■ **R:BASE 5000 equivalent**

None

Data security

■ **Description**

Unlike many database programs for microcomputers, R:BASE System V offers command options that permit you to limit access to your data. Without these commands, anyone can access and modify your database. Protecting your data from unauthorized use can be important: You may want to prevent unauthorized viewing of sensitive data (for example, payroll data), or you may want to restrict the activities of certain users (for example, temporary personnel).

■ **Procedure**

R:BASE offers three types of passwords:

☐ Database or owner password (OWNER command)

☐ Table modify password (PASSWORDS command followed by MPW)

☐ Table read-only password (PASSWORDS command followed by RPW)

You define passwords at the D> prompt in DEFINE mode or in Definition EXPRESS. Passwords can be as many as eight characters and can include blanks if the word is inside quotation marks. After passwords are defined, they control access to the database from Application EXPRESS, Definition EXPRESS, and FileGateway. In other words, you must specify the correct passwords to use these modules with tables that have passwords associated with them. Details for setting passwords in these modules are given in *Application EXPRESS, Definition EXPRESS*, and *FileGateway*.

Note, however, that data entry forms are not controlled by passwords defined for other tables, even if those tables are accessed by the form. You must define passwords for data entry forms in Forms EXPRESS or in DEFINE mode. Similarly, you can assign passwords to the REPORTS table. You can use the same password for multiple tables.

Owner passwords: You define the owner password with the OWNER command in the DEFINE mode or in Definition EXPRESS. If a database already has an owner password defined, the following commands will work only after you enter the correct password: DEFINE, RELOAD, UNLOAD, EXPAND, REDEFINE, REMOVE COLUMN, REMOVE. These commands allow you to modify the database structure, including deleting or changing the password. Therefore, only those persons responsible for managing the design and operation of the database should have access to the owner password. The equivalents of these commands in Definition EXPRESS and FileGateway also require an owner password. Enter the password with the USER command at the R> prompt or at the appropriate prompt in a menu-driven application.

Table passwords: You must define an owner password before you define table passwords. If you have not defined an owner password, the table passwords are ignored. You define table passwords with the PASSWORDS command in the DEFINE mode or in Definition EXPRESS. Table passwords allow you to restrict access to individual tables. This is convenient if you need to provide unlimited access to certain tables but want to restrict access to others. Table passwords are also entered with the USER command.

There are two types of table passwords: modify (MPW) and read-only (RPW). If a table requires a modify-table password, you must enter this password before you can change any data. If a table requires a read-only table password, you must enter the password before you can display the data in the table. If both modify and read-only table passwords are defined, the table will not be displayed when you issue a LIST command until the OWNER password is entered.

See: *DEFINE, Definition EXPRESS, OWNER,* and *PASSWORDS*

See also: *USER*

Caution: Always write down your owner password and keep it in a safe place! If you cannot remember the owner password, you cannot modify a protected database without assistance from Microrim.

■ **Comments**

Although R:BASE System V offers more protection than most microcomputer database programs, the level of protection does not compare with security measures on mini and mainframe computers and on some other microcomputer operating systems. This lack of security is not a flaw in R:BASE, but rather it is inherent in the MS-DOS operating system.

Despite all the password protection available in R:BASE, someone could simply delete the entire database from either the DOS prompt or with the DELETE command in R:BASE. Or, someone could playfully or maliciously rename the database. In other words, if someone wants to sabotage your work, he or she can do it despite the elaborate password scheme in R:BASE.

Here are some suggestions for protecting your databases:

☐ Use the MS-DOS ATTRIB command (MS-DOS 3.0 and later versions) to make your backup database files read-only (see your MS-DOS manual for details). Keep in mind, however, that you cannot open a database whose files are assigned the read-only attribute, nor can you copy data to read-only files. You must reset the file attribute to copy new data to the backup files or to use the files in R:BASE. For further protection, keep the *ATTRIB.COM* file on a separate disk.

☐ For applications requiring a high level of security, use the options in Application EXPRESS that prevent a user from exiting to the R> prompt with the Escape key. This denies the user access to the R:BASE command language (see *Application EXPRESS*).

☐ Use an MS-DOS *AUTOEXEC.BAT* file to start R:BASE and use an *RBASE.DAT* initial file to start your R:BASE application. You also can set the last command in the *AUTOEXEC.BAT* file to change to a directory that does not contain sensitive data. (For more information, see your MS-DOS user's manual and *Application EXPRESS*.)

☐ Back up your database frequently, and store the backups in a safe place (see *Backing up data*).

These measures are not foolproof, but they will at least discourage an intruder, while helping you prevent accidental loss of your data.

Data types

Columns and variables in R:BASE are assigned data types that specify the kind of data that will be stored in them. You specify the column data types when you define the database structure. You can specify variables explicitly with the SET VARIABLE command, or implicitly, by setting the variable equal to an initial value. R:BASE then assigns the variable the data type represented by the initial value. For further information, see *Variables*.

R:BASE System V uses the following data types:

Data Type	Description
CURRENCY	Used for dollar or foreign currency amounts to a maximum of 23 digits. Each currency value uses eight bytes of storage space.
DATE	The default format is MM/DD/YY. Hyphens also can be used as delimiters. Date values use four bytes of storage.
DOUBLE	Double precision real numbers are useful in situations requiring a high degree of numeric accuracy. However, double precision values require twice the storage space (eight bytes) of single precision numbers. See *REAL* below. The range of double precision numbers is $\pm 10^{\pm 307}$
INTEGER	Whole numbers in the range of $\pm 999,999,999$. Each uses four bytes of storage.

(continued)

Data Type	Description
NOTE	Note columns can contain as many as 4092 characters of text. Note columns require a storage space of four bytes plus the number of bytes of text.
REAL	Real numbers are in single precision format in the range of $\pm 9.0 \times 10^{\pm 37}$. Single precision numbers require four bytes of storage. Numbers with more than six digits are displayed in scientific notation ($1.23456E-7$, for example).
TEXT	Text columns can contain as many as 1500 characters of text. The default column width is eight characters, and the required storage space varies with the specified column width.
TIME	The default time format is HH:MM:SS. The time value uses four bytes of storage.

Here are some general comments on selecting data types:

☐ If computations will not be performed on numeric data, use the TEXT data type. For example, Zip Codes are five-digit numbers, but you gain no advantage by specifying an integer data type for the Zip Code column. However, there are significant advantages to specifying a TEXT data type. First, you can specify a five-character column width, which helps reduce data entry errors. An integer column has a default width that you cannot change. Second, you can use character string functions (see *WHERE*) to extract certain Zip Codes, for example, all that start with *941*.

The same considerations apply to noncomputed numeric quantities such as ID numbers, phone numbers, and Social Security numbers.

☐ You cannot store values of one data type in a column or variable that was previously defined as a different data type. If you want to use a variable to hold a different data type, use the CLEAR command or the SET VARIABLE command to reset the data type.

You can change the data type of a column, but you run the risk of losing data if the previously defined data type cannot be converted to the new data type (i.e., if you try to change data from TEXT to a DATE data type).

Changes between integer, real, double, and currency data types work without problems. However, when you convert decimal values to the integer data type they are truncated to their integer value.

You also can convert text column values that consist of numbers to the integer data type. However, values containing alphabetic characters are converted to null values.

For further information about changing column data types, see *REDEFINE*.

☐ The NOTE data type is useful for storing large blocks of text such as memos or comments. Unlike the TEXT data type, the NOTE data type is a *variable length* column that stores the complete text rather than a specified column width. Note, however, that the NOTE data type cannot be used in expressions.

See: *Columns, Database structure, Date and time arithmetic, Definition EXPRESS, Expressions, REDEFINE, SET characters and keywords,* and *Variables*

■ **R:BASE 5000 data types**
R:BASE 5000 does not support the DOUBLE and NOTE data types. The CURRENCY data type is called DOLLAR in R:BASE 5000.

Database structure

■ **Description**
The database structure (also called the schema) consists of the definitions of all the columns and tables of your database. If you execute the LIST ALL command, the structure of your database is displayed. Consider the following output from the LIST ALL command:

```
Table: PROPOSAL        No lock(s)
Read Password: No
Modify Password: No

Column definitions
# Name      Type      Length          Key    Expression
1 PROPNUM   INTEGER
2 DESCRIPT  TEXT      25 characters
3 AMOUNT    CURRENCY
4 PROB      REAL
5 CLINUM    INTEGER

Current number of rows:      4

Table: CLIENT          No lock(s)
Read Password: No
Modify Password: No

Column definitions
# Name      Type      Length          Key    Expression
1 CLINUM    INTEGER
2 CLINAME   TEXT      25 characters
3 STREET    TEXT      25 characters
4 CITY      TEXT      20 characters
5 STATE     TEXT       2 characters
6 ZIP       TEXT       5 characters
7 PHONE     TEXT      12 characters

Current number of rows:      5
```

(continued)

```
Table: FORMS            No lock(s)
Read Password: No
Modify Password: No

Column definitions
# Name      Type     Length          Key     Expression
1 FNAME     TEXT        8 characters yes
2 FDATA     TEXT       46 characters

Current number of rows:      42

Table: REPORTS          No lock(s)
Read Password: No
Modify Password: No

Column definitions
# Name      Type     Length          Key     Expression
1 RNAME     TEXT        8 characters yes
2 RDATA     TEXT       80 characters

Current number of rows:      37
```

Each table in the database is listed along with the characteristics of each column in that table. Note the FORMS and REPORTS tables. These are tables supplied by R:BASE when you create a data entry form or a report. For additional information about these tables, see *Tables and TABLES*.

You can back up the database structure with either the BACKUP or UNLOAD command. The database structure is stored in the file *dbname1.rbf*, where *dbname* is the database name. Never separate this file from the other two *.RBF* files that make up the database (see *Filenames and structure*).

For more information on designing the database structure, see *Definition EXPRESS* and *DEFINE*.

See also: *BACKUP, Columns, EXPAND, RBDEFINE, RELOAD, REMOVE, RENAME,* and *UNLOAD*

Date and time arithmetic

Operations involving dates and time are performed with the DATE and TIME data types and the system variables, *#DATE* and *#TIME*. R:BASE System V also provides a comprehensive set of date and time functions that are described in a separate entry (see *Date and time functions*). The default date and time formats are MM/DD/YY and HH:MM:SS. See *Date and time functions* and *SET characters and keywords* for information about alternative date and time formats.

The system variables, *#DATE* and *#TIME*, store the current date and time as set by your computer system. Whether you manually enter the current date and time or have a clock/calendar installed in your computer, it's important to ensure that your system operates with the current date and time. Otherwise, the system variables will contain incorrect values.

These system variables can be treated like any other variable in R:BASE. To check the current date and time, use the SHOW VAR command:

```
SHOW VAR #DATE
SHOW VAR #TIME
```

Entering these commands displays the date and time respectively.

A useful application of *#DATE* and *#TIME* is the *stamping* of the date or time on information when it is entered into the database. If you need to know the date when information was entered, include a computed column in your table that records the system date in each new row.

For example, let's say you have a table for creating client invoices. As each invoice is entered, you also can have R:BASE enter today's date in an associated computed column. Here is the table structure for the *INVOICE* table:

```
Table: INVOICE           No lock(s)
Read Password: No
Modify Password: No

Column definitions
# Name      Type      Length        Key    Expression
1 CLINUM    INTEGER                 yes
2 INV-NUM   TEXT       8 characters
3 ENTRDATE  DATE                           .#DATE
4 DUE       CURRENCY
5 PREVBAL   CURRENCY
6 TOTAL     CURRENCY                       'prevbal' + 'due'
7 FORWHAT   TEXT      50 characters
8 PAID      TEXT       1 characters

Current number of rows:       4
```

Note that the third column, the *ENTRDATE* column, is a computed column that stores the value of *#DATE* (indicated by the period in front of *#DATE*; see *Variables*). As each row is entered, the current value of *#DATE* is automatically stored in the *ENTRDATE* column.

With the date stamped on each invoice row, you can easily keep track of overdue bills. For example, you could check which invoices are unpaid and more than 30 days old by typing the following SELECT command:

```
SELECT CLINUM ENTRDATE TOTAL FROM INVOICE WHERE +
(.#DATE - ENTRDATE) > 30 AND PAID FAILS
```

Entering this displays the following:

```
CLINUM    ENTRDATE TOTAL
---------- -------- ----------------
       47 09/06/86     $6,290.00
       35 09/06/86     $2,065.00
```

In this example, the expression (.*#DATE* − *ENTRDATE*) > 30 tells R:BASE to subtract the value stored in *ENTRDATE* from the current system date. If the result is greater than 30, and the *PAID* column *FAILS* (for example, has a null value), the invoice meets the selection criteria that labels it as overdue. The above SELECT command would be even more convenient if it were stored in a keyboard macro (see *PLAYBACK* and *RECORD*).

The above example illustrates one form of date arithmetic, in which one date value is subtracted from another. You can also add or subtract integers to and from date or time values. Integers represent the number of days in date operations and the number of seconds in time operations. Here are two examples of date and time computations:

Type:

```
R>SET VAR duedate = (.#DATE + 30)
R>SHOW VAR duedate
09/15/87
```

to display the date 30 days from the current date.

Type:

```
R>SHOW VAR #TIME
13:54:58
```

to display the time. Then, type:

```
R>SET VAR newtime = (.#TIME + 600 )
R>SHOW VAR newtime
14:05:07
```

to display the new time.

In each case, we add days or seconds to an existing date or time value. Note that in the second example, we add 10 minutes (600 seconds) to the system time. The difference between the displayed values of *#TIME* and the variable *newtime* is not exactly 10 minutes because of the time that elapsed between issuing the commands.

■ **R:BASE 5000 equivalent**

R:BASE 5000 also provides the system variables *#DATE* and *#TIME* and similar date and time arithmetic. However, since R:BASE 5000 does not support computed columns (see *Columns*), more programming is required to accomplish tasks such as date stamping.

Date and time functions

Date and time functions serve two main purposes:

☐ they convert integers to date or time format; and

☐ they extract part of a date or time, such as the day of the week or the number of seconds.

R:BASE System V provides 8 date functions and 4 time functions. There are more date functions simply because there are more ways to express the date.

Date functions: The *RDATE()* function (month,day,year) converts the integer values within parentheses to the R:BASE internal date format (MM/DD/YY). For example, *RDATE(1,1,85)* becomes 01/01/85.

IDAY(), *IMON()*, and *IYR()* extract the integer value from the date for the day, month, and year respectively. *IDWK()* extracts an integer for the day of the week based on *one* for Monday, *two* for Tuesday, and so on. *TDWK()* and *TMON()* extract the text day of the week and the text name for the month, respectively. Finally, *JDATE()* extracts the Julian date for 1900-1999 only. All of these functions are illustrated in the following command file:

```
SET ECHO OFF
SET VAR vdate TO .#DATE       *(Initialize variable vdate)
WHILE vdate EXISTS THEN
  NEWPAGE
  FILLIN vdate USING "PLEASE ENTER A DATE (mm/dd/yy): " AT 5,5
  IF vdate FAILS THEN
    BREAK
  ENDIF
  *(Set date function variables)
  SET VAR vjdate = (JDATE(.vdate))
  SET VAR vday = (IDAY(.vdate))
  SET VAR vmon = (IMON(.vdate))
  SET VAR vyr = (IYR(.vdate))
  SET VAR vweek = (TDWK(.vdate))
  SET VAR vmonth = (TMON(.vdate))
  SET VAR vweeknum = (IDWK(.vdate))
  *(Concatenate vweek and vmonth)
  SET VAR daymonth = (.vweek + "," & . vmonth )
  WRITE "This date is " AT 7,5
  SHOW VAR daymonth AT 7,18   *(Display day of week and month)
  SHOW VAR vday AT 7,38       *(Display integer for day)
  WRITE "," AT 7,48
  SHOW VAR vyr AT 7,50        *(Display integer for year)
  WRITE "In Julian format, this date is: " AT 9,5
  SHOW VAR vjdate AT 9,37     *(Display Julian date)
  WRITE "It is month number " AT 11,5
  SHOW VAR vmon AT 11,25      *(Display month number)
  WRITE "The day of the week is number" AT 13,5
  SHOW VAR vweeknum AT 13,34  *(Display weekday number)
  WRITE "Press any key to continue" AT 15,3
  PAUSE
ENDWHILE
```

Here is an example of the output from this command file:

```
PLEASE ENTER A DATE (mm/dd/yy): 12/25/87

This date is Friday, December          25,        1987

In Julian format, this date is:     87359

It is month number          12

The day of the week is number          5
```

Press any key to continue

The Julian date format reports the year as the first two digits and the day number of the year as the last three digits. (In the above example, December 25 is the 359th day of the year.) The Julian date is available only for the twentieth century. If you input an earlier or later date, the Julian date function displays a null value.

Time functions: The time functions, *IHR()*, *IMIN()*, and *ISEC()*, simply display the integer value for hours, minutes, and seconds respectively. *RTIME(hours, minutes, seconds)* converts the integers within the parentheses to the internal R:BASE time format (HH:MM:SS). For more information about time formats, see *SET characters and keywords*.

Running the following command file demonstrates the use of all four time functions:

```
SET ECHO ON        *(Displays each line as it executes)
SHOW VAR #TIME     *(Display current time)
17:53:10
SET VAR vhour = IHR(.#TIME)  *(Store the hour in variable vhour)
SHOW VAR vhour               *(Display vhour)o
        17
SET VAR vmin = IMIN(.#TIME)  *(Store minutes in variable vmin)
SHOW VAR vmin                *(Display vmin)
        53
SET VAR vsec = ISEC(.#TIME)  *(Store seconds in variable vsec)
SHOW VAR vsec                *(Display vsec)
        10
CHKDSK                       *(Execute CHKDSK to see how long it
                               takes to complete)

  30203904 bytes total disk space
  17485824 bytes available on disk

    655360 bytes total memory
    129456 bytes free
SET VAR elapsed =  .#TIME - RTIME(.vhour,.vmin,.vsec)
SHOW VAR elapsed
        1
 Switching input back to keyboard
R>
```

The elapsed time for the completion of CHKDSK is about 1 second, depending on the type of computer you are using. Note that R:BASE cannot report times in fractions of a second. Any time value less than one second is reported as 0.

You can time any R:BASE operation by using the above command file and simply changing the command to be timed. This capability is useful for testing the performance of various approaches to extracting data from a table, for example. To do this, we can simplify the above command sequence:

```
SET VAR oldtime = .#TIME
CHKDSK                                    *(Time the CHKDSK command)
SET VAR elapsed = .#TIME - .oldtime
SHOW VAR elapsed
```

You also can transform the command line for CHKDSK into a variable expression so that you can enter any command when you execute the command file. For an illustration of this, see *RUN*.

■ **R:BASE 5000 equivalent**
None

DEFINE

■ **Syntax**

```
DEFINE ⌈        ⌉
        ⌊ dbspec ⌋
```

■ **Description**
DEFINE is more accurately described as a command *mode* than as a command. In DEFINE mode, you not only define the columns and tables of your database, but you also define additional characteristics and specific functions, including optional rules and passwords.

For more information about database design, see *Definition EXPRESS*.

■ **Procedure**
To enter DEFINE mode, type DEFINE at the R> prompt. At the D> prompt, you can then enter commands to define your database, line by line, according to the DEFINE mode command structure. The following commands are valid in DEFINE mode:

```
COLUMNS
OWNER
PASSWORDS
RULES
TABLES
END (end DEFINE mode and return to R> prompt)
```

The following example shows the definition of the *INVOICE* table in the *CONSULT* database:

```
R>DEFINE CONSULT
 Database exists
 Begin R:BASE Database Definition
D>OWNER none
D>COLUMNS
D>CLINUM    INTEGER KEY
D>INV-NUM   TEXT 8
D>ENTRDATE =.#DATE
D>DUE       CURRENCY
D>PREVBAL   CURRENCY
D>TOTAL = 'PREVBAL' + DUE
D>FORWHAT   TEXT 50
D>PAID      TEXT 1
D>TABLES
D>INVOICE WITH CLINUM INV-NUM ENTRDATE DUE PREVBAL TOTAL +
D>FORWHAT PAID
D>PASSWORDS
D>RPW FOR INVOICE  IS NONE
D>MPW FOR INVOICE  IS NONE
D>RULES
D>"Client # does not exist in CLIENT table" CLINUM IN INVOICE +
D>EQA CLINUM IN CLIENT
D>END
 End R:BASE Database Definition
R>
```

Command lines following a valid DEFINE mode command are interpreted as part of that command until another valid DEFINE mode command is encountered. For example, the lines following the COLUMNS command are interpreted as column definitions until the TABLES command is encountered.

The definition of columns must precede the definition of tables. All columns must be associated with a table. In this example, a single table called *INVOICE*, which contains all the previously defined columns, was defined. You can define up to 80 tables and a total of 800 columns. If you are defining a new table in an existing database, you do not need to redefine existing columns that you wish to include in the new table.

The RULES command in the above example specifies that client numbers entered in the *INVOICE* table must match existing client numbers in the *CLIENT* table. For more information about the RULES command, see *RULES* and *Definition EXPRESS*.

■ **Comment**

A bit of R:BASE history might be helpful in understanding the use of DEFINE. DEFINE mode represents the original method of defining databases in R:BASE 4000. The problem with this approach is that DEFINE has virtually no method of error recovery if you make a mistake. You are faced with starting the definition over again.

Well aware of this, Microrim introduced Application EXPRESS with R:BASE 5000, which, in addition to generating menu-driven applications, allowed columns and tables to be defined using a convenient full-screen editing system. With this major improvement, DEFINE was needed only for defining passwords and rules.

R:BASE System V has rendered DEFINE essentially obsolete with the introduction of Definition EXPRESS. All the characteristics of a database can be defined from within Definition EXPRESS. Unless you enjoy terse, unforgiving command modes that have no error recovery, there is no reason to use DEFINE mode except for defining very small databases or for making minor changes, such as changing a password.

Despite this, R:BASE still uses DEFINE internally to create databases that you define with Definition EXPRESS and databases created from backed-up files or from FileGateway. Also, the UNLOAD and BACKUP commands store the database definition as a list of DEFINE mode commands.

■ **R:BASE 5000 equivalent**
DEFINE

Definition EXPRESS

■ **Syntax**
Select Definition EXPRESS from the RBSYSTEM menu.

You also can execute RBDEFINE at the R> prompt if you entered R:BASE from the System menu.

```
RBDEFINE ┌──────┐
         └ exec ┘
```

If you entered R:BASE from the MS-DOS prompt, you must exit R:BASE. You can then execute RBDEFINE from MS-DOS:

```
RBDEFINE ┌────┐ ┌─────┐ ┌─────┐ ┌─────┐ ┌─────┐ ┌──────┐
         └ -R ┘ └ -Fn ┘ └ -Bn ┘ └ -Mn ┘ └ -Tn ┘ └ exec ┘
```

The *-R* option suppresses display of the R logo. The *-F* and *-B* options modify the foreground and background colors if you are using a color monitor. *-M* and *-T* modify other monitor characteristics. (See the R:BASE System V Installation Guide for further information on monitor options.) The *exec* option lets you specify an *exec* file that runs when you start RBDEFINE (see *RECORD* and *PLAYBACK*).

■ **Description**

Definition EXPRESS provides a convenient menu-driven system that lets you assign and modify the characteristics and functions of your database. You can create or modify column and table definitions, database and table passwords, and data entry rules. From within Definition EXPRESS, you also can access Forms EXPRESS, Reports EXPRESS, and the MS-DOS commands that are supported by R:BASE.

Definition EXPRESS performs all of the functions of the DEFINE mode commands. For both novice and experienced users, it is generally more convenient to create and modify databases in Definition EXPRESS rather than in the DEFINE mode.

■ **Procedure**

Although creating a database with Definition EXPRESS is quite straightforward, database design can be complicated and requires careful consideration. Before we look at the details of Definition EXPRESS, here are some guidelines that can help you design a database:

Start with pencil and paper: Sketch the format and content of the reports you expect to produce from your database. Work through each report, writing down the names and data types of columns that you want to include. When defining text columns, allow enough space to accommodate the largest anticipated entry. However, do not make text columns unnecessarily large (see *Columns* and *Data types*).

Keep in mind that all output from the database can be considered a report. For example, an invoice is a type of report. Ask yourself, what columns will I need to produce such an invoice?

Ask questions: Write down the questions that you will ask the database. These questions are called *queries*. Determine if you will need computed columns to answer any of these queries. For example, a query requesting the age of an invoice requires a computed column that subtracts the invoice date from the current date (see *Date and time arithmetic*).

Group related columns into separate tables: Data that will change frequently should be grouped separately from data that is permanent. For example, clients' names and addresses should be grouped separately from invoice data. To see why, let's assume that paid invoices are deleted after one year. If a client's name and address are kept in the same table as the invoice data, you will also delete this client information when you delete the invoice.

Another reason to group names and addresses separately from invoices is to reduce the amount of data entry required. If a name and address are part of the invoice table, you will have to enter them every time there is a new invoice. If the name and address of the client are in a separate table, you can retrieve this data when you print the invoice (see *REPORTS, Relational commands,* and *VIEW*).

The client/invoice relationship is an example of the *one-to-many* relationship that is discussed in the R:BASE documentation. There can be many invoices for one client, but not many clients for one invoice.

Share columns to combine data: If you plan to combine data from separate tables, the tables must be related to each other with a common column. The invoice example above needs a common column in the *INVOICE* table and in the name/address (*CLIENT*) table. The best choice is a unique number, for example, the client number. The client name would be a bad choice because you may have several clients with the same name.

Now to the details that you'll need to implement your design. The key functions of Definition EXPRESS are shown below:

Key	*Description*
PgDn	Moves from table or view name to column names.
PgUp	Moves from column names to table or view name.
Tab	Moves right one column.
Shift-Tab	Moves left one column.
Home	Moves to first column.
End	Moves to first empty column.
Left/right arrow	Moves left or right one character.
Ins	Inserts a blank.
Del	Deletes a character.
Backspace	Erases the character to the left.
Ctrl-right arrow	Moves to end of column or table name.
Ctrl-left arrow	Moves to first space in a column or table name.
Enter	Enters name and moves right one column.
ESC	Enters name and ends table editing.
F1	Adds a blank column to the left of the current column.
F2	Deletes the current column.
F3	Displays the database structure.
F5	Discards all changes to the current column name.
Shift-F5	Discards all changes to the current table.
Ctrl-Break	Discards unsaved work.

Before you use Definition EXPRESS, take a look at its main menu:

```
                          Definition EXPRESS
      Copyright (C) 1983,1984,1985,1986 by Microrim, Inc. (Ver. 1.00 PC-DOS)

    ┌══════════════════Definition EXPRESS Main Menu══════════════════┐
    │         (1)  Define a new database                             │
    │         (2)  Modify an existing database definition            │
    │         (3)  DOS functions                                     │
    │         (4)  Exit from Definition EXPRESS                      │
    └────────────────────────────────────────────────────────────────┘
```

[ENTER] Choose   [F10] Help

When you select item *1* to create a new database, you are prompted for the database name (which must be seven letters or less) and then presented with a screen for specifying your first table. The screen for the *INVOICE* table is shown in the following figure:

```
Enter or change the column names

┌───────────┐    An asterisk (*) identifies key columns
│  INVOICE  │    A plus sign (+) identifies computed columns
└───────────┘

┌─────────┬─────────┬──────────┬──────────┬──────────┬──────────┬──────────┐
│*CLINUM  │ INV-NUM │ ENTRDATE │ DUE      │ PREVBAL  │ TOTAL    │ FORWHAT  │
├─────────┼─────────┼──────────┼──────────┼──────────┼──────────┼──────────┤
│ INTEGER │ TEXT  8 │+DATE     │ CURRENCY │ CURRENCY │+CURRENCY │ TEXT  50 │
├─────────┼─────────┼──────────┼──────────┼──────────┼──────────┼──────────┤
│         │         │          │          │          │          │          │
└─────────┴─────────┴──────────┴──────────┴──────────┴──────────┴──────────┘
    ┌══════════════════════Choose column data type══════════════════┐
    │  TEXT   DATE   NOTE   COMPUTED                                  │
    └────────────────────────────────────────────────────────────────┘
Enter expression value:
.#DATE
```

[ESC] Discard   [F3] Review   [F5] Reset value   [F10] Help   [Shift-F10] More
Database CONSULT --- Table invoice --- Column   3
```
```

The column *ENTRDATE* is a computed column that records the current date. Enter the expression for the computed column in the space provided when you select *computed column*. A computed column is indicated by a + (plus sign) preceding the data type description. (See *Columns* for more information about computed columns.)

The *CLINUM* column is a key column, which is indicated by an asterisk preceding the column name. When you define a column, you have the option to specify it as a key. Keys allow R:BASE to find information faster and can increase performance in operations involving the *WHERE* clause. (See *BUILD KEY* and *Keys*.)

When you complete the first table, press ESC to display the Database Definition menu:

```
╔══════════════════════Database Definition Menu═══════════════════════╗
║          (1)  Tables                                                 ║
║          (2)  Views                                                  ║
║          (3)  Passwords                                              ║
║          (4)  Rules                                                  ║
║          (5)  Forms                                                  ║
║          (6)  Reports                                                ║
║          (7)  Return to Definition EXPRESS Main Menu                 ║
╚══════════════════════════════════════════════════════════════════════╝



[ENTER] Choose    [ESC] Done    [F3] Review    [F10] Help
Database CONSULT
```

From this menu, you can add or modify the characteristics represented by the menu options. If your database requires several tables, your next step will be to add these tables to the database. The Database Definition menu is the first menu you see when you select *Modify an Existing Database Definition* from the Main menu.

Use the *Views* option to add a view to your database. A view is a combination of columns from a maximum of five tables. A view can be used only for displaying and querying data. Views are discussed in detail in the *VIEW* entry. An example of defining a view in Definition EXPRESS follows:

```
Choose a table to include in the view
```

| INVFORM | | | | | | |

PREVBAL	TOTAL	FORWHAT	PAID	CLINAME	STREET	
INVOICE	INVOICE	INVOICE	INVOICE	CLIENT	CLIENT	

INVOICE	CLIENT			

```
                        Choose the columns to include from CLIENT
      CITY  STATE  ZIP  PHONE  (Reset)
```

```
[ENTER] Choose    [ESC] Done    [F1] Insert    [F2] Delete    [Shift-F10] More
Database CONSULT --- View invform --- Column      11
```

The view, called *INVFORM*, combines columns from the *INVOICE* and *CLIENT* tables. Simply select the columns from each table that you want to include in the view. Tables combined in a view must have a common column.

To add or change database and table passwords, use the *Passwords* option. For more information about defining and modifying passwords, see *Data security*, *PASSWORDS*, and *OWNER*.

Use the *Rules* option to add rules that govern the range or type of data that may be entered in a specific table. For example, you might require that the client number entered in the *INVOICE* table have a corresponding number in the *CLIENT* table. This rule is important because we plan to retrieve the client name and address from the *CLIENT* table. If the client number does not exist in the *CLIENT* table, there's no point in entering an invoice in the *INVOICE* table. The rule definition screen for our example looks like this:

```
Rule message:  Client does not exist in client table
```

	Column	Table	Operator	Value/Column	Table
	CLINUM	INVOICE	EQA	CLINUM	CLIENT

```
══════════════════════Choose column to validate═══════════════
 CLINUM  INV-NUM  ENTRDATE  DUE  PREVBAL  TOTAL  FORWHAT  PAID
```

```
[ENTER] Choose    [ESC] Done    [F3] Review    [F10] Help
Database CONSULT --- Table invoice  --- Rule          1
```

First, enter the message that will appear if you break the rule (e.g., if you enter a client number that does not exist in the *CLIENT* table). Next, select the column and table that the rule will check. In the example, this is the *CLINUM* column in the *INVOICE* table. Then specify the rule that the column will be checked against. In this case, the value entered in the *CLINUM* column in the *INVOICE* table must equal (EQA) a *CLINUM* value in the *CLIENT* table. For more information about rules, see *RULES*. See also *WHERE* for a list of valid R:BASE operators (such as EQA) in conditional clauses.

The design of forms and reports is discussed in *FORMS* and *REPORTS*.

■ **Comments**

You also can use Definition EXPRESS to modify databases that contain data.

Caution: Modifications made in Definition EXPRESS can affect the integrity of your data. When you remove tables or columns, you delete the data in them. When you change columns to data types that are incompatible with existing data, you also delete the data. For example, changing a text column to a date column converts the data to null values.

Always be sure to back up the database before you make modifications (see *Backing up data*).

Note that you cannot modify existing column names in tables that are part of a view. You first must delete the view.

See: *DEFINE, DOS commands in R:BASE, EXPAND, OWNER, PASSWORDS, REDEFINE, RENAME, RULES,* and *VIEW*

■ **R:BASE 5000 equivalent**

You can define your database in the R:BASE 5000 version of Application EXPRESS. The interface is the same as in Definition EXPRESS, except that the capabilities in R:BASE 5000 are more limited. You cannot modify the characteristics of databases that contain data. In addition, views and computed columns are not supported. See *Application EXPRESS.*

DELETE

■ **Syntax**

```
DELETE DUPLICATES FROM tblname

DELETE KEY FOR colname IN tblname

                        ┌─ tblname WHERE condlist ─┐
DELETE ROWS FROM ───────┤                          ├───
                        └──────── #n ──────────────┘
```

■ **Description**

You can use the DELETE command in three ways:

☐ To delete duplicate rows from a table

☐ To delete a column key

☐ To delete selected rows from a table

A duplicate row is a row in which all column values identically match the column values in another row, including uppercase and lowercase characters (JONES and Jones are not identical values). Duplicate rows usually occur when you import data from disk files (see *FileGateway*), or after you execute the UNION or the JOIN command.

For information about column keys, see *Keys* and *BUILD KEY*. You can re-insert deleted keys with the BUILD KEY command.

You must specify the rows you want to delete with a *WHERE* clause, unless you are using DELETE with the SET POINTER command (the #*n* option).

- **Procedure**

  In contrast to similar functions in other database programs, the DELETE command in R:BASE actually deletes the row or key from the table. You cannot recover deleted rows. However, deleting rows will not decrease the size of your database files: To recover storage space from deleted rows, you must *pack* the database (see *PACK* and *RELOAD*).

  Here are some examples of how to use the DELETE command:

```
R>SELECT ALL FROM CLIENT
  CLINUM    CLINAME                 STREET                    CITY
  --------- ----------------------- ------------------------- ---------------
          1 Johnson and Anderson Co. 101 Howard Street        San Francisco
          2 Cal Gas and Electric    1000 Main Street          Oakland
          3 Power Research Associates 205 Elmwood Avenue       San Francisco
          4 Stone Construction Co.  100 Oak Street            Oakland
          5 Ohio Electric Power Co. 101 Birch Street          Cincinnati
          2 Cal Gas and Electric    1000 Main Street          Oakland
          3 Power Research Associates 205 Elmwood Avenue       San Francisco
          3 Power Research Associates 205 Elmwood Avenue       San Francisco
R>DELETE DUPLICATES FROM CLIENT
3 row(s) have been deleted from CLIENT
R>DELETE ROWS FROM CLIENT WHERE CLINUM EXISTS
5 row(s) have been deleted from CLIENT
R>DELETE KEY FOR CLINUM IN CLIENT
R>
```

  Note that the second DELETE command uses the EXISTS operator to delete all rows in the table.

- **Comments**

  Duplicate rows can wreak havoc in your database, particularly when you compile statistical information. You will get incorrect results from a table with duplicate rows. Check your data for duplicate rows periodically. The DELETE DUPLICATES command executes faster if at least one of the columns is a key column (see *Keys*).

  DELETE also can be used as an MS-DOS command (DELETE *filename*), but this usage is not documented in the R:BASE manual (see *ERASE* and *DOS commands in R:BASE*).

  Caution: Always back up your database before you use the DELETE commands.

  See: *BUILD KEY, ERASE, PACK,* and *REMOVE*

- **R:BASE 5000 equivalent**
  DELETE DUPLICATES
  DELETE KEY
  DELETE ROWS

DIR

■ **Syntax**

```
DIR filespec
```

■ **Description**

DIR displays the files in the specified drive and directory. The DIR command is virtually identical to the MS-DOS DIR command. You can use wildcard characters to display files with specific character strings, and you can specify drive or path designations to display files on drives or directories other than the default drive or current directory.

■ **Procedure**

Here are two examples of the DIR command that use wildcard characters:

```
R>DIR C:\RBFILES\*.EXE

Volume in drive C has no label
Directory of C:\RBFILES

RBASE     EXE   347808   7-18-86   3:26p
RBSYSTEM  EXE    13696   7-17-86  10:17a
RCONVERT  EXE    78848   7-15-86  10:21p
RBDEFINE  EXE   285184   7-17-86   4:35p
EXPRESS   EXE   259584   7-17-86  12:05p
FORMS     EXE   324320   7-18-86   5:06p
REPORTS   EXE   281424   7-17-86   5:39p
GATEWAY   EXE   332464   7-16-86   9:38a
CODELOCK  EXE    59904   7-15-86  10:12p
RBEDIT    EXE    48640   7-15-86  10:09p
UNLOAD    EXE    46646   7-11-86   8:05p
PROMGEN   EXE    15236   7-10-86   9:38a
DEFGEN    EXE    10634   6-24-86   7:51a
       13 File(s)   11251712 bytes free

R>
```

```
R>DIR TEST*.*

Volume in drive C has no label
Directory of C:\RBFILES\DATA

TEST            128   9-26-86   3:54p
TEST1     RBF  1277  10-15-86   2:43p
TEST2     RBF     1  10-15-86   2:43p
TEST3     RBF     1  10-15-86   2:43p
        4 File(s)   11251712 bytes free

R>
```

The first example displays all files in the *RBFILES* directory that have the extension *.EXE*; the second displays all files starting with *TEST*. Issuing the DIR command without file or drive specifiers displays all the files in the current directory.

The DIR command output is identical to the output from the MS-DOS DIR command and includes the file size in bytes, the date and time of the last modification, the total number of files, and the available disk space.

See: *DOS commands in R:BASE*

■ **R:BASE 5000 equivalent**
DIR

DISPLAY

■ **Syntax**

```
DISPLAY scrnname ┬──────────────┬
                 └ IN procfile ┘
```

■ **Description**
The DISPLAY command displays a block of text on the screen. In the command's structure, *scrnname* can be either an ASCII text file or a screen block in a procedure file (*procfile*) created by CodeLock. (ASCII text files can also be displayed with the TYPE command.)

■ **Procedure**
The primary purpose of the DISPLAY command is to display information that requires no response. A help screen is an example of the kind of text you would display with the DISPLAY command. Use the CHOOSE or the FILLIN command to display menus or other messages that require a response.

Note that Application EXPRESS provides a convenient option that lets you include help screens in applications. You might find Application EXPRESS more convenient for some tasks.

■ **Example**
When requested, this command file displays a help screen:

```
CLS
SET VAR dchoice TO N
FILLIN dchoice USING "Do you need help? (Y or N): " AT 5,5
IF dchoice EQ "Y" THEN
  DISPLAY DISPLAY.TXT
  PAUSE
ENDIF
```

The Help menu text is stored in the file *DISPLAY.TXT*. Executing this command file displays the following screen:

```
Do you need help? (Y or N): Y



                     Help Screen

This is a database for consultants who need to keep track of client
proposals, invoices and personnel. If you have never used this data-
base before, please enter your ID Number at the prompt.

Press any key to continue.
```

Note that *Press any key to continue* is part of the display text. The PAUSE command in the command file tells R:BASE to display the text until a key is pressed (see *PAUSE*).

The text file also can be incorporated into a procedure as a screen block. (For details, see *Procedure files* and *CodeLock*.)

See: *CHOOSE, FILLIN, TYPE,* and *WRITE*

■ **R:BASE 5000 equivalent**
DISPLAY *scrnname IN procfile* AT *scrnrow*

The *AT scrnrow* clause lets you specify the screen row at which the display should start. However, it can be used only with screen blocks in procedure files. Note that the *AT scrnrow* option is not supported in version 1.1 of R:BASE System V.

DOS commands in R:BASE

The MS-DOS operating system (and IBM's version of MS-DOS) provides commands for handling files, directories, and disk drive operations. R:BASE provides a subset of the MS-DOS commands. Although the commands in this subset are part of the R:BASE command language, they function almost exactly like their MS-DOS counterparts. R:BASE supports the following MS-DOS commands:

Command	Description
CHDIR or CD	Changes the current directory.
CHDRV or *d*:	Changes the default drive.
CHKDSK	Checks disk space and system memory.

(continued)

90

Command	Description
COPY	Copies files.
DIR	Lists the contents of a directory.
ERASE or DELETE	Erases files.
MKDIR or MD	Creates a new directory.
RENAME	Renames files.
RMDIR or RD	Deletes or removes a directory.
TYPE	Displays the contents of an ASCII file.

Note that the above commands may be abbreviated to their first three or four letters, like any other R:BASE command (see *Command structure*). For further information on these commands, see the entry for each command.

You can also use the ZIP command to execute MS-DOS programs from within R:BASE. The ZIP command executes any MS-DOS file with an extension of *.EXE* or *.COM*. For example, to format a disk in drive B from within R:BASE, issue the following command:

```
ZIP FORMAT B:
```

For more information about executing MS-DOS programs, see *ZIP*.

- **R:BASE 5000 equivalent**
R:BASE 5000 supports the same MS-DOS commands as R:BASE System V, with the exception of the ZIP command.

EDIT

- **Syntax**

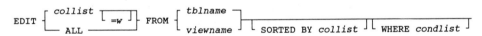

- **Description**
The EDIT command lets you modify or delete existing data in a table, using a full screen editing format.

- **Procedure**
To edit rows selectively, specify a *WHERE* condition. Use the *SORTED BY* clause to specify the order in which rows are displayed; either individual columns or *ALL* columns may be selected for editing. If you omit the *WHERE* clause, all rows in the table are made available for editing.

In contrast to editing with forms, the EDIT command lets you edit all selected rows and columns simultaneously. You can scroll through the rows or move the highlight horizontally to see columns that extend past the screen. Note, however, that you can scroll backward only 50 rows. (See *EDIT USING* and *FORMS.*)

When you select individual columns, you can use the $=w$ operator to specify a column display width other than the column's default width.

The key functions of the EDIT command are shown below:

Key	Function
F2	Deletes the current row.
F5	Resets the edited value to its original value. Reset works only when the column highlight has not been moved.
Tab	Moves the column highlight one column to the right.
Shift-Tab	Moves the column highlight one column to the left.
Left/right arrow	Moves the cursor to the left or right within the column highlight.
Up/down arrow	Moves the column highlight up or down one row.
Ctrl-left arrow	Moves the column highlight to the end of the row.
Ctrl-right arrow	Moves the column highlight to the beginning of the row.
Home	Moves the column highlight to the upper left column on the screen.
End	Moves the column highlight to the lower right column on the screen.
PgUp	Moves up a page (screen) of data.
PgDn	Moves down a page (screen) of data.
Del	Deletes the character at the cursor position.
Ins	Inserts a space at the cursor position.

The EDIT command is most commonly used with the *ALL* and *SORTED BY* clauses, as shown in the following example. Type:

```
EDIT ALL FROM EMPLOYEE SORTED BY EMPID
```

to display the following:

```
        Update  Press [ESC] when done, [F2] to delete, [F5] to reset   More→
   EMPID      FRSTNAME        LASTNAME         DEPT     SALARY         HIREDATE LAS
   ---------- ---------------- ---------------- -------- --------------- -------- ---
          1 James           Wilson           SLS      $25,000.00 08/15/83 04/
          2 Marjorie        Lawrence         SLS      $25,000.00 01/26/82 07/
          3 Barbara         Graham           ADMIN    $18,000.00 07/15/85 04/
          4 Paula           Stanton          Oper     $32,000.00 08/03/81 02/
          5 Franklin        Johnson          Mktg     $37,500.00 05/15/82 06/
          6 Robert          Smith            Dev      $45,000.00 04/01/84 11/
          7 Karen           Howard           Sls      $45,000.00 04/01/84 11/
          8 Sebastian       Lancaster        Trn      $35,000.00 11/15/82 10/
          9 Roland          Hanover          Oper     $45,000.00 10/15/81 07/
         10 Lenore          Fowler           Dev      $23,000.00 04/15/86 08/
         11 Clara           Anderson         Sls      $30,000.00 08/15/83 04/
         12 Lawrence        Butler           Dev      $35,000.00 02/26/82 01/
         13 Sean            ONeil            Admin    $36,000.00 11/15/85 04/
         14 John            Baker            Mktg     $30,000.00 04/03/81 03/
         15 Adele           Larson           Dev      $50,000.00 12/15/82 06/
         16 Laurie          Culbertson       Dev      $25,000.00 01/01/84 05/
         17 Dixie           Devereaux        Sls      $45,000.00 11/01/84 05/
```

All rows in the *EMPLOYEE* table are available for editing or deleting, and they are sorted and displayed by *EMPID*. Note the words *Update* and *More* in the top row. The bold *Update* indicates that the current highlighted column has been edited. Use the F5 key to reset the column to its original value. The *More* box indicates that there is more data (to the right, in this case). For quick horizontal movement through the table, use Tab to move to the right and Shift-Tab to move to the left. For quick vertical movement through the table, use PgUp to show the previous page and PgDn to show the next page.

The basic editing keys are Del, Ins, and F2. Use Del to delete individual characters and Ins to insert spaces for additions. The F2 key deletes the currently highlighted row.

Cautions: The F5 reset function will not restore the original value to a column entry if you move the column highlight to another column. The reset function also does not restore deleted rows.

The above example illustrates the use of the *ALL* clause. The following demonstrates another use of the *EDIT* command:

```
EDIT EMPID=3 FRSTNAME=10 LASTNAME=10 DEPT SALARY HIREDATE +
   FROM EMPLOYEE SORTED BY EMPID
```

This command line selects the *EMPID, FRSTNAME, LASTNAME, DEPT, SALARY,* and *HIREDATE* columns, specifies column widths, and displays the following formatted data table:

```
                    Press [ESC] when done, [F2] to delete, [F5] to reset
     EMP FRSTNAME    LASTNAME   DEPT    SALARY           HIREDATE
     --- ---------- ---------- ------- ---------------- --------
      1  James      Wilson     SLS        $25,000.00 08/15/83

      2  Marjorie   Lawrence   SLS        $25,000.00 01/26/82

      3  Barbara    Graham     ADMIN      $18,000.00 07/15/85

      4  Paula      Stanton    Oper       $32,000.00 08/03/81

      5  Franklin   Johnson    Mktg       $37,500.00 05/15/82

      6  Robert     Smith      Dev        $45,000.00 04/01/84

      7  Karen      Howard     Sls        $45,000.00 04/01/84

      8  Sebastian  Lancaster  Trn        $35,000.00 11/15/82
```

With the column width settings, you can adjust columns to put more on the screen at one time. You can easily store a long command, as in the example, in a macro or in a command file. (See *RECORD* and *PLAYBACK.)*

■ Comments

The EDIT command is the most convenient method of editing single tables. Of course, you also can use forms for editing. (See *FORMS* and *EDIT USING.)*

To edit multiple tables simultaneously, you must use FORMS and EDIT USING. Note that you can use the EDIT command only with views that represent a single table (see *VIEW*).

See: *BROWSE, Command files, EDIT USING, ENTER, SORTED BY,* and *WHERE*

■ R:BASE 5000 equivalent

EDIT

EDIT USING

■ Syntax

```
EDIT USING formname ┬─────────────────┬ ┬──────────────────┬ ┬────────────┬
                    └ SORTED BY collist ┘ └ WHERE condlist ┘ └ AT scrnrow ┘
```

■ Description

Note: We strongly recommend that before reading this entry you read the *FORMS* entry.

The EDIT USING command lets you modify data using a form previously created with the FORMS command.

- **Procedure**

You can selectively edit rows by using a *WHERE* clause. Include a *SORTED BY* clause to specify the order in which rows are displayed. If you use a multiple-table form, the *SORTED BY* and *WHERE* clauses apply only to the first table in the form.

In contrast to the EDIT command, which lets you edit multiple rows simultaneously, EDIT USING lets you edit only one row at a time. However, if your form includes multiple tables with tiers, you can edit multiple rows simultaneously in the tiered region. For more information about multiple-table forms and tiered regions, see *FORMS*.

EDIT USING can be used only with an existing form to edit existing data. The characteristics of a form cannot be altered with the EDIT USING command. However, you can add new rows to a table from an edited form by selecting the *Add new* menu option, if this option is available. Menu options are described below.

When you edit a form with the EDIT USING command, the form displays the first available row of data from the first table and, if applicable, secondary rows from additional tables in the form. Each entry in the form is called a field and the current field is highlighted. The following shows a typical form:

```
┌──────────────────────────────────────────────────────────────────────┐
│ Edit  Save  Add new  Delete  Reset  Previous  Next  Quit               │
└──────────────────────────────────────────────────────────────────────┘


                        CLIENT DATA ENTRY FORM

            Client Number: 1
              Client Name: Johnson and Anderson Co.
                   Street: 101 Howard Street
                     City: San Francisco
                    State: Ca
                      Zip: 94101
       Phone (xxx-xxx-xxxx): 415-397-8892

         ┌────────────────────────────────────────────────────────┐
         │                    Client Invoices                     │
         │ Invoice No.    Date      Amount    Prev. Bal.  Total Due   Paid │
         │ 001         10/22/86   $3,000.00   $345.00    $3,345.00    y │
         │ 002         10/22/86   $7,898.00   $0.00      $7,898.00    y │
         │                                                        │
         │                                                        │
         └────────────────────────────────────────────────────────┘
```

This form is an example of a multi-table form. The client-invoice part of the form is a tiered region that can display multiple rows simultaneously.

The key functions of the EDIT USING command are shown in the following table:

Key	Description
F2	Deletes the contents of the highlighted field.
Shift-F2	Deletes to the end of the field from the cursor position.
F4	Turns the repeat function on and off. The repeat function repeats the last typed character when you press the right or the left arrow key.
F5	Resets the edited value to its original value. Reset works only when the cursor is in the highlighted field.
F7	Displays the previous row in the current table.
F8	Displays the next row in the current table.
F9	Moves the cursor to the first field in the next table.
F10	Displays an R:BASE or custom help screen (see *FORMS*).
Shift-F10	Displays additional key descriptions.
Ins	Inserts a space at the cursor position.
Del	Deletes the character at the cursor position.
Up/down arrow	Moves the cursor to the previous or the next line of a multiple-line field.
Tab	Moves the highlight to the next field in the current row.
Shift-Tab	Moves the highlight to the previous field in the current row.
Enter	Moves the highlight to the next field in a row. If the highlight is at the last field in a row it moves to the next table. In tiered regions, the highlight moves from the last field of the current row to the first field of the next row.
PgUp/PgDn	Moves to the previous or the next page in a multi-page form.
ESC	Returns to the last menu or to the R> prompt.
Left/right arrow	Moves the cursor to the left or right within the highlight.
End	Moves the cursor to the end of the highlight.

The menu options for editing the form are listed at the top of the form. However, some forms may not include all options, depending on how the form was designed.

Here is a summary of menu options:

Option	Description
Edit	Select to begin editing the form.
Save	Saves the changes to the row currently displayed and then displays the next row.
Add new	Enters the current data in the form as a new row in the table, leaving the original row unchanged.
Delete	Deletes the current row in the form from the table and clears the row from the form.
Reset	Resets the edited values in the current row of the form to their original values. Reset works only if you have not saved the edited changes.
Previous	Displays the previous row of the first table in the form.
Next	Displays the next row of the first table in the form.
Quit	Quits the form and returns to the previous menu or to the R> prompt.

See: *EDIT, ENTER, FORMS, SORTED BY,* and *WHERE*

■ **R:BASE 5000 equivalent**
EDIT USING

EDIT USING is similar in R:BASE 5000. However, multiple-table forms are not supported (see *FORMS*).

ENTER

■ **Syntax**

ENTER ⌐────────⌐ *formname* ⌐────────────────⌐└ AT *scrnrow* ⌐
    └ USING ┘   ├ FOR *n* ROWS ──┤
                        └ FROM *filespec* ┘

■ **Description**

Note: We strongly recommend that you read the entry for *FORMS* before reading this entry.

ENTER is primarily used for entering new data into a previously created form (see *FORMS*). You also can use ENTER with the *FROM filespec* option to import a fixed-field ASCII file into R:BASE. (This also is a function of FileGateway.)

■ **Procedure**

You can limit the number of rows to be entered with the *FOR n ROWS* clause, where *n* is an integer. If you know in advance how many rows you will enter, the *FOR n ROWS* clause makes data entry more accurate. In command files, you can limit entry to one row and then perform other actions on the entered row. (See the example below.)

The *AT scrnrow* option lets you place a form on the screen at a row other than the top row, which is the default screen location.

Although the ENTER command enters new data into the tables represented by the form, you cannot use ENTER to make changes to the form itself. If you use the master lookup option, you can edit existing rows with the ENTER command. However, the EDIT USING command offers more flexibility for editing existing data with a form. See *FORMS* for information about designing and modifying forms.

The following screen shows a typical session with the ENTER command:

```
┌──────────────────────────────────────────────────────────────────────┐
│ Add  Duplicate  Edit again  Discard  Quit                              │
└──────────────────────────────────────────────────────────────────────┘


                         CLIENT DATA ENTRY FORM

                 Client Number: 7
                   Client Name: Maynard Robinson
                        Street: 100 Oak Street
                          City: San Jose
                         State: Ca
                           Zip: 93421
          Phone (xxx-xxx-xxxx): 408-467-9090

        ┌──────────────────────────────────────────────────────────────┐
        │                       Client Invoices                          │
        │ Invoice No.    Date      Amount     Prev. Bal.   Total Due  Paid│
        │ 7-001       10/23/86   $400.00     $0.00        $400.00      n  │
        │                                                                │
        │                                                                │
        │                                                                │
        └──────────────────────────────────────────────────────────────┘
```

This form serves two tables. The client-number field in the first table (*CLIENT*) is assigned the master lookup function so that existing rows can be displayed. The second table (*INVOICE*) is set up as a tiered region so that you can enter multiple invoice rows corresponding to a single client number in the client table. See *FORMS* for more information about multiple-table forms.

The key functions in the ENTER mode are listed in the following table:

Key	Description
F2	Deletes the contents of the highlighted field.
Shift-F2	Deletes to the end of the field from the cursor position.
F4	Turns the repeat function on or off. The repeat function repeats the last typed character when you press the right or the left arrow key.
F5	Resets the edited value to its original value. Reset only works when the cursor is in the highlighted field.
F7	Displays the previous row in multiple-row regions.
F8	Displays the next row in multiple-row regions.
F9	Moves the cursor to the first field in the next table.
F10	Displays an R:BASE or custom help screen (see *FORMS*).
Shift-F10	Displays additional key descriptions.
Ins	Inserts a space at the cursor position.
Del	Deletes the character at the cursor position.
Up/down arrow	Moves the cursor to the previous or the next line of multiple-line fields.
Tab	Moves the highlight to the next field in the current row.
Shift-Tab	Moves the highlight to the previous field in the current row.
Enter	Moves the highlight to the next field in a row. If the highlight is at the last field in a row it moves to the next table. In tiered regions, the highlight moves from the last field of the current row to the first field of the next row.
PgUp/PgDn	Moves to the previous or the next page in a multi-page form.
ESC	Returns to the last menu or to the R> prompt.
Left/right arrow	Moves the cursor to the left or right within the highlight.
End	Moves the cursor to the end of the highlight.

The top line of the form displays the menu options. Depending on how the form was designed, not all of these options may be included in the form (see *FORMS*). Here is a summary of the menu options:

Option	Description
Add	Adds the current data in the form as a new row (or rows) in the corresponding table (or tables).
Duplicate	Copies the current data in the form as a new row, but leaves the original data on the screen. This feature is useful for entering repetitive data because values that do not change can be used for the next row.
Edit again	Returns the cursor to the form for further editing before saving the data.
Discard	Clears the highlighted row from the screen. (In multiple-row regions, you are asked if you want to discard all rows.)
Quit	Ends the ENTER session and returns to the previous menu or to the R> prompt.

Command file example: Like any other command in R:BASE, the ENTER command can be used in a command file. The example below shows the use of ENTER and the *FOR n ROWS* clause:

```
ENTER CLIENT FOR 1 ROW
SET VAR vcount = CLINUM IN INVOICE WHERE COUNT EQ LAST
CLS
COMPUTE vnotpaid AS COUNT CLINUM FROM INVOICE WHERE CLINUM EQ +
  .vcount AND PAID EQ "N"
IF vnotpaid GT 3 THEN
  WRITE "Warning! This CLIENT has over 3 unpaid invoices!" at 3,5
ENDIF
WRITE "press any key to continue" at 5,4
PAUSE
```

This command file processes one new client row and then checks the number of unpaid invoices for that client number. If a client has more than three unpaid invoices, the following screen is displayed:

```
Warning! This client has over 3 unpaid invoices!

press any key to continue
```

The above command file could be inserted into a WHILE loop so that the entry procedure repeats until you exit the loop.

The ENTER command enters one row in the client table using the form shown earlier in this section. Note that the row specifier *only applies to the first table in the form.* In this case, only one new client, but many invoices, can be added to the tables.

When you enter an existing client number in the first table, the *FOR n ROWS* clause is ignored because you are not adding a new row to the *CLIENT* table. The rest of the command file still executes when you exit the form, but only the invoices for the last entered client number are checked (*WHERE COUNT EQ LAST*).

The above discussion is clarified in the *FORMS* entry, which discusses master lookups of existing rows and multiple-table forms.

Fixed-field data entry with the ENTER command: You can enter fixed-field data into an R:BASE table by using the ENTER command and a form. (If the record length in your fixed-field file is greater than 79 characters, the following method will not work. Use FileGateway instead.) Briefly, here are the steps you must follow to enter a fixed-field file with the ENTER command:

1) Create a table that has the same column widths (defined in the same order) as in the fixed-field file.

2) Create a data entry form that has no text but just contains the column locations. The locations should be next to each other, like this:

```
S        ES            ES        ES              E
```

Again, you must locate the columns on the form in the same order as they are in the fixed-field file. See *FORMS* for further details on locating columns.

3) Let's assume the form is called *FIXFIELD* and the fixed field file is called *DATA.EXT*. To load the file with data, open the appropriate database and enter the following command:

```
ENTER FIXFIELD FROM DATA.EXT
```

See: *EDIT USING, FileGateway, FORMS, LOAD,* and *WHILE*

■ **R:BASE 5000 equivalent**
ENTER

To enter record lengths greater than 79 characters, you must write a program that splits the record into two parts. See pages 12-16 of the R:BASE 5000 User's Manual for a program that performs this function.

ERASE

- **Syntax**

```
ERASE filespec
```

- **Description**

The ERASE command deletes a file (or files) from the default drive and current directory or from a drive and directory that you specify.

- **Procedure**

The ERASE command performs the same function as the MS-DOS ERASE command. For example, the following command deletes the three files of the *TEST* database:

```
ERASE TEST?.RBF
```

This command uses the wildcard character *?* to delete all files with a four- or five-character filename starting with the word TEST and having the *.RBF* extension. You can use the asterisk (*) wildcard character to include multiple file extensions:

```
ERASE TEST*.*
```

This command deletes all files beginning with the word *TEST*, regardless of the remaining characters.

Caution: The ERASE command deletes your files! Be sure you test the effect wildcard characters have on the command by first performing a DIR with the wildcard pattern before you delete the specified file or files. We also recommend that you own a utility for recovering deleted files (e.g., The Norton Utilities).

- **Comment**

You can substitute DEL or DELETE for the ERASE command.

- **R:BASE 5000 equivalent**

ERASE
or
DEL

Error messages

■ **Description**

There are several hundred error messages in R:BASE System V, so it's not practical to list them here. All the error messages are listed in the R:BASE documentation. Also, see the file *ERRVAL.DOC* on the R:BASE system disks.

It is important to note, however, that R:BASE error messages may be turned on or off with the SET ERROR MESSAGE command. When error messages are off, illegal commands or other data-handling errors are not reported on the output device (usually the screen). Unless fatal errors occur that cause R:BASE to abort (such as writing to an open floppy disk drive), R:BASE appears to be operating normally in spite of detected errors. This may be desirable in menu-driven applications or in other routines developed for inexperienced users. In many cases, errors may occur that do not affect the overall operation of a command file.

For example, let's say your command file loads a backup file back into a database. When you execute an INPUT or RESTORE command, some errors may occur because the backup data includes commands that attempt to redefine existing columns or tables. However, these errors actually have no effect on the success of the restore operation. The errors are reported and then the data is loaded into the database normally. For inexperienced users, however, these error messages can be quite disconcerting and might even prompt them to abort the operation because they think it is not working properly. In these situations, error messages should be turned off by including a SET ERR MESS OFF command in the command file.

If you run an application developed with Application EXPRESS, error messages are turned off by default. When you return to the R> prompt to continue with other work, error messages remain turned off until you issue the SET ERR MESS ON command.

There is a distinction between error messages and diagnostic messages. Diagnostic messages report the result of an R:BASE operation. *Database exists* and *40 row(s) have been deleted from EMPLOYEE* are examples of diagnostic messages. Diagnostic messages are turned off with the SET MESSAGE OFF command. Diagnostic messages also are turned off by default in Application EXPRESS applications.

For a detailed discussion of error trapping with error variables, see *SET ERROR VARIABLE*.

EXIT

■ **Syntax**

```
EXIT
```

■ **Description**

Use EXIT to leave R:BASE and return to the RBSYSTEM menu (see *RBSYSTEM*). If you started R:BASE from MS-DOS, EXIT returns you to the MS-DOS prompt.

Caution: Always use EXIT to terminate a session with R:BASE. Never use Ctrl-Break or Ctrl-Alt-Del or turn off the computer to leave R:BASE. If you do, new data or changes to existing data might not be saved. However, if your computer system locks up, you will have no choice but to reboot the computer. If you are working on a local area network, check with other users before rebooting the computer.

■ **R:BASE 5000 equivalent**

EXIT

EXPAND

■ **Syntax**

```
EXPAND tblname WITH colname
                            =expression    datatype
                                                    length
```

■ **Description**

The EXPAND command adds a column to a table.

Database design is usually a dynamic process. A database requires changes as you become more familiar with its requirements. As you work with a database, you might discover that you need an additional computed column or that you left out an important piece of data. The EXPAND command lets you add columns that meet new requirements.

■ **Procedure**

If the column you want to add already exists in another table in the database, simply specify the column name. If you are adding a new column, use the *expression* or *datatype* options to define the column. With the exception of computed columns, the expanded column initially contains no data, even if it is an existing column that contains data in another table.

For example, suppose you omitted the *PAID* column in your initial definition of the *INVOICE* table. You can easily add it with the following command:

```
EXPAND INVOICE WITH PAID TEXT 1
```

This defines the *PAID* column as a text data type with a character length of one. (See *Columns* and *Data types* for more information on defining columns).

Defining a computed column is also straightforward with the EXPAND command. To add a computed column that calculates the age of existing invoices, type:

```
EXPAND INVOICE WITH INVCEAGE = (.#DATE - ENTRDATE)
```

In this case, the new column *INVCEAGE* computes the difference between the current date and the column *ENTRDATE*, which stores the date the invoice was entered. See *Date and time arithmetic* for further discussion. See *Columns* for more information about computed columns.

■ **Comments**

Keys cannot be defined with the EXPAND command and are not transferred from existing columns. Use the BUILD KEY command to define keys.

The UNION command offers an alternative but less convenient method of adding columns.

Caution: The EXPAND command requires that you have enough disk space to store a temporary table during its operation. Repeated use of the EXPAND command also increases the file size of your database and reduces usable storage space. Use the PACK command periodically to remove unusable disk space. (Be sure your database is backed up before you issue the PACK or RELOAD command.)

See: *BUILD KEY, Columns, PACK, REDEFINE,* and *UNION*

■ **R:BASE 5000 equivalent**

EXPAND

EXPRESS (Application EXPRESS)

■ **Syntax**

Select Application EXPRESS from the RBSYSTEM menu.

You also can execute EXPRESS at the R> prompt if you entered R:BASE from the RBSYSTEM menu.

```
EXPRESS ⌐ exec ⌐
```

If you entered R:BASE from the MS-DOS prompt, you must exit R:BASE. You can then execute EXPRESS from MS-DOS:

EXPRESS ⌐ -R ⌐ -Fn ⌐ -Bn ⌐ -Mn ⌐ -Tn ⌐ exec ⌐

The *-R* option suppresses display of the R logo. The *-F* and *-B* options modify the foreground and background colors if you are using a color monitor. *-M* and *-T* modify other monitor characteristics. See the R:BASE System V Installation Guide for further information on monitor options. The *exec* option lets you specify an *exec* file that runs when you start EXPRESS from MS-DOS (see *RECORD* and *PLAYBACK*).

■ **Description**
The EXPRESS command starts Application EXPRESS.

See: *Application EXPRESS, PLAYBACK,* and *RECORD*

■ **R:BASE 5000 equivalent**
Definition EXPRESS

Expressions

In R:BASE System V, an expression is a mathematical or text-string operation that calculates a value. Expressions can involve columns, functions, variables, or constants.

The following commands can include expressions:

CHANGE
For example:

```
CHANGE SALARY TO (110 % SALARY) IN EMPLOYEE WHERE EMPID EXISTS
```

The expression (110 % SALARY) increases the value in the SALARY column by 10% for each row that has a value in the EMPID column.

COLUMNS
For example:

```
YEARS = (NINT((.#DATE - HIREDATE)/365))
```

The computed column expression calculates the difference between the current date (.#DATE) and the column value *HIREDATE* and divides this result by 365 to calculate the number of years of employment. Note that the *NINT()* function rounds off real numbers to the nearest integer (see *Conversion functions*).

COMPUTE

For example:

```
COMPUTE contrib AS SUM (0.05 * SALARY) FROM EMPLOYEE
```

The sum of the expression (0.05 * SALARY) is calculated and stored in the variable *contrib* (see *COMPUTE*).

EXPAND

For example:

```
EXPAND RT-TRI WITH HYPOT = (SQRT(('SIDE1')**2 + ('SIDE2')**2))
```

The *HYPOT* column is a computed column set equal to the square root of the sum of the squares of the two legs of a right triangle (Pythagorean Theorem). This example demonstrates the use of the *SQRT()* function and exponentiation (**). For more information, see *Arithmetic and mathematical functions*.

REDEFINE

For example:

```
REDEFINE BONUS TO (IFLT(YEARS,2,0,(2 % SALARY)))
```

The *BONUS* column is redefined to equal the expression defined by the logical *IFLT()* function. If *YEARS* is less than 2, then *BONUS* is 0. Otherwise, *BONUS* is 2% of the annual salary (see *Logical functions*).

SELECT

For example:

```
SELECT EMPID SALARY ((.#DATE - HIREDATE)/365) FROM EMPLOYEE
```

Here, the expression ((.#DATE − HIREDATE)/365) is one of the values selected from the *EMPLOYEE* table.

SET VARIABLE

For example:

```
SET VAR initvar = (SMOVE(.fname,1,1,.initvar,1))
```

The expression uses the *SMOVE()* function to move character strings from one variable to another (see *String manipulation functions*). The condition clause of an IF, WHERE, or WHILE statement also can include an expression:

IF

For example:

```
IF .vsalary GT (1.5 * .vminsal) THEN ...
```

The variable *vsalary* is compared to the expression (1.5 * *vminsal*), which is 1.5 times the value of the variable *vminsal*.

WHERE

For example:

```
WHERE BONUS LT (2 % SALARY)
```

The *BONUS* column is compared to expression (2 % *SALARY*).

WHILE

For example:

```
WHILE (.frstname & .lastname) eq "Joe Brown" THEN ...
```

The expression (.*frstname* & .*lastname*) concatenates the values of the variables *frstname* and *lastname* and is compared to the text string "Joe Brown".

Notice in the above examples that a period precedes the arguments. These are *dotted variables* and indicate that the *current value* of the variable is required. For example, *#DATE* is the system variable that stores the current date. The current value of *#DATE* is represented by .*#DATE*, and is treated like any other valid date value. Similarly, .*frstname* represents the current value of the variable *frstname*. For more about dotted variables, see *Variables*.

The following operators can be used in expressions:

Operator	Description
+ or −	Unary plus or minus (e.g., − SQRT(4) = −2)
**	Exponentiation
*	Multiplication
/	Division
%	Percentage
+	Addition
−	Subtraction
+	Concatenation with no separating space
&	Concatenation with a separating space

The order of precedence of the above operators is as follows:

1. Expressions inside internal parentheses
2. Functions
3. Unary + or −
4. Exponentiation
5. Multiplication or division from left to right
6. Percent
7. Addition or subtraction

If you have any doubt about the order of precedence in a complex expression, use parentheses around the parts of the expression that should be evaluated together. The following example shows how the order of precedence can affect results:

```
SET VAR result REAL
SET VAR result = (5 * 4 - 2);   SHOW VAR result
     18.
SET VAR result = (5 * (4 - 2)); SHOW VAR result
     10.
SET VAR result = SQRT(16) / 2;   SHOW VAR result
     2.
SET VAR result = SQRT(16 / 2);   SHOW VAR result
2.828427
```

Caution: Note the following when working with expressions:

☐ Expressions can contain a maximum of 160 characters and a total of 50 operators and operands. A total of 25 columns and variables is allowed per expression. Expressions can have as many as 75 nesting levels.

☐ Each table can have a total of 10 computed columns.

☐ Columns can be enclosed with single quotes (e.g., *'HIRE-DATE'*) to denote that the argument is a column. In the case of *HIRE-DATE*, the single quotes are required because the hyphen in *HIRE-DATE* would be interpreted as a subtraction operation.

☐ COMPUTE cannot be used with text expressions.

☐ NOTE columns cannot be used in expressions or as computed columns.

☐ Variables used repeatedly in expressions should be explicitly set to the desired data type. For example, if we did not specify the variable *result* in the above example as a REAL data type, the last square root operation would give the wrong answer because the first *SET VAR* command would set *result* to the INTEGER data type (see *Variables* and *Data types*).

☐ REDEFINE cannot be used on a column that is part of a computed column definition (see *REDEFINE*).

☐ Enclose text expressions in parentheses.

☐ Enclose functions in parentheses as a general rule. Numeric expressions, such as the *SQRT()* function, work without enclosing parentheses. Text expressions, such as the *SMOVE()* function, will not work without surrounding parentheses.

☐ Null values are not treated as numeric values in expressions, unless you issue the SET ZERO ON command. The default is SET ZERO OFF, in which case expressions involving null values are not evaluated and are left null.

■ Comments

Many examples of expressions can be found throughout this book. In particular, see the entries for commands that use expressions (listed earlier in this entry). Also see the entries for the various functions (*Arithmetic and mathematical functions, Conversion functions, Date and time functions, Financial functions, Logical functions, String manipulation functions,* and *Trigonometric functions*).

■ R:BASE 5000 equivalent

Expressions are limited in R:BASE 5000. Parentheses are not supported, thus limiting expressions to one operator. In addition, computed columns and the SuperMath functions available in R:BASE System V are not included.

FileGateway

■ Syntax

Select FileGateway from the RBSYSTEM menu.

You also can execute GATEWAY at the R> prompt if you entered R:BASE from the System menu.

GATEWAY ⌐ *exec* ⌐

If you entered R:BASE from the MS-DOS prompt, you must exit R:BASE. You can then execute GATEWAY from MS-DOS:

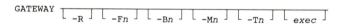

GATEWAY ⌐ -R ⌐ ⌐ -F*n* ⌐ ⌐ -B*n* ⌐ ⌐ -M*n* ⌐ ⌐ -T*n* ⌐ ⌐ *exec* ⌐

The *-R* option suppresses display of the R logo. The *-F* and *-B* options modify the foreground and background colors if you are using a color monitor. The *-M* and *-T* options modify other monitor characteristics. See the R:BASE System V Installation Guide for further information on monitor options. The *exec* option lets you specify an *exec* file that runs when you start GATEWAY.

■ Description

FileGateway is a separate module in R:BASE System V that lets you transfer data to and from other file formats. FileGateway does not convert the original data file to another format but instead makes a copy of the existing file in another format. In other words, when you finish, you still have the original file in its original format as well as a second file that contains the converted data.

■ **Procedure**

The Import and Export menus of FileGateway are shown in the following screens:

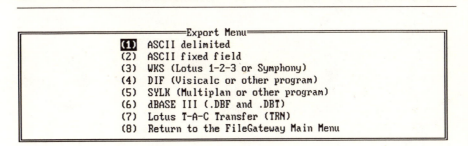

```
═══════════════════════Import Menu═══════════════════════
     (1)  ASCII delimited
     (2)  ASCII fixed field
     (3)  WKS, WK1, WRK (Lotus 1-2-3 or Symphony)
     (4)  DBF (dBASE II or dBASE III)
     (5)  pfs:file
     (6)  DIF (Visicalc or other program)
     (7)  SYLK (Multiplan or other program)
     (8)  Lotus T-A-C Transfer (TRN)
     (9)  Return to the FileGateway Main Menu
```

[Ctrl-Break] Abort   [F3] Display   [F10] Help   [Shift-F6] Options

```
═══════════════════════Export Menu═══════════════════════
     (1)  ASCII delimited
     (2)  ASCII fixed field
     (3)  WKS (Lotus 1-2-3 or Symphony)
     (4)  DIF (Visicalc or other program)
     (5)  SYLK (Multiplan or other program)
     (6)  dBASE III (.DBF and .DBT)
     (7)  Lotus T-A-C Transfer (TRN)
     (8)  Return to the FileGateway Main Menu
```

[Ctrl-Break] Abort   [F3] Display   [F10] Help   [Shift-F6] Options

FileGateway is basically simple to use. First, select the appropriate file type from the Import or Export menu. If you are importing data, select the file to import from those listed on the screen, or enter a new filename. Then specify the database and table into which the data will be imported. If you select an existing table, the structure of the table must match the sequence and field widths of the data you are importing. If you select a new table, FileGateway presents the File Conversion Editor, which helps you create the table.

For example, the following screen shows the File Conversion Editor during the conversion of an ASCII delimited file to a new R:BASE table:

```
════════════════════════════File Conversion Editor══════════
  To change the name, type, or length of a field, move the cursor to the
  field and type in the new information. Do not change sample values.
  Up, Dn, Lt, Rt, PgUp, PgDn, Home, End  Move the cursor between fields
    + . . . . . . . . . . . . . . . . .  Get next record of sample data
    ESC . . . . . . . . . . . . . . . .  When changes are complete
```

```
 Field name    Data type    Maximum length    Sample values
 ----------    ---------    --------------    -----------------------------
  FLD18001     INTEGER                        200
  FLD18002     TEXT              8            Harry
  FLD18003     TEXT              8            Miller
  FLD10004     TEXT             19            1203 N.E. 23rd Ave.
  FLD18005     TEXT              8            Seattle
  FLD18006     TEXT              8            WA
  FLD18007     INTEGER                        98106
  FLD18008     TEXT              8            651-9099
  FLD18009     INTEGER                        209

  [Ctrl-Break] Abort   [F3] Display   [F10] Help   [Shift-F6] Options
  DATABASE: CONCOMP   TABLE: NEWSLREP   IMPORT FILE: SALESREP.DEL
```

The sample data is taken from a row in the file to be imported. FileGateway supplies the field names (column names) shown in the example. You can change the names to any valid R:BASE column name. If you use a column name that already exists in your database, the data type and column width (if applicable) are supplied because they have been previously defined.

After you define the table, load the data from the import file. If the data includes date fields, FileGateway prompts you to select from a list of valid date formats as shown in the following screen:

```
╔══════════Select date format(s) - Press [ESC] when done══════════╗
║ (YY)YY/MM/DD  DD/MM/(YY)YY  DD/Mon(th)/(YY)YY  Mon(th) DD, (YY)YY ║
║ Mon(th)  Serial  (Reset)                                         ║
╚══════════════════════════════════════════════════════════════════╝


       MM/DD/(YY)YY




[Ctrl-Break] Abort    [F3] Display    [F10] Help    [Shift-F6] Options
 DATABASE: CONCOMP   TABLE: COMPORD   IMPORT FILE: COMPORD.WK1
```

You can select multiple but not conflicting date formats. For example, the formats *MM/DD/YY* and *DD/MM/YY* conflict with each other. If you select conflicting date formats, a warning message is displayed. The Serial date format is used to convert date values from Symphony and Lotus 1-2-3.

After you select the date formats, FileGateway loads the data into your table. Data that does not conform to the structure of your table is placed in an exception file (*EXCEPT.DAT*), which you can either edit and then add to the table, or discard.

Exporting data is simply a matter of selecting the appropriate file type from the Export menu and then specifying the database and table from which you are exporting. Depending on the file type you are exporting to, you may have to supply additional parameters. To export to spreadsheet files, for example, you must specify the cell range in the spreadsheet.

You also can include sorting and conditional criteria for the rows to be exported. An example of selecting conditional criteria is shown in the following screen:

```
══════════Choose an operator to combine conditions══════════
 AND   OR   AND NOT   OR NOT   (Done)   (Undo Last)
```

	Column	Operator	Value
	EMPID	GT	10

```
[Ctrl-Break] Abort    [F3] Display    [F10] Help    [Shift-F6] Options
DATABASE: CONCOMP   TABLE: SALESREP
```

When working with FileGateway, press F10 for help or press Shift-F6 to invoke the Options menu. From the Options menu, you can review the contents of a database, display files, run a program using the ZIP command, set rules to *ON* or *OFF*, enter passwords, or execute MS-DOS commands.

The remainder of this section provides information on specific file types.

ASCII delimited files: Here is an example of a typical ASCII delimited file:

```
200,Harry,Miller,"1203 N.E. 23rd Ave.",Seattle,WA,98106
201,Julie,Harrison,"9932 S.E. 17th St.",Kent,WA,98307
202,Lawrence,Barton,"123 S. 48th St.",Renton,WA,98209
```

Each row in an ASCII file normally corresponds to a record or row in a database. Each line ends with a carriage return and a line feed, which are called end-of-record markers. If you omit the end-of-record marker, data is read as one long line of data.

Each column or field is separated by a comma, which is called a delimiter. Since spaces are also considered delimiters, it is necessary to enclose fields that include spaces with quotes. In rare instances, you may have to use a delimiter other than a comma, so FileGateway provides an option for changing the delimiter both for importing and exporting ASCII delimited files.

ASCII fixed-field files: Here is an example of a typical fixed-field file:

```
X3030 Box-Single Drive w/Hard Disk2006/02/87 7:56:0006/04/87
X3050 Box-512K-Dual Drive-Portable 506/03/8715:37:0006/06/87
X3040 Box-256K-Dual Drive-Portable1706/04/8715:29:0006/10/87
X2010 Monitor-Monochrome-12        1106/05/8710:28:0006/09/87
```

Each field in a fixed-field file has a fixed length. There are no delimiters. In this example, the first field is six characters, the second field is 28 characters, and so forth. As you can see from *Monitor-Monochrome-12*, trailing blanks are added to characters that do not fill up the entire field length.

FileGateway makes it easy to import and export fixed-field files. A sample record is placed on the screen and you mark the beginning and ending positions of each field. When importing fixed-field data, the tricky part is identifying the beginning and ending of the fields. In the above example, the third field is two characters. It would be easy to mistakenly assign three characters to this field. You must be familiar with the data to import it correctly.

Spreadsheets: FileGateway can transfer data directly to and from Lotus 1-2-3 and Symphony files. FileGateway also supports the DIF and SYLK file formats, which allow the transfer of data from any spreadsheet that can convert its data files to one of those formats. Multiplan spreadsheets can be converted to the SYLK format. Visicalc, SuperCalc, VP-Planner, and many other spreadsheet programs support the DIF file format.

Before you import from Lotus 1-2-3, Symphony, or SYLK files, note the coordinates of the upper-left and lower-right cells that bound the data area. In Lotus 1-2-3 or Symphony files, also note the coordinate of the row or column containing labels. You can use these labels as R:BASE column names.

The column/row format of SYLK and DIF files must be maintained when transferring data to R:BASE. In other words, rows and columns in Multiplan or Visicalc will correspond to rows and columns in R:BASE. With Lotus 1-2-3 or Symphony, however, you have the choice of orienting the spreadsheet data by row or column. For example, a row of data in 1-2-3 can be imported as a column in an R:BASE table. Similarly, you can export R:BASE columns as rows to a 1-2-3 spreadsheet.

Spreadsheet formulas cannot be converted. You can use computed columns in R:BASE, however, to duplicate spreadsheet formulas that apply to a single row. For example, if a spreadsheet formula adds the values of two cells in a single row and places the sum in a third cell in the same row, you can duplicate the process with a computed column in R:BASE. Because formulas that use cell values from other spreadsheet rows have no equivalent computed column expression, you must use other techniques in R:BASE to duplicate the formulas (see *COMPUTE*).

Databases: FileGateway lets you directly import pfs:FILE and dBASE II and III data files. In each case, the conversion is straightforward. There are some differences in data types between R:BASE and dBASE. dBASE uses a single numeric data type for integers, real numbers, and currency values. Dates in dBASE are treated as a character data type. The logical data type (T or F) has no direct equivalent in R:BASE and is converted as a text data type. Memo fields are converted to the R:BASE NOTE data type.

The FileGateway File Conversion Editor assigns R:BASE data types that seem to best fit the type of data contained in the dBASE file. You can change these data types if you wish.

A pfs:FILE form is imported as a row in a table. The labels on the form are used as column names if they are eight characters or less in length. Longer labels are not used, and you are prompted to enter a new column name. A pfs:FILE form may not exceed 4096 characters and cannot include attachments. If you need to preserve the information in an attachment, redesign the form to include this information in the form itself.

■ **Comments**

You can record your actions in FileGateway as an *exec* file (see *RECORD* and *PLAYBACK*). This feature is convenient if you perform a particular file transfer frequently. At the FileGateway Main menu, press Shift-F7 to begin recording. After you enter a filename for the *exec* file, proceed normally with your file conversion. To allow entry of other database or data filenames in future sessions, include a variable designator by entering an & when prompted for a filename. The & tells the *exec* file that you want to enter the filename manually. Then, every time you execute the *exec* file, it prompts you for the filename that you wish to use. Press Shift-F7 again to end the recording.

You can replay an *exec* file from the FileGateway Main menu by pressing Shift-F8. From the R> prompt or the MS-DOS prompt, issue the GATEWAY command with the *exec* filename appended (GATEWAY *exec*). For more detailed information, see *GATEWAY*.

Caution: There is no facility in FileGateway for exporting or importing large data files (greater than 360 KB) to or from multiple floppy disks. The best alternative is to make enough room on the hard disk to accommodate the exported or imported data file. You can then use the MS-DOS BACKUP or RESTORE commands (or equivalent backup utilities) to copy the file to or from multiple floppy disks.

Another possibility when exporting large R:BASE tables is to break them into smaller sections using the PROJECT command and then to use FileGateway to export the smaller sections.

■ **R:BASE 5000 equivalent**

A less powerful version of FileGateway is included in R:BASE 5000. This version imports only data and ASCII fixed-field files. In addition, most of the command line options, such as executing MS-DOS programs and running an *exec* file, are not included in R:BASE 5000.

Filenames and structure

MS-DOS files: MS-DOS filenames may not exceed eight characters plus an optional file extension of a maximum of three characters. The name and the extension must be separated by a period (e.g., *TESTING.TXT*).

R:BASE files: R:BASE files can be divided into three general categories:

1. Database files

2. Application and procedure files

3. Command and text files

1. Database files. When you define a database, you assign a name of a maximum of seven characters. R:BASE then creates three files for the database. Each of the three files has a number (1, 2, or 3) appended to the filename and the file extension *.RBF*. For example, suppose you name your database *PERSONL*. R:BASE then creates the following three files:

> *PERSONL1.RBF*—contains the database structure
> *PERSONL2.RBF*—contains the data that you enter
> *PERSONL3.RBF*—contains keys

These three files must always be kept in the same directory on your disk.

2. Application and procedure files. In Application EXPRESS, application names can be a maximum of eight characters. Application EXPRESS creates three files when you define an application, and they are assigned specific file extensions by default. For example, if you define an application called *PERSONL*, Application EXPRESS creates the following three files:

> *PERSONL.APP*—ASCII version of application file
> *PERSONL.API*—Internal file used by the EXPRESS
> *PERSONL.APX*—Binary version of the application file

These files are discussed in greater detail in the entry for *Application EXPRESS*.

Procedure files created with CodeLock are assigned the default extension of *.PRC*. You have the option, however, of changing this extension when you are prompted for the procedure name (see *CodeLock* and *Procedure files*).

3. Command and text files. You can assign any MS-DOS filename to a command or text file. We recommend, however, that you use the extension *.CMD* for command files and *.TXT* for text files.

One special type of command file is the optional R:BASE initial command file, also called the start-up file. This file must always be named *RBASE.DAT* and must reside on the directory from which you start R:BASE. If you create an *RBASE.DAT* file, it is automatically executed when you start R:BASE. See *Application EXPRESS* and *Command files* for more discussion of the *RBASE.DAT* file.

For more information on file maintenance and backup, see *BACKUP, COPY, PACK, RELOAD,* and *UNLOAD.* For more information on the different file types, see *ASCII characters and files, Application EXPRESS, Command files, DEFINE,* and *Definition EXPRESS.*

FILL

- **Syntax**

FILL

- **Description**
Use the FILL command with the LOAD command to enter NULL values (-0-) into empty columns. If you have a table of five columns, for example, but you enter only data for the first three columns, the FILL command assigns NULL values to the remaining columns. To understand the use of the FILL command, you first must be familiar with the LOAD command.

The opposite of the FILL command is the NOFILL command, which prevents data from being loaded unless values exist for all columns.

- **Procedure**
Use the FILL command with LOAD at the L> prompt or when you use LOAD to load an external file. Loading from an external file is the most common use of LOAD. For example, assume we have a table, called *TEST*, that contains four columns; *VAL1, VAL2, VAL3,* and *VAL4* (all INTEGER data types). To load data into *TEST* from the keyboard using LOAD, type the following:

```
R>LOAD TEST
 Begin R:BASE Data Loading
L>FILL
L>10,20,30
L>END
```

The fourth column, *VAL4,* is assigned a *NULL* value. Keep in mind that only columns at the end of the sequence are automatically filled. You must explicitly include the *NULL* value for inner columns (e.g., L>10,-0-,20,30).

Now, let's say you want to load TEST from an ASCII file, *TESTFILE*, which contains only two values (e.g., 10,20). The following FILL command assigns null values to *VAL3* and *VAL4*:

```
R>LOAD TEST FROM TESTFILE; FILL
```

See: *LOAD* and *NOFILL*

- **R:BASE 5000 equivalent**
FILL

FILLIN

- **Syntax**

```
FILLIN varname USING "message"
                             ├─ AT scrnrow scrncol ─┤
```

- **Description**

Use the FILLIN command in command files to accept input from the keyboard. FILLIN displays *message* on the screen and waits for the user to enter a value from the keyboard. The value is then stored in the variable, *varname*. The message may be either a string of text surrounded by double quotes or a dotted variable. You can specify the screen location for the FILLIN prompt message by including the *AT scrnrow, scrncol* clause. If you omit this clause, the message displays at the cursor position.

- **Procedure**

The FILLIN command provides a convenient method for accepting a response to a request for specific information. Requests such as *Please enter an ID Number:* or *Enter the database to work on:* are generally handled with the FILLIN command. The CHOOSE command usually is more convenient for accepting a menu selection. However, the FILLIN command can also be used with menus that are displayed from text files with the DISPLAY command.

For example, let's say you have a custom menu in a text file. To keep things simple, the text file, called *MENU.TXT*, looks like this:

```
1) Open a database
2) List all files
3) Quit
```

To display the menu and prompt for a selection, the FILLIN command is used with the following block of commands:

```
CLS
SET VARIABLE vnum INTEGER
DISPLAY MENU.TXT
FILLIN vnum USING "Enter 1, 2, or 3: " AT 7,10
```

The result of this command block looks like this:

```
1) Open a database
2) List all files
3) Quit



        Enter 1, 2, or 3:
```

The example illustrates how you can use the DISPLAY and FILLIN commands together. You can, of course, create much more elaborate custom menus. Note that the variable *vnum* stores a NULL value when you press ENTER without making a selection. Follow this command block with a series of IF statements to determine which action to perform next. See *CHOOSE* for further discussion of menu design.

FILLIN is used often in the command file examples in this book. In particular, see the command files in the entries for *Arithmetic and mathematical functions* and *Date and time functions*.

Caution: If you do not explicitly set the data type of the variable used in the FILLIN command, the variable assumes the data type of the first value that is entered. For example, if you enter 2 the first time the FILLIN command is used, the variable is set to INTEGER. Later text entries cause an error. It is, therefore, a good idea to set the variable data type explicitly before issuing the FILLIN command (see *SET VARIABLE*). In the example above, *vnum* is set to the INTEGER data type in the second line.

See: *CHOOSE* and *DISPLAY*

■ **R:BASE 5000 equivalent**
FILLIN

Financial functions

■ **Description**
R:BASE System V provides a comprehensive set of financial functions for calculating equal payments, time periods, interest rates, and present and future values. See *Functions* for a general description of available functions.

The R:BASE financial functions listed in the table below all represent standard formulas. These formulas can be found in textbooks on accounting or engineering economics, such as *Principles of Engineering Economy,* Grant, Ireson, and Leavenworth (New York: Wiley, 1976), and *Basic Accounting and Cost Accounting,* Grant and Bell (New York: McGraw-Hill, 1964).

These financial functions accept various combinations of the following arguments. The terms used in many accounting and economics texts are given in parentheses:

pmt—payment amount (A)
int—periodic interest rate (i%)
per—number of compounding periods (n)
pv—present value (P)
fv—future value (F)

Function	Description
FV1(pmt,int,per)	Calculates the future value of a series of equal payments.
FV2(pv,int,per)	Calculates the future value of the investment.
PV1(pmt,int,per)	Calculates the present value of a series of equal payments.
PV2(fv,int,per)	Calculates the present value of the investment.
PMT1(int,per,pv)	Calculates the required periodic payment to pay off the investment.
PMT2(int,per,fv)	Calculates the required periodic payment to accrue the investment.
RATE1(fv,pv,per)	Calculates the periodic interest rate required to return the future value.
RATE2(fv,pmt,per)	Calculates the periodic interest rate required to return the future value.
RATE3(pv,pmt,per)	Calculates the interest rate required to return the series of equal payments of the given payment amount.
TERM1(pv,int,fv)	Calculates the number of compounding periods required to accrue the future value based on the present value and interest rate.
TERM2(pmt,int,fv)	Calculates the number of compounding periods required to accrue the future value based on the payment and interest rate.

(continued)

Function	Description
TERM3(pmt,int,pv)	Calculates the number of compounding periods required to pay off the investment (e.g., reduce the present value to 0) based on the payment and interest rate.

It is important to understand the relationship between the periodic interest rate and the compounding period. For example, if the *annual* interest rate is 12% and it is compounded daily, then the *periodic* interest rate is 0.12/365. Similarly, if the compounding period is daily, then the number of compounding periods is the number of days over which you are calculating the result. Payment amounts are always equal in a series based on the number of compounding periods. When using financial functions, make sure that your units of time are consistent for all of the arguments.

To clarify the above discussion, let's perform a simple calculation by hand. The basic formula for calculating future value (*fv*) based on a present investment (*pv*) at a given interest rate (*int*) is given as:

```
fv = pv(1 + int)per
```

If you deposit $5,000.00 today at 10% interest, compounded daily, how much will you have in the account one year from now? The answer is:

```
fv = 5000(1 + 0.10/365)365
   = 5000(1.0003)365
   = $5578.50
```

Using the R:BASE *FV2()* function, the above equation would look like this:

```
FV2(5000,(.12/365),365)
```

Database example: Financial functions are extremely useful for defining computed columns that provide calculations based on other columns in the table. For example, suppose you are a car salesperson and want to present your customers with various payment plans. The table for calculating payments might look like this:

```
Table: CARPMTS          No lock(s)
Read Password: No
Modify Password: No

Column definitions
# Name      Type      Length      Key   Expression
1 CARCOST   CURRENCY
2 MONTHNUM  INTEGER
3 INTRATE   REAL
4 PAYMENT   CURRENCY                     PMT1(('INTRATE'/12),
                                         'MONTHNUM','CARCOST')
```

In this example, the *PAYMENT* column is a computed column that calculates the required monthly payment based on the cost of the car, the number of months needed to pay off the car (assuming there is no downpayment), and the interest rate. Note that the interest is entered as an annual rate but is converted to monthly interest in the computed column expression.

Here is a sample session using the command LOAD WITH PROMPTS and the *CARPMTS* table:

```
Press [ESC] to end, [ENTER] to continue
CARCOST  (CURRENCY):15000
MONTHNUM (INTEGER ):48
INTRATE  (REAL    ):.10

Press [ESC] to end, [ENTER] to continue
CARCOST  (CURRENCY):20000
MONTHNUM (INTEGER ):60
INTRATE  (REAL    ):.09

Press [ESC] to end, [ENTER] to continue
CARCOST  (CURRENCY):60000
MONTHNUM (INTEGER ):72
INTRATE  (REAL    ):.10

Press [ESC] to end, [ENTER] to continue
End R:BASE Data Loading
R>SELECT ALL FROM CARPMTS
   CARCOST        MONTHNUM  INTRATE  PAYMENT
   -------------- --------- -------- ----------------
       $15,000.00        48     0.1           $380.44
       $20,000.00        60    0.09           $415.17
       $60,000.00        72     0.1         $1,111.55
R>
```

Program example: The following command file illustrates the use of financial functions to update a *LOAN* database. Here is the structure of the *LOAN* table and some typical values:

```
Table: LOAN            No lock(s)
Read Password: No
Modify Password: No

Column definitions
# Name      Type       Length        Key    Expression
1 AMTOWED   CURRENCY
2 LOAN      CURRENCY
3 UPDATE    DATE
4 LOANDATE  DATE
5 INTRATE   REAL
6 LOAN-NUM  INTEGER                  Yes
7 CLINUM    TEXT       5 characters

SELECT LOAN-NUM=2 CLINUM=2 AMTOWED LOAN INTRATE LOANDATE UPDATE +
   FROM LOAN
   LO CL AMTOWED    LOAN        INTRATE  LOANDATE UPDATE
   -- -- ---------- ----------  -------- -------- --------
    1  1 $4,589.53  $5,000.00       0.17 11/11/85 11/08/86
    2  2 $6,970.25  10,000.00       0.15 01/01/86 11/08/86
    3  3 $4,408.99  $5,000.00       0.15 11/08/85 11/08/86
```

Note that the titles for *LOAN-NUM* and *CLINUM* are truncated (see *SELECT*).

When you enter a new loan into the table, the *AMTOWED* column and the *LOAN* column should have identical values, as should the *LOANDATE* column and the *UPDATE* column. As the loan is paid off, the *AMTOWED* and *UPDATE* columns are updated to reflect the current amount owed and the date of the last payment. The payment is not actually recorded in the table; instead, it is entered when the command file is executed and then used to update the *AMTOWED* column.

Here is the command file for updating the *LOAN* table:

```
OPEN PERSONL
SET MESS OFF
SET ERR MESS OFF
SET VAR vloan# INTEGER
SET VAR vloan# = 0
SET VAR vpaid CURRENCY
SET VAR vnowowed CURRENCY
WHILE vloan# EXISTS THEN
  CLS
  WRITE "Loan Update Program" AT 1,20
  FILLIN vloan# USING "Enter Loan Number to Update: " AT 3,20
  IF vloan# FAILS THEN
    SET MESS ON
    SET ERR MESS ON
    BREAK
  ENDIF
  SET POINTER #1 p1 FOR LOAN WHERE LOAN-NUM EQ .vloan#
  IF p1 EQ 0 THEN
    SET ZERO ON
    FILLIN vpaid USING "Enter amount of payment or <Enter> IF 0: " +
      AT 5,20
    SET VAR vowed TO AMTOWED IN #1
    SET VAR vint TO INTRATE IN #1
    SET VAR vdate TO UPDATE IN #1
    SET VAR vnowowed = (FV2(.vowed,(.vint/365),(.#DATE - .vdate)) - .vpaid)
    CHANGE AMTOWED TO .vnowowed IN #1
    CHANGE UPDATE TO .#DATE IN #1
    SET VAR textowed = (CTXT(.vnowowed))
    WRITE "The amount now owed on this loan is: " AT 8,20
    SHOW VAR textowed AT 8,58
    WRITE "Press any key to continue" AT 10,20
    PAUSE
  ELSE
    WRITE "Loan number not found, press any key to continue" AT 5,20
    PAUSE
  ENDIF
ENDWHILE
```

The following screen shows a session in which this command file was run:

```
Loan Update Program

Enter Loan Number to Update: 3

Enter amount of payment or <Enter> if 0: 400


The amount now owed on this loan is:  $4,408.99

Press any key to continue
```

Let's look at the main features of this command file. First, the loan numbers are entered into the variable *vloan#* with the FILLIN command. If you press Enter at the loan number prompt, it is entered as *NULL* (i.e., *FAILS*) and the program terminates. For more information about *FAILS*, see *WHERE*. Second, the SET POINTER command finds the loan number you entered and prompts you to enter a payment (*vpaid*). Note that the program issues a SET ZERO ON command so that null values are interpreted as 0.

The command file sets the variables *vowed*, *vint*, and *vdate* to the corresponding column values in the *LOAN* table. Next, it calculates the variable *vnowowed* using the *FV2()* financial function. The current value of the principal is calculated before the new payment, *vpaid*, is subtracted. Finally the *AMTOWED* and *UPDATE* columns are updated, and the text conversion function *CTXT()* displays the final result.

You can easily transform the above loan table and update program into a savings table and update program by adding the variable *vpaid* rather than subtracting it and by changing the word owed to saved.

■ **R:BASE 5000 equivalent**
None

FORMS (Forms EXPRESS)

■ **Syntax**
Select Forms EXPRESS from the RBSYSTEM menu.

You also can execute FORMS at the R> prompt if you entered R:BASE from the RBSYSTEM menu.

```
FORMS ┬──────────┬┬─────────┬
      └ formname ┘└ tblname ┘
```

If you entered R:BASE from the MS-DOS prompt, you must exit R:BASE. You can then execute FORMS from MS-DOS:

FORMS ⌐── ⌐── ⌐── ⌐── ⌐──
        └ -R ┘└ -Fn ┘└ -Bn ┘└ -Mn ┘└ -Tn ┘

The -R option suppresses the display of the R logo. The -F and -B options modify the foreground and background colors if you are using a color monitor. The -M and -T options modify other monitor characteristics. See the R:BASE System V Installation Guide for further information on monitor options.

The options for appending a form name (*formname*) and the table name (*tblname*) are only available when executing FORMS from the R> prompt with an open database.

■ **Description**

Forms EXPRESS is an R:BASE System V module that lets you create forms for data entry and editing. A computerized form is analogous to the paper form that you fill out as an application or questionnaire. In fact, the data from most paper forms is ultimately transferred to a computerized database.

Creating a form: There are four main steps involved in creating a form:

1. Learn the format and tools used with forms.
2. Create the text and format of the form.
3. Locate the columns and variables on the form.
4. Add customized features, if necessary.

Format and tools. When you design data entry forms that correspond to existing handwritten forms, make them as similar to the handwritten versions as possible. Users can enter data more accurately and efficiently if the blanks on the screen, called fields in R:BASE, have a layout similar to those on the paper form.

Although you can enter and edit data using the R:BASE commands LOAD and EDIT, forms created with Forms EXPRESS give you much greater control of the data entry and editing processes. Forms EXPRESS offers these advantages:

Full screen editing and line drawing. You can use the entire screen to design a form. You can include explanatory text, highlights, and boxes to customize the appearance of the form. In addition, you can divide the screen into windows or use multiple screens to enter data into large tables that require multiple displays of different data entry fields.

Multiple table data entry and editing. With a form you can simultaneously enter or edit data in as many as five tables. Each table in the form must share a common column with at least one other table in the form.

Multiple row display. Forms EXPRESS provides a feature called a tiered region, which lets you display and enter multiple rows from a table. A tiered region is particularly useful when one row in a master table is connected to many rows in a secondary table.

Use of variables and expressions. Forms do not limit you to directly entering or editing data; you can use variables and expressions to perform calculations or to look up data to display on a form.

Data entry and editing control. Forms let you completely control the data entry and editing processes. You can customize the form's menu options, and you can specify the characteristics of individual fields on the form. For example, you can specify that individual fields be *edit-only* or *display-only.* You also can assign characteristics to the tables that the form accesses. For example, you can specify that new rows cannot be added or that rows cannot be replaced or deleted.

Forms in R:BASE are classified either as *table forms* or as *variable forms.* A table form is associated with a table in a database. A variable form is used only to enter data into variables. (The variable form is a remnant of R:BASE 5000.) With R:BASE System V, you probably will not need to use variable forms. For more information about variable forms, see *R:BASE 5000 commands.*

The function keys help you create forms. The following table lists the key functions in Forms EXPRESS:

Key	Description
F1	Inserts a line above the current line.
F2	Deletes the current line.
Shift-F2	Deletes the current field.
F3	Displays defined variables and columns from the current table (or from other tables if you press F3 again). If the cursor is in a field, F3 displays the field name and its data type.
F4	Turns the repeat function on and off. The repeat function lets you repeat the last character you typed by pressing any cursor key.

(continued)

127

Key	Description
Shift-F4	Duplicates tiers in the current region and lets you enter or edit multiple rows. Also removes duplicate tiers from a current multi-tiered region.
F5	Resets form, table, or field characteristics to their original status.
F6	Locates or relocates a field.
F7	Moves from the current table to the previous table.
F8	Moves from the current table to the next table.
F9	Expands or contracts the size of the region.
F10	Displays context-sensitive help screen.
Shift-F10	Displays more function key descriptions.
Ins	Inserts a space at the cursor position.
Del	Deletes the character at the cursor position.
Left/right arrow key	Moves the cursor left or right one character.
Ctrl-Right arrow	Moves the cursor to column 80.
Ctrl-Left arrow	Moves the cursor to column 1.
Tab	Moves the cursor 10 spaces to the right.
Shift-Tab	Moves the cursor 10 spaces to the left.
Home	Moves the cursor to the top of the page or region.
End	Moves the cursor to the end of the page or region.
PgUp/PgDn	Moves the cursor to the previous or the next page in a multi-page form.
ESC	Quits the current activity and displays the FORMS Definition menu.

After you open a database and start Forms EXPRESS from the R> prompt, the first menu you see is the Forms Option menu. Otherwise, the main Forms EXPRESS menu is displayed.

From the Forms Option menu, you can edit or create a form, list forms, and duplicate (copy) or remove forms. The *Copy* option is useful for making duplicates to test modifications on a working form. You also can use it to create separate forms for data entry and editing. The *Remove* option deletes a form from your database.

Text and format of the form. To edit or create a form, select *Edit/Create* from the Forms Option menu. When you create a new form, R:BASE gives you the option of customizing form and table characteristics. (In general, it's best to customize after you design the form.)

After you select *Edit/Create,* you see the following screen:

```
============================Form Definition Menu============================
  Edit  Expression  Customize  Draw
```

You use this menu to design the form. First, select the *Edit* option and type the text that will appear on your form. To add lines, select the *Draw* option. (If you are in Edit mode, press ESC and then select the *Draw* option.) Then use the *Expression* option to define new variables and expressions and change or reorder existing expressions. Finally, use the *Customize* option to customize form, table, and variable characteristics.

Caution: Do not use the top two lines of the screen to display text in your form. These lines are reserved for the data entry menu of the ENTER command and the Edit menu of the EDIT USING command. These menus overwrite any text you place in the top two lines.

Locate columns and variables. Before we look at multi-table forms and other advanced features of Forms EXPRESS, let's look at a simple example that illustrates how to create a basic data entry form and how to use calculated variables and the line-drawing feature.

This sample form lets you enter values for the legs of a right triangle (*SIDE1* and *SIDE2*) and then calculates the hypotenuse. The example uses the *RT-TRI* table of the *TRIG* database (see *Trigonometric functions*). The *RT-TRI* table contains the following columns:

```
Table: RT-TRI          No lock(s)
Read Password: No
Modify Password: No

Column definitions
# Name     Type     Length      Key    Expression
1 SIDE1    REAL
2 SIDE2    REAL
3 HYPOT    REAL                         (SQRT (('SIDE1')**2
                                         + ('SIDE2')**2))

4 ANGLE1   REAL                         (ASIN
                                         ('SIDE1'/'HYPOT') /
                                         (2 * .#PI) * 360)

5 ANGLE2   REAL                         (ACOS
                                         ('SIDE1'/'HYPOT') /
                                         (2 * .#PI) * 360)
```

Note that *HYPOT, ANGLE1,* and *ANGLE2* are all computed columns, and that you must enter only *SIDE1* and *SIDE2.* The following screen shows the design of a simple form that enters *SIDE1* and *SIDE2* and displays the calculated hypotenuse.

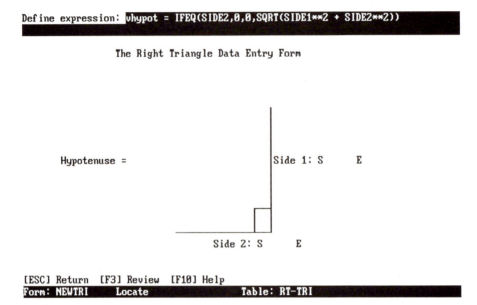

Define expression: `vhypot = IFEQ(SIDE2,0,0,SQRT(SIDE1**2 + SIDE2**2))`

The Right Triangle Data Entry Form

Hypotenuse =   Side 1: S   E

                               Side 2: S   E

[ESC] Return [F3] Review [F10] Help

Form: NEWTRI   Locate   Table: RT-TRI

The screen shows the form in Edit mode. The *Draw* option was used to draw the lines for the sides of the triangle. (Unfortunately, diagonal lines are not supported by the *Draw* option.) The fields for *SIDE1* and *SIDE2* were located with the F6 key. When you press F6, you are prompted to enter the variable or column to locate. Press F3 at any time to review the columns of the table or variables that you have already defined.

When you enter a column or variable name, R:BASE prompts you to enter an expression for the column or variable and lets you customize the field characteristics. Because *SIDE1* and *SIDE2* are simply numbers that you enter, they do not require an expression. These fields also do not require customized field characteristics, which are discussed later in this entry.

To locate a field on the form, move the cursor to the appropriate location and press *S*. Then move the cursor to the end of the field and press *E*. You can make the field shorter than its default length but not longer. For long text fields, continue a field on the next line by entering *W* rather than *E* on the continuation line. Note that the order in which you locate the fields determines the order in which you can access these fields when using the form. You can, however, change the order as we will discuss later in this entry.

Note that the above screen shows the process of defining an expression for the variable *vhypot*. The expression uses both the logical function *IFEQ()* and the *SQRT()* function. The *IFEQ()* function sets the hypotenuse to 0 unless a non-zero value is entered for *SIDE2*. If *SIDE2* is not equal to zero, then the hypotenuse is equal to the *SQRT()* expression (the Pythagorean theorem).

You might wonder why the example uses a variable (*vhypot*) rather than the computed column *HYPOT* to display the hypotenuse on the form. This question brings up an important concept in forms design. The values that you enter in a form are not actually recorded in the database until you select the appropriate menu item to save the data. This means that, even though you enter values for *SIDE1* and *SIDE2*, these values are not available for calculation by the *HYPOT* column until you save the row. The *vhypot* variable, however, can use the current values of *SIDE1* and *SIDE2* immediately to calculate the hypotenuse.

To clarify the above discussion, let's look at the form as it appears when you enter data using the ENTER command:

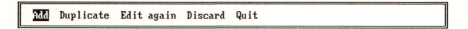

The Right Triangle Data Entry Form

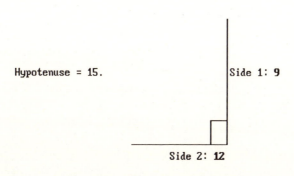

Hypotenuse = 15.   Side 1: **9**

Side 2: **12**

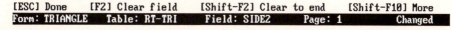

```
[ESC] Done    [F2] Clear field    [Shift-F2] Clear to end    [Shift-F10] More
Form: TRIANGLE    Table: RT-TRI    Field: SIDE2    Page: 1    Changed
```

When you enter values for *SIDE1* and *SIDE2*, the value of the hypotenuse is immediately calculated and displayed on the screen. If you use the computed column, *HYPOT*, the hypotenuse is not calculated until you select *Add* or *Duplicate* from the data entry menu. *Duplicate* displays the correct value for the hypotenuse because it saves the values and leaves them on the screen.

Add, however, saves the values in the fields and then replaces them with blanks for the next new row, so you never see the correct hypotenuse value. For more details see *ENTER*.

This example illustrates a multi-table form and a master search. Many database applications involve *one-to-many relationships*, as they are called in the R:BASE documentation. For example, our *CONSULT* database contains a list of clients (the *CLIENT* table), each differentiated by a client number, and a list of invoices (the *INVOICE* table), each connected to a single client. Obviously, you can have many invoices for a single client. You cannot, however, have many clients for a single invoice. This relationship is called a one-to-many relationship. The listing below shows the columns from the *CLIENT* and *INVOICE* tables:

```
Table: CLIENT          No lock(s)
Read Password: Yes
Modify Password: Yes

Column definitions
# Name    Type     Length         Key    Expression
1 CLINUM  INTEGER
2 CLINAME TEXT     25 characters
3 STREET  TEXT     25 characters
4 CITY    TEXT     20 characters
5 STATE   TEXT      2 characters
6 ZIP     TEXT      5 characters
7 PHONE   TEXT     12 characters

Current number of rows:      10


Table: INVOICE         No lock(s)
Read Password: No
Modify Password: No

Column definitions
# Name    Type     Length         Key    Expression
1 CLINUM  INTEGER                 yes
2 INV-NUM TEXT      8 characters
3 ENTRDATE DATE                          .#DATE
4 DUE     CURRENCY
5 PREVBAL CURRENCY
6 TOTAL   CURRENCY                       'PREVBAL'+'DUE'
7 FORWHAT TEXT     50 characters
8 PAID    TEXT      1 characters

Current number of rows:      14
```

Note that the tables are related by the common column *CLINUM*.

The standard procedure for using these two tables is to display a client on the screen and then edit the client's existing invoices or enter new invoices. A form designed for this operation is shown in the following screen:

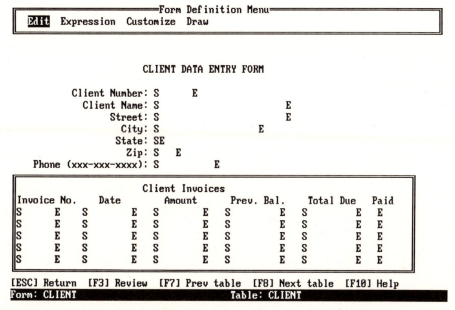

The upper portion of the form presents the client information from the *CLIENT* table. The *Client Name* field on the form uses an expression, which is based on the entered client number, to search for the information from the *CLIENT* table:

```
CLINAME = CLINAME IN CLIENT WHERE CLINUM = CLINUM
```

Note that this expression involves only columns. The expression looks for the column *CLINAME* in the table *CLIENT*, where the entered client number equals an existing client number. The *CLINAME* expression is executed when you enter a client number. If the client number exists, the client name and *all the other fields from that row* are displayed on the form. In other words, you only need to perform the search once for a single row, not for each column in the row. These searches can be used only with the ENTER command. The EDIT USING command automatically displays existing rows.

If you enter a nonexistent client number, R:BASE assumes it is a new entry. When you define the lookup expression, however, you can make it more specific. There are two options for lookups: You can provide a default value for the target column if the lookup fails, or you can require that the existing value be entered (i.e., "the lookup must succeed"). If you use the second option in the above example, you cannot enter new clients in the form. In this case, you could use the form only to enter new invoices.

After you specify the remaining fields of the client part of the form, press the F8 key to begin defining the next table in the form, the *INVOICE* table. This part of the form is defined as a multi-tiered region. To create a multi-tiered region, select *Customize* from the Form Definition menu and select the table characteristics. The following screen displays these characteristics:

```
Press [ESC] when done
                        Table Characteristics

Do you want to add new rows to the table? ..............................  [Yes]

Do you want to replace existing rows in the table? .....................  [Yes]
     Is the replace automatic when the user leaves the row? ............. [Yes]

Do you want to delete rows from the table? ............................. [Yes]
     Restrict the delete to the current table? ......................... [Yes]

Is this table on the MANY side of a ONE-to-MANY relationship? .......... [Yes]

Do you want to define a region? ........................................ [Yes]
     Do you want a border around the region? ........................... [Yes]
     How many lines in the border - enter 1 or 2: 2
     Do you want custom colors for the region? ......................... [No ]
     Foreground color: _____  Background color: _____
     (Press [ENTER] for a color palette)



[ESC] Done  [F5] Reset  [F10] Help  [↑] Up  [↓] Down
Form: CLIENT      Customize table          Table: INVOICE
```

The *INVOICE* table is on the *many* side of a *one-to-many* relationship. Select this characteristic to display multiple rows on the form. To define a region, select *Yes*. Then use the cursor to set the boundaries of the region. After you define the region, press any key to return to the table characteristics screen. Then select the option to draw a border around the region.

At this point, consider the other *Table Characteristics* options. You can prevent rows from being replaced or deleted and you can specify that no new rows be added. A *No add* option is not appropriate for the invoice part of the form, but it might be useful for the client table of a form designed to log only new invoices.

After you define a region, press ESC, choose *Edit,* and press the F6 key to position the fields for that region in a single row. The term applied to a single row in the region is a *tier.* To make the region multi-tiered, press Shift-F4. This duplicates the row in the rest of the region. Here is how a form looks when used to edit existing invoices:

```
┌──────────────────────────────────────────────────────────────────┐
│ ┌─────┐                                                            │
│ │Edit │ Save  Add new  Delete  Reset  Previous  Next  Quit         │
│ └─────┘                                                            │
└──────────────────────────────────────────────────────────────────┘


                      CLIENT DATA ENTRY FORM

         Client Number: 1
           Client Name: Johnson and Anderson Co.
                Street: 101 Howard Street
                  City: San Francisco
                 State: Ca
                   Zip: 94101
   Phone (xxx-xxx-xxxx): 415-397-8092

┌──────────────────────────────────────────────────────────────────┐
│                      Client Invoices                               │
│ Invoice No.    Date      Amount      Prev. Bal.    Total Due   Paid│
│ 001          10/22/86   $3,000.00    $345.00       $3,345.00    y  │
│ 002          10/22/86   $7,898.00    $0.00         $7,898.00    y  │
│ 003          10/22/86   $343.00      $600.00       $943.00      n  │
│                                                                    │
└──────────────────────────────────────────────────────────────────┘
```

When you select the customized form, use the F7 and F8 keys to move between the two tables. Note that a region is like a window. If there are more rows than will fit in the region at one time, they will scroll into the window as you move the cursor through the rows.

It is important to realize that while you are in ENTER mode, no existing invoices are displayed. The lookup expression displays the client information, but the invoice region only lets you enter new rows.

Multiple page forms. To create multiple page forms, press PgDn when you are in Edit mode. Note, however, that fields and regions may *not* extend across form pages.

Customized features. In the client/invoice example, we used the *Table Characteristics* option to customize the *INVOICE* table for use in a multi-tiered region. You also can customize field and form characteristics. Here is the Field Characteristics screen:

```
Press [ESC] when done
                          Field Characteristics

Will new data be entered in the field? ................................. [No ]

Can the user change the data displayed in the field? ................... [No ]
      Restrict changes to the current table? ........................... [N/A]

Do you want to display a default value in the field? ................... [No ]
      Enter the default value OR #DUP to use the previous row value
 _____


Do you want custom colors for the field? .............................. [No ]
      Foreground color: _____   Background color: _____
      (Press [ENTER] for a color palette)




 [ESC] Done  [F5] Reset  [F10] Help  [↑] Up  [↓] Down
 Form: TRIANGLE   Column      Field: HYPOT      Type: REAL      Table: RT-TRI
```

The Field Characteristics screen lets you impose special restrictions on individual fields. Note that the *Restrict changes to the current table* option is applicable only to columns that are common to other tables in the form. Choosing this option prevents changed column values from affecting other tables in the form that contain the same column. The default for this option is *Yes.*

To leave the previous row values on the screen, use the *#DUP* option. This feature is useful for forms that contain fields that do not generally change from row to row.

Now, let's look at the Form Characteristics screen:

```
Press [ESC] when done
                           Form Characteristics

Assign passwords for this form? ........................................ [N/A]
      Read-only password: _____      Modify password: _____
Clear the screen before form use? ..................................... [Yes]
Clear the screen after form use? ...................................... [Yes]
Display a status line during form use? ................................ [Yes]
Do you want custom colors for the form? ............................... [No ]
      Foreground color: _____   Background color: _____
      (Press [ENTER] for a color palette)

Do you plan to use the form with the ENTER command? ................... [Yes]
      Do you want to change the menu? ................................. [No ]
 ┌──────────────────────────────────────────────────────────────────────┐
 │  Add  Duplicate  Edit again  Discard  Quit                             │
 └──────────────────────────────────────────────────────────────────────┘

Do you plan to use the form with the EDIT command? ................... [Yes]
      Do you want to change the menu? ................................. [No ]
 ┌──────────────────────────────────────────────────────────────────────┐
 │  Edit  Save  Add new  Delete  Reset  Previous  Next  Quit              │
 └──────────────────────────────────────────────────────────────────────┘
[ESC] Done  [F5] Reset  [F10] Help  [↑] Up  [↓] Down
Form: TEST        Customize form
```

Form characteristics let you assign passwords to restrict access to the form. Note that these passwords override any assigned table passwords. The *clear screen* and *status line* options are generally left as they are. However, when you use a command file to display a text file on one part of the screen and the form on the other, turn off the clear screen function. To suppress the status line, which displays the form name and function key instructions at the bottom of the form and the *ESC when done* reminder at the top of the screen, turn off the *status line* function.

Also of interest are the options that let you modify the menus displayed with the ENTER and EDIT USING commands. The most common use of these options is to remove the *Delete* or *Add New* options from the Edit menu to restrict their use.

Changing a form: Forms EXPRESS makes it easy to change any aspect of a form. However, to make changes in a region, you must first remove duplicated tiers by pressing Shift-F4. After you make your changes, press Shift-F4 again to reduplicate the tier. You can make changes only in the current table. To change the current table, use the F7 and F8 keys.

In the Edit mode, you can relocate, delete, and insert fields as well as edit the text in a form. To relocate a field or redefine its characteristics, move the cursor to the beginning of the field and press F6. Answer the prompts to change field characteristics and relocate the field. You can always change your mind and reply with *No* to both these options, or you can cancel the operation by pressing ESC at any time.

To delete an existing field, select the Edit mode from the Form Definition screen. Move the cursor to the field you wish to delete and press Shift-F2. You also can delete fields containing expressions by selecting *Expressions* from the Form Definition screen and then deleting the expression. You can, of course, change an existing expression rather than delete it.

To insert a field while you are in the Edit mode, move the cursor to the desired location and press F6. Note, however, that new fields are entered last on the form unless you change the *field order.* To change the field order, select *Customize* and then *Field Order.* All fields on your form are displayed in numbered sequence. Simply change the numbering sequence to suit your needs. You also can reorder expressions and tables in your form with the *Expressions* and *Customize* options.

You must reorder expressions if you use a variable that is defined in an expression later in the sequence. Expressions are executed in sequence starting with the first listed expression. If the first expression uses a variable value that is defined in the fourth expression, for example, you will get an error.

Regions can be expanded or contracted by pressing the F9 key with the region as the current table. Again, remove duplicate tiers before you modify the region.

Another feature worth mentioning is the use of the *Customize* option to rename and delete tables in the form. Note that these functions do not affect the tables in the database, but only the table names in the form. These functions are helpful if you want to use the same form or part of the form with different tables.

See: *EDIT USING, ENTER, Expressions,* and *Variables*

- **R:BASE 5000 equivalent**
R:BASE 5000 table forms can be used only to enter and edit data in a single table. Although variables and expressions are not supported, you can use a variable form within a command file for multiple table data entry (see *R:BASE 5000 commands*). If you need to work with multiple tables in a form, we strongly recommend that you upgrade to R:BASE System V.

Functions

■ **Description**

R:BASE System V provides one of the most comprehensive sets of functions available for a microcomputer-based database program. Functions in R:BASE System V are divided into the following categories:

Arithmetic and mathematical
Conversion
Date and time
Financial
Logical
String manipulation
Trigonometric

Consult the above entries for details and for examples of the use of each function. For additional examples of the use of functions see *Expressions.*

A function consists of the reserved R:BASE word for that function (e.g., *SQRT, AVE*) followed by one or more *arguments* within parentheses. The argument may, unless otherwise noted, consist of a constant, a dotted variable, an expression, or a column name. Column names can be used as arguments only in cases where the context or syntax of the command includes the table in which the column name belongs.

For example, you cannot use a column name as an argument to a function used in the SET VARIABLE command because the syntax of the command does not let you reference a table. You can, on the other hand, use a column name as an argument with the COMPUTE command, because the expression in the COMPUTE command is interpreted as a computed column. In the case of the SET VARIABLE command, you can get around the problem by first setting a variable equal to the column value and then using the variable as the argument of the function, as follows:

```
SET VAR vcount TO SAMPNUM IN SAMPLES WHERE COUNT EQ LAST
SET VAR vcount = SQRT(.vcount)
```

Here, *vcount* is set equal to the value of the column *SAMPNUM* in the *SAMPLES* table. Then the *SQRT()* function is used with the value of *vcount* as the argument. It also could be handled as follows:

```
COMPUTE vcount AS SUM (SQRT(SAMPNUM)) FROM SAMPLES
```

■ **R:BASE 5000 equivalent**

R:BASE 5000 does not include functions. If you are using R:BASE 5000 and performing many calculations, upgrading to R:BASE System V can make your life much easier.

Function keys

■ **Description**

The function keys (F1 through F10) are assigned a variety of functions depending on the R:BASE module with which you are working (Forms EXPRESS, RBEDIT, etc.). Although there is some consistency in the assignments, function keys often perform different operations in different R:BASE modules.

The following table shows the actions of the function keys. For actions that apply to specific modules, the module is noted in parentheses.

Function Key	Description
F1	Inserts a line (FORMS/REPORTS/RBEDIT).
	Inserts a column (Definition EXPRESS).
	Inserts an option (Application EXPRESS).
Shift-F1	Defines function key assignments with Alt and Ctrl keys.
F2	Deletes a line (FORMS/REPORTS/RBEDIT).
	Deletes a row (EDIT).
	Deletes a column (Definition EXPRESS).
	Deletes an option (Application EXPRESS).
	Erases the current field in a form (ENTER/EDIT USING).
Shift-F2	Deletes a field (FORMS/REPORTS).
	Deletes a text block (RBEDIT).
	Erases from the cursor to the end of the field (EDIT/ENTER).
F3	Displays defined columns and variables.
	Displays the menu tree (Application EXPRESS).
Shift-F3	Displays the custom key map (see Shift-F1).
F4	Toggles the repeat function for repeating characters.
	Toggles pen up/pen down drawing function (FORMS/REPORTS).
Shift-F4	Duplicates/removes multiple tiers in a region (FORMS).
F5	Resets a row to its original value (EDIT).
	Resets a field value (EDIT USING/ENTER).
	Resets a column definition (Definition EXPRESS).

(continued)

140

Function Key	Description
F5	Resets an option definition (Application EXPRESS).
	Resets characteristics (FORMS).
Shift-F5	Resets a table value (Application EXPRESS).
F6	Locates/relocates fields (FORMS/REPORTS).
Shift-F6	Options menu (FileGateway).
	Marks a text block (RBEDIT).
F7	Moves the cursor to the previous table (FORMS).
	Moves the cursor to the previous section (REPORTS).
	Moves the cursor to the previous row (ENTER/EDIT USING).
Shift-F7	Records an *exec* file.
F8	Moves the cursor to the next table (FORMS).
	Moves the cursor to the next section (REPORTS).
	Moves the cursor to the next row (ENTER/EDIT USING).
Shift-F8	Plays back an *exec* file.
F9	Expands regions (FORMS).
	Expands sections (REPORTS).
	Moves the cursor to the next table or region (ENTER/EDIT USING).
F10	Help.
Shift-F10	Help for defining key maps (see Shift-F1).
	Toggles the function key display at the bottom of the screen.

■ Defining your own function keys

You can define your own function key actions with the Alt and Ctrl keys. This is called *defining your own key map*. It should be emphasized, however, that these key assignments are valid only during the current R:BASE session. When you quit R:BASE, your key definitions are deleted. This limitation diminishes the usefulness of personalized key maps. However, if you use the Record/Playback feature to record the steps for defining the function keys in a file, you can then play the file back to redefine the function keys (see *RECORD* and *PLAYBACK*).

To define your function key combinations, press Shift-F1. You are then prompted to press the keys you want to define. The keys must include the Ctrl or Alt key followed by a function key, F1 through F10. Then enter an action to a maximum of 512 characters. Press Shift-F1 again to end the function key definition. Embed this operation inside a Record session so that you can easily recall it the next time you start R:BASE.

■ **R:BASE 5000 equivalent**
Function keys F1 through F5 and F10 perform essentially the same functions in R:BASE 5000. The function keys F6 through F9 are not used. There also is no provision for defining function keys.

GATEWAY

■ **Syntax**
Select FileGateway from the main System menu.

You also can execute GATEWAY at the R> prompt if you entered R:BASE from the System menu.

```
GATEWAY ┬─────┬
        └ exec ┘
```

If you entered R:BASE from the MS-DOS prompt, you must exit R:BASE. You can then execute GATEWAY from MS-DOS:

```
GATEWAY ┬───┬ ┬───┬ ┬───┬ ┬───┬ ┬───┬ ┬─────┬
        └ -R ┘ └ -Fn ┘ └ -Bn ┘ └ -Mn ┘ └ -Tn ┘ └ exec ┘
```

The -*R* option suppresses display of the R logo. The -*F* and -*B* options modify the foreground and background colors if you are using a color monitor. The -*M* and -*T* options modify other monitor characteristics. See the R:BASE System V Installation Guide for further information on monitor options. The *exec* option lets you specify an *exec* file that runs when you start GATEWAY.

■ **Description**
The GATEWAY command starts the FileGateway module.

See: *FileGateway, PLAYBACK,* and *RECORD*

■ **R:BASE 5000 equivalent**
None

GOTO

■ **Syntax**

GOTO *lblname*

■ **Description**

Use the GOTO command in command files to skip to another line in the file and continue the procedure from that line.

■ **Procedure**

Specify the line to which the program skips with the LABEL command. The label name you use in the GOTO command must correspond to a label name specified in a LABEL command. This LABEL command may either follow or precede the GOTO command. R:BASE searches for the label name starting from the GOTO command to the end of the file, and if it does not find it, continues the search from the top of the file.

The GOTO command is useful for skipping blocks of commands that do not need to be executed. For example, if you decide to quit an application somewhere in the middle of the command file, you do not need to execute the rest of the commands. With the GOTO command, you can skip to the end of the file, clear variables, and exit.

GOTO also is commonly used to repeat the display of a menu. The command files generated by Application EXPRESS provide a good example of this use. Here is an excerpt from the main application file discussed in the Application EXPRESS entry:

```
$COMMAND
CONSULT
SET MESSAGE OFF
OPEN CONSULT
   .
   .
   .
LABEL startapp
NEWPAGE
CHOOSE pick1 FROM Main IN CONSULT.APX
IF pick1 EQ -1 THEN
   NEWPAGE
   DISPLAY Help IN CONSULT.APX
   WRITE "Press any key to continue "
   PAUSE
   GOTO startapp
ENDIF
IF pick1 EQ 0 THEN
   GOTO endapp
ENDIF
   .
   .
   .
LABEL endapp
CLEAR pick1
RETURN
   .
   .
   .
```

The first IF statement block checks to see if you have pressed F10 for Help, which sets the variable *pick1* to *-1*. If you have, the help text is displayed. When you press a key to continue, the GOTO command tells the program to skip to *startapp*. This sequence causes the main menu to be displayed again. Note that the label *startapp* precedes the GOTO command.

The second use of the GOTO command occurs if the variable *pick1* is *0*, which means that ESC has been pressed. In this case, GOTO tells the program to skip to the label *endapp*. The variable *pick1* is cleared and the RETURN command terminates the execution of the command block or file. Note that the complete command file contains 40 lines of code between the GOTO *endapp* and LABEL *endapp* statements.

The above example is not restricted to command files generated in Application EXPRESS. You also can use the same commands and programming structures in your own command files.

See: *Command files, IF, LABEL, Procedure files,* and *Programming*

■ **R:BASE 5000 equivalent**
GOTO

HELP

■ **Syntax**

```
HELP ┌─────────┐
     └ cmdname ┘
```

■ **Description**
The HELP command activates the R:BASE Help mode.

■ **Procedure**
Typing HELP and a command name displays information about that command and then returns you to the R> prompt. If you execute HELP without appending a command, the screen prompt changes to H>, and you request information about any command by simply entering that command. You can also activate the Help mode by pressing the F10 key at the R> prompt. To exit from the Help mode, type: END.

Here is the screen you see when you enter the HELP command:

```
══════════════════════════════HELP══════════════════════════════
Help is available for these database management tasks:

    1 - Define a new database
    2 - Modify an existing database structure
    3 - Add rows to a table
    4 - Look at table values, or information about table values
    5 - Modify values in a table
    6 - Create a new table from old tables
    7 - Look at and modify R:BASE status values
    8 - Manage drives, paths, files, and databases
    9 - Build command files and R:BASE applications

At the H> prompt below, enter:
▪ A number (1 through 9) to display help for that task
▪ COMMANDS to list the R:BASE commands with help available
▪ An R:BASE command name to display help for that command
▪ ARGUMENTS to list commonly used syntax arguments
▪ SUPERMATH to list R:BASE functions
```

```
For additional HELP text, enter a command name. To leave HELP, enter END.
For the previous help menu press [ESC]
H>END
R>
```

- **R:BASE 5000 equivalent**

  HELP

IF

- **Syntax**

```
IF conditionlist THEN
      then-block
ENDIF
```

```
IF conditionlist THEN
      then-block
ELSE
      else-block
ENDIF
```

- **Description**

  The IF statement gives a command file procedure the ability to select alternative actions depending on specified conditions.

■ **Procedure**

In its simplest form, the IF statement consists of a condition followed by one or more commands and the *ENDIF* clause. If the condition is met (i.e., it is true), the program executes the commands inside the IF statement. Execution then continues at the line immediately following the *ENDIF* clause. If the condition is not met (i.e., it is false), the program skips the commands inside the IF statement and executes the line immediately following the *ENDIF* clause.

If the *IF* condition is false and the optional *ELSE* clause is specified, the program executes the commands following the *ELSE* clause. As in the other cases, the program resumes execution at the line immediately following the *ENDIF* clause.

A *condition* is a combination of variables and operators that together form a logical statement. A logical statement also can include functions and expressions. The *conditionlist* can consist of a single logical statement or as many as ten statements connected by the operators AND, OR, AND NOT, or OR NOT. You also can use the following conditional operators in a logical statement:

EXISTS, FAILS, CONTAINS
EQ (=), NE (<>), GT (>), GE (> =), LT (<), LE (< =)

For further information about these operators, see *Operators*.

Typically, IF statements are used to take a course of action that depends on the value of a variable, usually provided by the user. For example, when you make a menu selection, the IF statements in the menu's command file determine which commands are executed. The following command file illustrates this situation:

```
CHOOSE vchoice FROM MENU1
IF vchoice EQ 1 THEN
   NEWPAGE
   FILLIN vpath USING "Enter Path or <Enter> to Quit: " AT 4,5
   IF vpath EXISTS THEN
      DIR .vpath
      WRITE "Press any key to continue"
      PAUSE
   ENDIF
ENDIF
```

When you select option 1 from *MENU1*, the variable *vchoice* is set to *1*. If *vchoice* equals *1*, R:BASE prompts you to enter a pathname for a directory listing. If the path exists, the directory is listed on the screen. This command block also illustrates the use of nested IF statements. You can nest IF statements inside other IF statements. R:BASE permits you to nest a maximum of nine levels of IF statements. Indent the commands within IF statements to make them easier to read.

A more complex example of the IF statement is shown in the following command file:

```
OPEN CONSULT
SET MESS OFF
SET ERR MESS OFF
SET VAR vloan# INTEGER
SET VAR vloan# = 0
SET VAR vpaid CURRENCY
SET VAR vnowowed CURRENCY
WHILE vloan# EXISTS THEN
  CLS
  WRITE "Loan Update Program" AT 1,10
  FILLIN vloan# USING "Enter Loan Number to Update: " AT 3,10
  IF vloan# FAILS THEN
    SET MESS ON
    SET ERR MESS ON
    BREAK
  ENDIF
  SET POINTER #1 p1 FOR LOAN WHERE LOAN-NUM EQ .vloan#
  IF p1 EQ 0 THEN
    SET VAR vclinum TO CLINUM IN #1
    SET POINTER #2 p2 FOR CLIENT WHERE CLINUM EQ .vclinum
    IF p2 EQ 0 THEN
      SET VAR vcliname TO CLINAME IN #2
      WRITE "The client in this loan transaction is: " AT 5,10
      SHOW VAR vcliname AT 5,50
      SET ZERO ON
      FILLIN vpaid USING "Enter amount of payment or <Enter> IF 0: " +
        AT 7,10
      SET VAR vowed TO AMTOWED IN #1
      SET VAR vint TO INTRATE IN #1
      SET VAR vdate TO UPDATE IN #1
      SET VAR vnowowed = (FV2(.vowed, (.vint / 365), +
        (.#DATE - .vdate)) - .vpaid)
      CHANGE AMTOWED TO .vnowowed IN #1
      CHANGE UPDATE TO .#DATE IN #1
      SET VAR textowed = (CTXT(.vnowowed))
      WRITE "The amount now owed on this loan is: " AT 9,10
      SHOW VAR textowed AT 9,48
      WRITE "Press any key to continue" AT 11,10
      PAUSE
    ELSE
      WRITE "This client does not exist -- check loan table! Press any key." +
        AT 7,10
      PAUSE
    ENDIF
  ELSE
    WRITE "Loan number not found, press any key to continue" AT 7,10
    PAUSE
  ENDIF
ENDWHILE
```

This command file is a modified version of the *Loan Update* command file found in the *Financial functions* entry. The major difference is that the command file searches for the client name for the entered loan number in a second table (the *CLIENT* table). The user must not only enter a valid loan number, but a corresponding valid client number must also exist. The program uses nested IF statements to check for these conditions.

The first IF statement checks to see if a loan number has been entered. If the condition *vloan# FAILS* is true, the user pressed Enter at the loan number prompt, and a null value was assigned to the variable *vloan#*. In this case, the program terminates with the BREAK command.

Of particular interest in this example is the use of the IF statements in conjunction with the SET POINTER command. The first pointer (*pointer #1*) is set for the *LOAN-NUM* column in the *LOAN* table. The variable *p1* in the SET POINTER command is set to *0* if the *WHERE* clause in the SET POINTER command is satisfied. In other words, *p1* is *0* as long as the program finds a valid loan number. If it does not, R:BASE sets *p1* to a non-zero value, and the IF statement is false. We can look at the basic structure of the first IF statement by extracting it from the main command file:

```
IF p1 EQ 0 THEN
   SET VAR vclinum TO CLINUM IN #1
   SET POINTER #2 p2 FOR CLIENT WHERE CLINUM EQ .vclinum
   .
   .      *(list of commands)
   .
ELSE
   WRITE "Loan number not found, press any key to continue" AT 7,10
   PAUSE
ENDIF
```

If the entered loan number is not found in the *LOAN* table, the command file displays the following message:

```
Loan Update Program

Enter Loan Number to Update: 565



Loan number not found, press any key to continue
```

If the entered loan number is valid, the variable *vclinum* is set to the value of *CLINUM* in the *LOAN* table. The second pointer (*pointer #2*) then looks up the client number in the *CLIENT* table. If it finds the number, variable *p2* equals *0* and the loan update proceeds. If it does not, the *CLIENT* number in the *LOAN* table does not have a counterpart in the *CLIENT* table and is not a valid number. The command file then displays the following message:

```
Loan Update Program

Enter Loan Number to Update: 3



This client does not exist -- check loan table! Press any key.
```

Although studying these IF statements may seem to be a tedious exercise, it is important because the IF and SET POINTER combination is one of the most powerful programming features of R:BASE.

■ **Comment**

IF conditions do not use column names because the logical statement cannot include the table to which the column belongs. To use a column value in a condition, you must use the SET POINTER and SET VARIABLE commands to assign the column value to a variable and then use the variable in the IF statement. For example, you can use the *LNAME* column from the *EMPLOYEE* table in a condition by first assigning its value to the variable *vlname*:

```
SET POINTER #2 p2 TO EMPLOYEE
SET VAR vlname TO LNAME IN #2
IF vlname EQ SMITH THEN
   .
   .     *(list of commands)
   .
ENDIF
```

Also note that the logical functions *IFEQ()*, *IFLT()*, and *IFGT()* offer an alternative, in some cases, to IF statements. For further information about these functions, see *Logical functions*.

Cautions: Be sure to end all IF statements with an ENDIF statement. Indent nested IF statements so you can easily locate corresponding ENDIF statements. Condition statements cannot be enclosed in parentheses. If you execute a command file and the screen suddenly displays an I> prompt, either an IF command lacks a corresponding ENDIF statement or ESC was pressed to exit the IF block abnormally. Type ENDIF to return to the R> prompt and then check the command file for missing ENDIF statements.

See: *Expressions, Functions, Logical functions, Operators, SET POINTER,* and *SET VARIABLE*

See also: *BREAK* and *Financial functions*

■ **R:BASE 5000 equivalent**

IF...THEN...ELSE...ENDIF

INPUT

■ **Syntax**

```
INPUT ⎧ filespec
      ⎩ KEYBOARD
```

■ **Description**

The primary function of the INPUT command is to restore data files created with the OUTPUT and UNLOAD commands. You also can use the INPUT command to enter R:BASE commands from an ASCII file rather than from the keyboard. However, when you use INPUT to execute command files in ASCII format, you cannot pass parameters as you can with the RUN command. We recommend that you use RUN for running command files because it enables you to execute both ASCII and encoded command files.

■ **Procedure**

The following example illustrates the INPUT command. Let's assume that you used the UNLOAD command to create a file called *LOAN.DAT* and that the file is on a floppy disk in drive A. At the R> prompt, type:

```
INPUT A:LOAN.DAT
```

This enters the contents of the *LOAN.DAT* file, line by line, into R:BASE. For further information on files created with UNLOAD, see *UNLOAD*.

■ **Comments**

If you use INPUT with a file that contains database definition commands for a database that already exists, errors will appear on the screen; the input file, however, will still execute successfully.

■ **R:BASE 5000 equivalent**

INPUT

See: *ASCII characters and files, Backing up data, CodeLock, OUTPUT, RUN,* and *UNLOAD*

INTERSECT

■ **Syntax**

```
INTERSECT tblname1 WITH tblname2 FORMING tblname3 ─┬─────────────────┬─
                                                   └ USING collist ┘
```

■ **Description**

The INTERSECT command forms a new table from two tables that have one or more common columns; it uses only the rows in which the common column values are identical. The primary purpose of the INTERSECT command is to combine information from two tables while omitting rows that do not have matching values.

■ **Procedure**

As an example, consider the following command sequence:

```
R>SELECT CLINUM LOAN-NUM FROM LOAN
  CLINUM     LOAN-NUM
  ---------- ----------
          1          1
          2          2
         67          3
R>SELECT CLINUM CLINAME FROM NEWCLI
  CLINUM     CLINAME
  ---------- -------------------------
          1 Johnson and Anderson Co.
          2 Cal Gas and Electric
          3 Power Research Associates
          4 Stone Construction Co.
          5 Ohio Electric Power Co.
R>INTERSECT LOAN WITH NEWCLI FORMING CHECK USING CLINUM LOAN-NUM CLINAME
  Successful intersect operation, 2 rows generated
R>SELECT ALL FROM CHECK
  CLINUM     LOAN-NUM   CLINAME
  ---------- ---------- -------------------------
          1          1 Johnson and Anderson Co.
          2          2 Cal Gas and Electric
R>
```

The *LOAN* table has a client number (67) that does not exist in the *NEWCLI* table. When the two tables are combined with the INTERSECT command, the row containing client 67 is not included in the new table. Note that a UNION command would include this row and insert null values in the corresponding columns from the *NEWCLI* table. The SUBTRACT command, however, would perform the opposite function of the INTERSECT command and include *only* the row containing client 67.

Note that if multiple common columns exist in the two tables, all values of the common columns listed in the *USING* clause must match for the intersection to take place.

■ **Comment**

The following guidelines can help you use the INTERSECT command most efficiently:

☐ For better performance, key the common column or columns in the second table (*tblname2*). In the above example, *CLINUM*, in the *NEWCLI* table, should be keyed.

☐ If one table is much larger than the other, make the smaller table the second table of the INTERSECT command and do not use keys.

☐ If both tables are large, name the table with the shorter row length first, and use a key in the common column of the second table.

■ **R:BASE 5000 equivalent**

INTERSECT

See: *APPEND, BUILD KEY, JOIN, Keys, PROJECT, Relational commands, SUBTRACT, UNION,* and *VIEW*

JOIN

■ **Syntax**

```
JOIN tblname1 USING colname1 WITH tblname2 ...

                  ... USING colname2 FORMING tblname3 ┌─────────────────┐
                                                       └ WHERE logicop ┘
```

■ **Description**

The JOIN command forms a new table from two existing tables, based on columns with the same data types and lengths. The JOIN command differs from other relational commands in that it is often applied to tables that do not have common columns.

■ **Procedure**

The comparison of *colname1* to *colname2* is defined by a *WHERE* clause followed by one of the logical operators EQ, NE, GT, GE, LT, or LE. If the *WHERE* clause is omitted, the default comparison operator is EQ (*colname1* EQ *colname2*). Note that this usage of *WHERE* is unique to the JOIN command.

The JOIN command is best understood by working through an example. Let's assume you are a financial consultant who must advise clients on what kinds of cars they can afford to buy. Your wealth of experience indicates that a buyer's annual salary should be at least twice the price of the car he or she intends to buy. Therefore, you set up two tables: the *CARCUST* table and the *CARLIST* table:

```
Table: CARCUST          No lock(s)
Read Password: No
Modify Password: No

Column definitions
# Name     Type      Length          Key    Expression
1 CLINUM   INTEGER
2 FRSTNAME TEXT       15 characters
3 LASTNAME TEXT       15 characters
4 SALARY   CURRENCY
5 SAL50%   CURRENCY                         .50*'SALARY'
6 HIREDATE DATE
7 SEX      TEXT        1 characters
8 INITIALS TEXT        3 characters

Current number of rows:    10
```

(continued)

```
Table: CARLIST          No lock(s)
Read Password: No
Modify Password: No

Column definitions
# Name      Type      Length          Key    Expression
1 MAKE      TEXT       15 characters
2 MODEL     TEXT        8 characters
3 PRICE     CURRENCY

Current number of rows:     16
```

The following screen shows sample data from these two tables:

```
R>SELECT ALL FROM CARLIST
  MAKE              MODEL     PRICE
  --------------    --------  ----------------
  Cadillac          Seville   $25,000.00
  BMW               525e      $27,000.00
  Renault           Alliance  $13,000.00
  Mercedes          280SE     $33,000.00
  Pontiac           Firebird  $22,000.00
  Volvo             760       $24,000.00
  Porsche           911       $40,000.00
  Chevrolet         Citation  $12,000.00
  Toyota            Tercel     $8,000.00
  Nissan            Stanza     $7,000.00
  Volkswagen        Bus       $10,000.00
  AMC               Jeep       $9,500.00
  Alfa Romeo        Firenze   $13,400.00
  Fiat              124        $8,800.00
  BMW               320i      $23,000.00
  Porsche           924       $16,000.00
R>SELECT ALL FROM CARCUST WHERE LIMIT EQ 2
  CLINUM    FRSTNAME        LASTNAME        SALARY            SAL50%
  --------- --------------- --------------- ----------------  ----------------
        1 Harold          Wilson          $27,500.00        $13,750.00
        2 Marjorie        Lawrence        $27,500.00        $13,750.00
R>
```

The *CARCUST* table contains information on your clients. The computed column *SAL50%* represents 50% of the client's annual salary. The *CARLIST* table tracks the make, model, and price of new cars. Your goal is to use a formula that presents each client with a list of new cars that he or she can afford.

To do this, use the JOIN command to combine the *CARCUST* table with the *CARLIST* table. Specify that *SAL50%* from the *CARCUST* table must be greater than or equal to *PRICE* from the *CARLIST* table. The following command sequence shows the results for clients *Smith* and *Graham*:

```
R>JOIN CARCUST USING SAL50% WITH CARLIST USING PRICE +
+> FORMING RANGECAR WHERE GE
 Successful join operation, 85 rows generated
R>SELECT LASTNAME SALARY MAKE MODEL PRICE FROM RANGECAR +
+> WHERE LASTNAME EQ "Graham" OR LASTNAME EQ "Smith"
 LASTNAME         SALARY           MAKE            MODEL      PRICE
 ---------------- ---------------- --------------- ---------- ----------------
 Graham           $19,800.00 Toyota               Tercel       $8,000.00
 Graham           $19,800.00 Nissan               Stanza       $7,000.00
 Graham           $19,800.00 AMC                  Jeep         $9,500.00
 Graham           $19,800.00 Fiat                 124          $8,800.00
 Smith            $49,500.00 Renault              Alliance    $13,000.00
 Smith            $49,500.00 Pontiac              Firebird    $22,000.00
 Smith            $49,500.00 Volvo                760         $24,000.00
 Smith            $49,500.00 Chevrolet            Citation    $12,000.00
 Smith            $49,500.00 Toyota               Tercel       $8,000.00
 Smith            $49,500.00 Nissan               Stanza       $7,000.00
 Smith            $49,500.00 Volkswagen           Bus         $10,000.00
 Smith            $49,500.00 AMC                  Jeep         $9,500.00
 Smith            $49,500.00 Alfa Romeo           Firenze     $13,400.00
 Smith            $49,500.00 Fiat                 124          $8,800.00
 Smith            $49,500.00 BMW                  320i        $23,000.00
 Smith            $49,500.00 Porsche              924         $16,000.00
 R>
```

Clearly, client *Smith* has a greater number of cars to choose from because she has a larger salary.

Notice that the JOIN command generates 85 rows from two tables that consist of 10 and 16 rows. The JOIN command generates a row for each occurrence that satisfies the *WHERE* clause. The higher the client's salary, the more rows will be generated for that client.

■ **Comment**

The output of the JOIN command is not elegant because it must generate enormous tables if the original tables are large themselves. JOIN is most useful for ad hoc reporting. To obtain the same output in a more elegant format, use the SET POINTER command in a command file.

The following guidelines can help you use the JOIN command most efficiently:

☐ For better performance, key the common column or columns in the second table (*tblname2*).

☐ If one table is much larger than the other, make the smaller table the second table in the JOIN command and do not use keys.

☐ If both tables are large, name the table with the shorter row length first, and use a key in the common column of the second table.

154

See: *APPEND, BUILD KEY, INTERSECT, Keys, PROJECT, Relational commands, SUBTRACT, UNION,* and *VIEW*

■ **R:BASE 5000 equivalent**

JOIN

Keys

■ **Description**

Most relational database programs provide some form of *indexing.* In general, indexing a database increases the speed of searches and sorts. In R:BASE, indexes are called *keys* and are used to enhance the performance of relational commands (UNION, INTERSECT, SUBTRACT, and JOIN) and any operation involving a *WHERE* clause. R:BASE does *not* provide an index function for maintaining a table in sorted order. To create a sorted table, use the PROJECT command with the *SORTED BY* clause.

You can define columns as key columns during database definition or at the R> prompt with the BUILD KEY command. It is more efficient to define a keyed column during database definition. If a table has many rows, the BUILD KEY operation can be quite slow. When you define a column as a key, the indexing information is stored in the third *.RBF* file, which has a 3 appended to its filename (e.g., *PERSONL3.RBF*).

Do not use keys indiscriminately. Assign them to columns that are frequently used in a *WHERE* clause or that are common columns among tables used in relational commands. Unnecessarily assigning keys slows down the performance of your database.

Here are some guidelines for using keyed columns:

☐ When you use keyed columns in a *WHERE* clause that involves multiple conditions, the last condition should include a comparison of the key column, using EQ, EQA, or =, and should be connected to the preceding condition by the logical AND operator (see *Operators*). For example, let's assume you have a keyed column *CLINUM* and a non-keyed column *AMOUNT*. Compare the following usages in a SELECT command:

Efficient usage:

```
SELECT ALL FROM PROPOSAL WHERE AMOUNT GT 20000 AND CLINUM EQ 1
```

Inefficient:

```
SELECT ALL FROM PROPOSAL WHERE CLINUM EQ 1 AND AMOUNT GT 20000
```

While the second command is correct, the benefit of using the keyed column is negated by placing it first in the *WHERE* clause.

☐ In relational commands, the *second table* named in the command should contain the keyed common column.

See: *BUILD KEY, DELETE, Filenames and structure, INTERSECT, JOIN, Relational commands, SUBTRACT,* and *UNION*

LABEL

■ **Syntax**

```
LABEL lblname
```

■ **Description**

The LABEL command specifies a destination for a GOTO command. It is used in command files to pass control to another command line.

■ **Procedure**

Both the GOTO and its corresponding LABEL commands must have the same label name, which can be a maximum of 8 characters long. The LABEL command can either follow or precede the GOTO command. R:BASE searches for the label name from the GOTO command to the end of the file; if it does not find the label, it continues the search from the top of the file.

In the following example, an IF statement includes a GOTO command that passes control to the label name, *end*, if the database does not exist. If the database exists, the IF block is ignored, and the commands in the WHILE loop are executed.

```
IF dbcheck NE 0 THEN
  WRITE "Sorry, database doesn't exist, press any key to continue."
  PAUSE
  GOTO end
ENDIF
WHILE done EQ N THEN
  .
  .      *(list of commands)
  .
ENDWHILE
LABEL end
```

For further discussion of GOTO and LABEL, see *GOTO*.

■ **R:BASE 5000 equivalent**

LABEL

156

LIST

■ **Syntax**

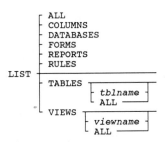

```
         ┌─ ALL
         ├─ COLUMNS
         ├─ DATABASES
         ├─ FORMS
         ├─ REPORTS
         ├─ RULES
LIST ────┤
         ├─ TABLES ──┬─ tblname ─┐
         │           └─ ALL ─────┘
         └─ VIEWS ───┬─ viewname ─┐
                     └─ ALL ──────┘
```

■ **Description**

The LIST command displays descriptive information about an opened database or lists the databases in the current directory.

With the exception of the LIST DATABASES option, all LIST options require that a database be open and therefore apply only to the current database. Here is a description of each option:

Option	Description
ALL	Lists all tables in the open database, their password status, current number of rows, column names, data types, computed column expressions, and key status.
COLUMNS	Lists all columns in the database in alphabetical order and includes which tables they belong to, their data types, computed column expressions, and key status.
DATABASES	Lists all databases in the current directory.
FORMS	Lists all form names defined for the open database.
REPORTS	Lists all report names defined for the open database.
RULES	Lists the rules defined for the open database and the rule checking status.
TABLES	Lists all tables in the open database, the number of columns, and the number of rows.
tblname or *viewname*	Lists the password status, defined columns, data types, computed column expressions, key status, and current number of rows for the specified table or view. (The number of rows is not applicable to views.)
VIEWS	Lists all view names defined for the open database.

The LIST command is helpful for getting a quick overview of the database. It enables you to review your column definitions, see what forms or reports have been defined, check the defined rules, and so on. Here are some examples of the results of some LIST options.

```
R>LIST RULES
(RULES     ) ON  Check data validation RULES
RULE 1          CLINUM IN INVOICE EQA CLINUM IN CLIENT
     Message:Client does not exist in client table

R>LIST TABLES

     Tables in the Database CONSULT

     Name    Columns   Rows         Name    Columns   Rows

     CLIENT      7       10          FORMS       2       78
     REPORTS     2       58          RATES       3        0
     ASSIGNED    4        0          EMPLOYEE   10       40
     RULES       8        2          VIEWS       3       11
     VIEWCOND    5        0          INVFORM    10      N/A
     INVOICE     8       16          PROPOSAL    6        4
     NEWINV      9       18          NEWONE     14       19
     LOAN        7        3          NEWCLI      7        5
     CHECK       3        2


R>LIST CLIENT

     Table: CLIENT          No lock(s)
     Read Password: Yes
     Modify Password: Yes

     Column definitions
     # Name      Type       Length        Key   Expression
     1 CLINUM    INTEGER
     2 CLINAME   TEXT       25 characters
     3 STREET    TEXT       25 characters
     4 CITY      TEXT       20 characters
     5 STATE     TEXT        2 characters
     6 ZIP       TEXT        5 characters
     7 PHONE     TEXT       12 characters

     Current number of rows:     10


R>LIST DATABASES

     Databases in current directory

     CLIENTS    PROPOSL    PERSONL    MSINDEX    CONSULT    RUNTEST
     TEMPNDX    CHARGES    TEST       SPRPROJ    TRIG       NEWTEST
     SAMPLE     CARPMTS
```

```
R>LIST FORMS

    Form      Table
    --------  --------
    CLIENT    CLIENT
    PROPOSAL  PROPOSAL
```

```
R>LIST REPORTS

    Report    Table
    --------  --------
    CLIENT    CLIENT
    NEWONE    NEWONE
    PROPOSAL  PROPOSAL
```

■ **Comment**

You can direct the output of the list command to a disk file or to the printer by issuing an OUTPUT command before you execute the LIST command.

For information on displaying the status of other database parameters, see *SHOW*.

See also: *OUTPUT*

■ **R:BASE 5000 equivalent**
LIST

LOAD

■ **Syntax**

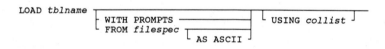

■ **Description**

LOAD is the basic R:BASE command for adding data to a table from the keyboard, from variables, or from external ASCII files. Although you can use LOAD to enter data from the keyboard, it is most frequently used for loading data into tables from variables or from external files. When entering data from the keyboard, use a data entry form; it is much more convenient and flexible than using the LOAD command.

■ **Procedure**

The LOAD command requires you to enter data in the *same order as the columns it will fill*. This requirement applies to all forms of data entry with the LOAD command. You can change the column order or omit columns to be entered by including the optional *USING* clause and listing the columns in the desired order. If you omit the *USING* clause, the order of the columns corresponds to the order in which the columns were defined when the table was created. Check the column definition order by issuing the LIST *tblname* command.

Using LOAD for keyboard data entry: There are two forms of the LOAD command for keyboard entry: LOAD and LOAD WITH PROMPTS. If you simply type LOAD followed by the table name, R:BASE switches to LOAD mode and displays an L> prompt. Enter column values in the same order that the columns are defined in the table. Separate entries with commas or blanks, and enclose text values that contain embedded blanks with quotes. Type END when you finish loading data. The process is shown in the following screen:

```
R>LIST CARLIST

    Table: CARLIST          No lock(s)
    Read Password: No
    Modify Password: No

    Column definitions
    # Name      Type      Length          Key    Expression
    1 MAKE      TEXT       15 characters
    2 MODEL     TEXT        8 characters
    3 PRICE     CURRENCY

    Current number of rows:       18

R>LOAD CARLIST
  Begin R:BASE Data Loading
L>Toyota,Camry,14000
L>Renault,"Le Car",6500
L>END
  End R:BASE Data Loading
R>
```

Clearly, there are more convenient methods for entering data from the keyboard. However, for quickly banging out a few rows, nothing is faster than LOAD. Once again, be sure to use the correct column order.

In the LOAD WITH PROMPTS format, R:BASE prompts you for each column you want to load. You do not even need to enclose embedded blanks with quotes. The following screen shows a session with LOAD WITH PROMPTS:

```
R>LOAD CARLIST WITH PROMPTS
 Begin R:BASE Data Loading

 Press [ESC] to end, [ENTER] to continue
 MAKE    (TEXT    ):Honda
 MODEL   (TEXT    ):Accord
 PRICE   (CURRENCY):9800

 Press [ESC] to end, [ENTER] to continue
```

Entering data from variables: In some situations, you may wish to load data into a table from variable values created by a command file. The following example is taken from the command file in the *Arithmetic and mathematical functions* entry. In that command file, which enters test data in a table called SAMPLES, the LOAD command loads data from computed variable values:

```
LOAD SAMPLES; .vcount .vsampmax .vsampmin .vsampave +
.vsampdev .vresult .vsampmod; END
```

Note the format of the LOAD command. The semicolons are command line separators. In other words, the two lines of code above actually consist of three commands: LOAD, the variable list, and END.

Entering data from external files: Use the LOAD command to load data from external ASCII delimited files. You can omit the *AS ASCII* option when you use the *filespec* option. Note that you also can use FileGateway to load ASCII delimited files. The advantage of the LOAD command is that the process is somewhat faster: You need only type in the command and need not make all the menu selections FileGateway requires.

Files loaded with the LOAD command must be delimited with commas or blanks. Text fields with embedded blanks must be enclosed with quotes. (Note, however, that you may use other characters as delimiters by changing the delimiter character with the SET DELIMITER command.) A typical ASCII delimited file looks like this:

```
200,Harry,Miller,"1203 N.E. 23rd Ave.",Seattle,WA,98106
201,Julie,Harrison,"9932 S.E. 17th St.",Kent,WA,98307
202,Lawrence,Barton,"123 S. 48th St.",Renton,WA,98209
```

Assuming that the above ASCII file has the name *TEXT.DAT* and is located on drive B, you would issue the following command to load this data file into the *CLIENT* table:

```
LOAD CLIENT FROM B:TEXT.DAT
```

The order of the data in the external file must coincide with the order of the defined columns in the table to be loaded. To change the order of column loading, include the *USING* clause in the LOAD command.

■ **Comments**

If you are loading from external files, you may wish to turn off RULES checking with the NOCHECK command. For additional options for handling null values with LOAD, see *FILL*.

Note that R:BASE truncates any values that exceed the defined column length. Similarly, extra data fields in the ASCII file are ignored during the LOAD process.

See: *ASCII characters and files, CHECK/NOCHECK, ENTER, FileGateway, FORMS,* and *SET characters and keywords*

■ **R:BASE 5000 equivalent**

LOAD

Logical functions

■ **Description**

For a general description of the functions available in R:BASE System V, see *Functions.* The three logical functions are:

Function	Description
IFEQ(*arg1,arg2,arg3,arg4*)	If *arg1* and *arg2* are equal, the function returns the value of *arg3*. Otherwise, it returns the value of *arg4*.
IFLT(*arg1,arg2,arg3,arg4*)	If *arg1* is less than *arg2*, the function returns the value of *arg3*. Otherwise, it returns the value of *arg4*.
IFGT(*arg1,arg2,arg3,arg4*)	If *arg1* is greater than *arg2*, the function returns the value of *arg3*. Otherwise, it returns the value of *arg4*.

These functions let you set up simple conditions for assigning a value to a column or variable without the use of a command file. The arguments can be non-text column values, variables, or expressions. You can create fairly complex conditions by embedding logical functions within logical functions.

■ **Examples**

Logical functions are useful for defining computed columns that depend on values in other columns. For example, if your employees' bonus amounts depend on their years of employment, you can define a computed column (*BONUS*) that determines such bonuses:

```
Table: EMPLOYEE           No lock(s)
Read Password: No
Modify Password: No

Column definitions
# Name      Type        Length        Key    Expression
1 EMPID     INTEGER                    yes
2 FRSTNAME  TEXT        15 characters
3 LASTNAME  TEXT        15 characters
4 DEPT      TEXT         5 characters
5 SALARY    CURRENCY
6 HIREDATE  DATE
7 YEARS     INTEGER                           (NINT((.#DATE-
                                              'HIREDATE')/365))
8 BONUS     CURRENCY                          (IFLT('YEARS',2,0,(2
                                              % 'SALARY')))
```

The *BONUS* column checks to see if the computed column *YEARS* is less than 2. If it is, the bonus is zero. Otherwise, the bonus is two percent of the employee's salary. The result of using this computed column is shown in the following screen:

```
R>SELECT EMPID YEARS SALARY BONUS FROM EMPLOYEE
  EMPID       YEARS       SALARY           BONUS
  ----------  ----------  ---------------- ----------------
          1           3   $25,000.00            $500.00
          2           5   $25,000.00            $500.00
          3           1   $18,000.00              $0.00
          4           5   $32,000.00            $640.00
          5           4   $37,500.00            $750.00
          6           3   $45,000.00            $900.00
          7           3   $45,000.00            $900.00
          8           4   $35,000.00            $700.00
          9           5   $45,000.00            $900.00
         10           1   $23,000.00              $0.00
         11           3   $30,000.00            $600.00
         12           5   $35,000.00            $700.00
         13           1   $36,000.00              $0.00
         14           6   $30,000.00            $600.00
         15           4   $50,000.00          $1,000.00
         16           3   $25,000.00            $500.00
         17           2   $45,000.00            $900.00
         18           4   $48,000.00            $960.00
         19           6   $25,000.00            $500.00
         20           1   $33,000.00              $0.00
More output follows - press [ESC] to quit, any key to continue
```

Note that we include the *YEARS* column in the table only for the sake of clarity. We could omit the *YEARS* column by including the *YEARS* calculation in the *BONUS* expression:

```
(IFLT((NINT((.#DATE-'HIREDATE')/365)),2,0,(2 % 'SALARY')))
```

You can create an even more complicated expression by embedding another logical function that calculates a bonus of three percent of the *SALARY* if years of employment is greater than 10. Assuming we keep the *YEARS* column, this function replaces the *(2% 'SALARY')* argument in the above expression and looks like this:

```
IFGT('YEARS',10,(3 % 'SALARY'),(2 % 'SALARY'))
```

Obviously, expressions with functions embedded in functions can become quite convoluted. They might become so complicated, in fact, that you forget how the expression works. On the other hand, you gain storage space and improved performance by combining as many calculated columns as possible. Complex expressions involve a tradeoff between efficiency and readability.

Logical functions also can be used in forms and reports and, of course, in command files. The FORMS entry presents an example in which an expression involves logical functions:

```
============================Expression Options============================
 Define  Customize lookups  Delete  Retype  Reorder


   1. DOUBLE  :  vhypot   =  IFEQ(SIDE2,0,0,SQRT(SIDE1**2 + SIDE2**2))
```

```
[ESC] Return  [F3] Review  [F7] Prev table  [F8] Next table  [F10] Help
Form: NEWTRI     Define expressions     Table: RT-TRI
```

This expression is used to determine the hypotenuse of a right triangle. The hypotenuse is reported as zero if a value for *side2* is not entered. See *FORMS* for further discussion of this example.

See: *Expressions, FORMS*, and *Functions*

MKDIR

- **Syntax**

MKDIR ⌐ *d:* ⌐ *pathname*

- **Description**

Use the MKDIR command to create new directories or subdirectories from within R:BASE. The MKDIR command is virtually identical to the MS-DOS MKDIR command.

- **Procedure**

The command abbreviation MD is permitted in R:BASE as well as in MS-DOS. Unlike MS-DOS, however, you must insert a space between MKDIR and the leading backslash of pathname. The drive designator is necessary only if you are creating a directory on another drive.

To create a directory called *\RBFILES\DATA* on the current drive, type the following at the R> prompt:

```
MKDIR \RBFILES\DATA
```

Cautions: We strongly recommend that you create separate subdirectories for separate applications. It's easier to back up and maintain files if related files are in their own directory. For example, you can use the COPY *.* command to copy all files of one application if they are the only files in the directory. If all your applications are stored in a single directory, however, backing up a single application is more tedious.

Above all, do *not* store applications in the main R:BASE directory, in which the R:BASE system files are located. If Microrim issues an update or a new version of System V, you will want to delete all of the system files in the main R:BASE directory so that you can copy the new version to a blank directory. This process is far more complicated if data files are mixed in with the R:BASE system files.

See: *CHDIR, DOS commands in R:BASE*, and *RMDIR*

- **R:BASE 5000 equivalent**
MKDIR

NEWPAGE

■ **Syntax**

```
NEWPAGE
```

■ **Description**

The NEWPAGE command sends a form feed to the output device. If the output device is the screen, NEWPAGE clears the screen. If the output device is the printer, NEWPAGE advances the paper to the top of the form.

■ **Procedure**

Generally, you use the NEWPAGE command in command files to clear the screen or during the execution of the file to start printing on a new page. For example, the following sequence sends a form feed to the printer before printing a data listing:

```
OUTPUT PRINTER
LIST ALL
NEWPAGE
OUTPUT SCREEN
```

■ **Comment**

Note that the CLS command is more appropriate for clearing the screen because it *always* clears the screen, regardless of the output device.

■ **R:BASE 5000 equivalent**

NEWPAGE

NEXT

■ **Syntax**

```
NEXT #n ┌─────────┐
        └ varname ┘
```

■ **Description**

Use the NEXT command with the SET POINTER command to move the pointer to the next row in the route number *#n*.

■ **Procedure**

In most cases, you use NEXT with the optional variable (*varname*) to detect when the pointer is unable to find a row in the route. The variable is set to *0* as long as the pointer finds a row. When all rows are found or no rows fit the conditions of the SET POINTER command, the variable is set to a non-zero

166

value. Therefore, you can test the value of the variable with an IF or WHILE statement to determine when to terminate commands that use a route (*#n*).

See *SET POINTER* for a complete description and for examples of the NEXT command.

- **R:BASE 5000 equivalent**
  NEXT

NOCHECK

- **Description**
  NOCHECK is the opposite of the CHECK command. These two commands turn the rules checking procedure off and on, respectively. They are used only with LOAD. For a complete description of these commands, see *CHECK/NOCHECK*.

- **R:BASE 5000 equivalent**
  NOCHECK

NOFILL

- **Description**
  NOFILL is the opposite of the FILL command. Use this command with the LOAD command to reject new rows until all columns in each row are assigned a value. For a complete description of the use of these commands see *FILL*.

- **R:BASE 5000 equivalent**
  NOFILL

OPEN

- **Syntax**

  ```
  OPEN dbspec
  ```

- **Description**
  The OPEN command opens an existing database. With the exception of copying, renaming, or deleting the database, you cannot perform any operations on a database until you open it.

- **Procedure**
  Only one database may be open at a time. You close a database if you open another database, define a new database, or issue a CLOSE or EXIT command.

167

You can open a database located in any drive or directory. To open a database in a directory other than the current one, include the pathname in the OPEN command. For example, the following command opens a database called *MEMOS* located in the *DATA**HISTORY* subdirectory in drive D:

```
OPEN D:\DATA\HISTORY\MEMOS
```

As a general rule, however, try to work with databases that are in the current directory. That way, you won't need to specify the pathname every time you generate command files or other output files that belong in the same directory as the database. In the above example, it is better practice to use the CHDRV and CHDIR commands to make *D:**DATA**HISTORY* the current directory, and then type:

```
OPEN MEMOS
```

See: *CHDIR, CHDRV, CLOSE, DEFINE, Definition EXPRESS,* and *EXIT*

■ **R:BASE 5000 equivalent**
OPEN

Operators

■ **Description**
R:BASE operators are used in expressions, in IF and WHILE statements, with the *WHERE* clause, and for rules definition. For the purposes of this discussion, we can group R:BASE operators into the following categories:

☐ *Value operators* compare variable or column values to a specified text or numeric value.

☐ *Column value operators* compare the value of one column to the value of another column.

☐ *Arithmetic operators* perform arithmetic operations such as addition and subtraction.

☐ *String operators* combine text values to form another text value.

☐ *Row count operators* control the row numbers to be involved in a database operation.

☐ *Boolean operators* control actions based on multiple conditions (AND, OR, AND NOT, OR NOT).

It is important to understand the distinction between value operators and column value operators. Value operators compare a variable or column to a value that you specify. For example, the clause *SALARY GT 10000* compares the value in the *SALARY* column to the value *10000*. The value can be any number or a variable value. For example, *SALARY GT .vminsal* compares the value of *SALARY* to the value currently contained in the variable *vminsal*. Note that the period preceding *vminsal* indicates the current value of the variable (see *Variables*).

On the other hand, the clause *SALARY GTA MINSAL* compares the value in the *SALARY* column to the value in the *MINSAL* column, which is another column in the same table. Column value operators always compare two column values in the same table and in the same row, unless you use them to define rules. In that case, you can specify columns in different tables. The letter *A* appended to *GT* indicates that it is a column value operator.

The operators in each category are discussed below:

Value Operators

Operator	Definition
EQ or =	equal
NE or <>	not equal
GT or >	greater than
GE or >=	greater than or equal to
LT or <	less than
LE or <=	less than or equal to
CONTAINS	contains a text string
EXISTS	contains data (value other than NULL)
FAILS	contains a NULL value (-0-)

Note that the wildcard operators * and ? can be used to compare text strings. For example, the clause *ZIPCODE EQ 941** is true for all values of *ZIPCODE* that start with *941*. You can also use the ? to represent a single character.

The *CONTAINS* operator is used primarily to find substrings of text data. For example, *ZIPCODE CONTAINS 941* looks for any occurrence of the string *941* in *ZIPCODE*.

EXISTS and *FAILS* check to see if a column or variable contains data or a NULL value. If the value is NULL, then *FAILS* is true. If there is data (zeros and blanks are considered data), then *EXISTS* is true. A column or variable contains a NULL value if no data has been entered for that column or variable.

NULL values are assigned to columns or variables if you press Enter without entering data when you use a data entry form or the LOAD WITH PROMPTS command. Similarly, NULL values are entered from external files when no data exists (see *FILL*). Many of the command file examples in this book use FAILS and EXIST to test for NULL values (see also *WHERE*).

Column Value Operators

Operator	Definition
EQA	equal
NEA	not equal
GTA	greater than
GEA	greater than or equal to
LTA	less than
LEA	less than or equal to

For examples of the use of column value operators, see *RULES*.

Arithmetic Operators

Operator	Description
+ or −	unary plus or minus (e.g., $-SQRT(4) = -2$)
**	exponentiation
*	multiplication
/	division
%	percentage
+	addition
−	subtraction

The order of precedence of the above operators is as follows:

1. expressions inside internal parentheses
2. functions
3. unary + or −
4. exponentiation
5. multiplication or division from left to right
6. percent
7. addition or subtraction

For a further discussion of the order of precedence, see *Expressions*.

String Operators

Operator	Description
+	concatenation (no separating space)
&	concatenation (adds a separating space)

To illustrate the use of these operators, suppose you have two variables, *vfname* and *vlname*, equal to *John* and *Smith* respectively. Here is what happens when you use the string operators with the two variables:

```
SET VAR vname = (.vfname + .vlname)
SHOW VAR vname
JohnSmith
SET VAR vname = (.vfname & .vlname)
SHOW VAR vname
John Smith
```

Row count operators: The two row count operators are *COUNT* and *LIMIT*. The *COUNT* operator selects rows according to the value specified in the *COUNT* clause. For example,

```
SELECT ALL FROM TBLNAME WHERE COUNT GT 100
```

selects all row numbers greater than 100. The value operators *EQ, NE, GT, GE, LT, LE* or their corresponding symbols ($=$, $<>$, $>$, $>=$, $<$, $<=$) can be used with the *COUNT* clause. The clause *COUNT EQ LAST* finds the last row.

The *LIMIT* operator limits the number of rows to be included in an operation. The LIMIT clause always uses the form *LIMIT EQ n*, where *n* is the number of rows. For example,

```
PRINT TESTRPT WHERE LIMIT EQ 5
```

prints only the first five rows of the report *TESTRPT*. The *LIMIT* operator lets you test commands before you apply them to the whole table. When printing mailing labels, for example, you can print a few rows to test the positioning of the labels in the printer before you print the whole table.

Boolean operators: The *Boolean* operators can combine as many as 10 conditions in a *WHERE* clause, IF statement, or WHILE statement.

Operator	Description
AND	Both conditions separated by *AND* must be true.
OR	One of the two conditions separated by *OR* must be true.
AND NOT	The first condition must be true and the second condition must be false.
OR NOT	Either the first condition must be true or the second condition must be false.

For example, the following two commands specify the same requirements:

```
SELECT ALL FROM EMPLOYEE WHERE SALARY GT 20000 OR HIREDATE LT 1/1/70
SELECT ALL FROM EMPLOYEE WHERE SALARY GT 20000 OR NOT HIREDATE GE 1/1/70
```

The salary must be greater than *20000* or the hire date must be before *1/1/70*.

The following IF condition is satisfied if *vlname* is equal to *Smith* and if *vfname* is not equal to *Tom*:

```
IF vlname EQ Smith AND NOT vfname EQ Tom THEN ...
```

See: *Expressions, IF, RULES, Variables, WHERE,* and *WHILE*

■ **R:BASE 5000 equivalent**

R:BASE 5000 supports all of the above operators. Note, however, that the *COUNT* operator works only with the value operator *EQ* (=).

OUTPUT

■ **Syntax**

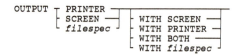

■ **Description**

The OUTPUT command directs the output from R:BASE to the screen, printer, a disk file, or any combination of these.

■ **Procedure**

You can specify only one disk file with the OUTPUT command. Valid output ports such as *COM1:* and *LPT2:* can be substituted for the word *PRINTER* in the syntax line, and *TERMINAL* can be substituted for *SCREEN*. The clause *BOTH* directs output to the printer and the screen. The order in which you specify output devices does not affect the operation of OUTPUT.

Output from R:BASE is in ASCII format and consists of the results of commands, diagnostic messages, and error messages. You control the output of messages with the SET MESSAGE and SET ERROR MESSAGE commands. Use the SET ECHO ON command to display commands as well as their results.

You can send all R:BASE operations to any combination of the output devices discussed above. After you finish sending output to a specified device, always redirect output back to the screen with the OUTPUT SCREEN command. When you direct output to a disk file, the file is not closed until you issue another OUTPUT command. Therefore, data sent to a disk file can be lost if you exit R:BASE without redirecting output again.

■ **Examples**

```
OUTPUT SCREEN WITH B:TEST.DTA
SELECT ALL FROM TESTTBL
OUTPUT SCREEN

OUTPUT PRINTER
PRINT TEST
OUTPUT SCREEN

OUTPUT B:BACKUP.DTA
UNLOAD DATA FOR EMPLOYEE SORTED BY EMPID
OUTPUT SCREEN
```

■ **Comments**

When you combine screen output with printer or file output (e.g., OUTPUT SCREEN WITH PRINTER), R:BASE pauses at the end of each screenful of data and requires you to press a key to continue. For printing large reports, it is generally more efficient to direct output only to the printer.

Use *OUTPUT filespec* before you back up data to a disk file with the BACKUP or UNLOAD command. Directing output to a disk file is also a convenient way to capture data in ASCII format so that you can add it to text documents from other software packages.

Caution: Be sure to issue the OUTPUT SCREEN command after you direct output to a disk file.

See: *BACKUP, Error messages, PRINT, SET ERROR VARIABLE,* and *UNLOAD*

■ **R:BASE 5000 equivalent**

OUTPUT

OWNER

■ **Syntax**

OWNER *password*

■ **Description**

Use the OWNER command in the DEFINE mode (at the D> prompt) to define an owner password. You also can define the owner password using Definition EXPRESS.

■ **Procedure**

The owner password gives password holders access to all parts of the database and allows them to execute any R:BASE command, including deleting or changing the password. If you do not issue an owner password, anyone can access the entire database.

If a database has an owner password, you can use the following commands only after you enter the correct password: DEFINE, RELOAD, UNLOAD, EXPAND, REDEFINE, and REMOVE. These commands modify the database structure. The equivalents of these commands in Definition EXPRESS and FileGateway also require you to use the owner password. Enter the password with the USER command at the R> prompt or at the appropriate prompt in a menu-driven application.

Passwords can be as long as eight characters and can include blanks if you enclose the password in quotes. To define a password, enter DEFINE mode by typing DEFINE at the R> prompt. Then type the command:

```
OWNER password
```

where *password* is your chosen owner password. If a password already exists, you must enter the USER command from the R> prompt before you can define a new password.

■ **Comments**

Only those persons responsible for managing the design and operation of the database should have access to the owner password. If you intend to use table passwords, you *must* define an owner password. For a complete discussion of database security, see *Data security*.

Caution: Write down your owner password and keep it in a safe place! If you forget the owner password, you must ask Microrim for assistance to modify the database.

See: *Data security, DEFINE, Definition EXPRESS, PASSWORDS,* and *USER*

■ **R:BASE 5000 equivalent**
OWNER

PACK

■ **Syntax**

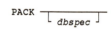

PACK
dbspec

■ **Description**

The PACK command recovers unusable disk space created by deleting rows or tables. For example, the DELETE, REMOVE, EXPAND, and REDEFINE commands create unusable disk space in the database files. If these commands are used frequently, the *2.RBF* file (e.g., *MYDATA2.RBF*) can become very large, even though it may contain little data. If the database has key columns, the *3.RBF* file also accumulates unusable disk space.

■ **Procedure**

To pack the current database, simply issue the PACK command. If you wish to pack a database other than the current one, append the database name (include a path, if necessary) to the PACK command.

Caution: Always be sure to back up the database before you issue the PACK command. If the PACK operation is interrupted by either human error or a computer malfunction, the database can be destroyed.

■ **Comment**

To conserve disk space and to improve the performance of a database, use the PACK command periodically, particularly if you frequently use the DELETE, REMOVE, EXPAND, and REDEFINE commands.

Note that the RELOAD command is similar to the PACK command. However, RELOAD creates a new set of *.RBF* files and, in addition to freeing disk space, optimizes the organization of the rows and tables on the disk.

See: *Backing up data, DELETE, Filenames and structure,* and *RELOAD*

■ **R:BASE 5000 equivalent**

PACK

PASSWORDS

■ **Syntax**

```
PASSWORDS

RPW ┐   ┌ tblname  ┐
    ├─ FOR ┤          ├ IS password
MPW ┘   └ viewname ┘
```

■ **Description**

Use the PASSWORDS command in DEFINE mode (at the D> prompt) to define modify and read passwords for tables. See *Data security* for a general discussion of passwords.

■ **Procedure**

You first must define an owner password before the PASSWORDS command will have any effect. Passwords also can be defined in Definition EXPRESS.

The modify password (MPW) allows only those who know it to enter or modify data in the table associated with the password. The read password (RPW) allows only those who know it to read data in the table associated with the password. The RPW password is effective only if both the owner and the MPW passwords have been previously defined.

After you define the MPW or RPW passwords, you must issue the correct password with the USER command before you can modify, or read, the associated table. If you don't know the password, R:BASE denies you access to the table. For example, if a table has only an MPW password, anyone can use BROWSE or SELECT to view the data. However, a user must enter a password to use the LOAD command.

Forms and reports require their own passwords, which override passwords defined for the tables associated with the forms or reports.

After you type DEFINE to enter the DEFINE mode, type *PASSWORDS* at the D> prompt. Then enter the following commands:

```
RPW FOR tblname/viewname IS password
MPW FOR tblname/viewname IS password
```

For example, the following sequence (in DEFINE mode) defines both owner and MPW passwords:

```
OWNER password
PASSWORDS
MPW FOR EMPLOYEE IS password
END
```

As with owner passwords, RPW or MPW passwords can be a maximum of eight characters and can include spaces if you enclose the word in quotes.

Caution: You can only change MPW or RPW passwords if you know the owner password. Be sure to write down the owner password and keep it in a safe place.

See: *Data security, DEFINE, Definition EXPRESS, OWNER,* and *USER*

- **R:BASE 5000 equivalent**
PASSWORDS

PAUSE

- **Syntax**

```
PAUSE
```

- **Description**
The PAUSE command stops the execution of a command file until you press a key. This function is useful for viewing data on the screen before continuing with the execution of the command file.

■ **Procedure**

PAUSE is normally preceded by a TYPE or WRITE command that displays a message prompting the user to press a key to continue. The PAUSE command itself does not display anything on the screen; it simply stops the cursor at its current position until you press a key.

You also can use PAUSE when you display a text file with the DISPLAY command. Add a *Press any key to continue* message to the end of the text file and follow the DISPLAY command with PAUSE.

■ **Example**

```
SET VAR vdate TO .#DATE
WHILE vdate EXISTS THEN
    .
    .      *(list of commands)
    .
    SHOW VAR vweeknum AT 13,34
    WRITE "Press any key to continue" AT 15,3
    PAUSE
ENDWHILE
```

This excerpt from a command file shows how to use the WRITE command with a PAUSE. The message *Press any key to continue* is displayed at row 15, column 3, and execution pauses until a key is pressed. Note that the WRITE message precedes the PAUSE command.

See: *DISPLAY, TYPE,* and *WRITE*

■ **R:BASE 5000 equivalent**

PAUSE

PLAYBACK

■ **Syntax**

```
PLAYBACK exec
```

■ **Description**

The PLAYBACK command repeats a sequence of keystrokes that was saved in an *exec* file with the RECORD command. For more information on recording and saving keystrokes, see *RECORD*.

■ **Procedure**

To play back a file, type:

```
PLAYBACK filename
```

at the R> prompt where *filename* is the name of the *exec* file. You also can press Shift-F8 at the R> prompt and then enter the filename when R:BASE prompts you for it.

- **Comment**
  Edit the contents of *exec* files with RBEDIT, the R:BASE text editor. For information on this procedure, see *RECORD*.

  See: *RECORD*

- **R:BASE 5000 equivalent**
  None

PRINT

- **Syntax**

```
PRINT rptname ┬─────────────────────┬ ┬────────────────────┬
              └ SORTED BY collist ┘ └ WHERE condlist ┘
```

- **Description**
  The PRINT command sends a report designed with Application EXPRESS or Reports EXPRESS to an output device. The output device can be the screen, the printer, or a disk file.

- **Procedure**
  When you issue the PRINT command without the optional *SORTED BY* or *WHERE* clauses, R:BASE prints all rows from the table associated with the report. The *SORTED BY* clause controls the order in which rows are printed; the *WHERE* clause selects specific rows to be printed.

  The following example sends a report called *EMPLOYEE* to the printer. The rows are sorted by *EMPID* and selected by specific salary criteria.

```
OUTPUT PRINTER
PRINT EMPLOYEE SORTED BY EMPID WHERE SALARY GE 30000 AND +
  SALARY LT THAN 40000
OUTPUT SCREEN
```

- **Comments**
  The default output device for PRINT (and other output commands) is the screen. As shown in the above example, use the OUTPUT command to direct a report to the printer.

  Note: If your report is designed for printer output (e.g., set to lines per page, condensed print, and so on), it may not look right when it is displayed on the screen. For further information on designing reports, see *REPORTS*.

  Caution: Use the *SORTED BY* clause carefully when you have *breakpoints* specified in your report. The report is sorted by these specified breakpoint columns. The *SORTED BY* clause overrides the breakpoint sort order. If you wish to sort additional columns in the report, specify the breakpoint columns first in the *SORTED BY* clause.

See: *OUTPUT, REPORTS,* and *TYPE*

- **R:BASE 5000 equivalent**
  PRINT

Procedure files

- **Description**
  A procedure file consists of sets of R:BASE commands, menu items, or screen text that are organized into command, menu, or screen *blocks*. In contrast to command files, procedure files are designed specifically to be translated into binary form by CodeLock, the R:BASE application file encoder. Application EXPRESS also generates procedure files that it translates into binary form. The concept of blocks is applicable only to procedure files. Command files, which are executed in ASCII format, are not organized in blocks.

  Procedure files let you organize all the components of your application into a single file. They provide a means for designing large applications in a modular fashion. You can start by writing small ASCII command and text files. After you test the files individually, use CodeLock to build them into a procedure file. Another major advantage of procedure files is that they are translated into binary format, which provides security from tampering, and, in some cases, improves performance.

  The basic structure of a procedure file looks like this:

```
$COMMAND
command_block name (eight characters or less)
list of R:base commands
   .
   .
   .
last command in command block
$MENU
menu_block name (eight characters or less)
COLUMN/ROW Menu title
menu choice 1
menu choice 2
   .
   .
   .
last menu choice
$SCREEN
screen_block name (eight characters or less)
screen text
   .
   .
   .
last line of screen text
```

The first line of each block must start with a dollar sign followed by the type of block (*COMMAND, SCREEN,* or *MENU*). The second line always gives the name of the block, which must be eight characters or less. A single procedure file can have up to 42 blocks.

The commands (or text) in each block are executed (or displayed) by R:BASE commands that call the *block name*. Command blocks are executed with the RUN command, menu blocks with the CHOOSE command, and screen blocks with the DISPLAY command. In most cases, the commands for executing the blocks are contained within a command block in the same procedure file. However, it is possible to run, choose, or display blocks from other procedure files. See *RUN, CHOOSE,* and *DISPLAY* for additional information about designing command, menu, and screen blocks, respectively.

■ **Example**

To illustrate the design and operation of procedure files, look at the following application, which enters and displays data. We used a text editor to create the procedure file in ASCII format; then we compiled it with CodeLock.

```
$COMMAND
MAINPROC                        *(Name of main command block)
*(WORKMEN.CMD -- COMPILE TO WORKMEN.PRC)
SET ERR MESS OFF
SET MESS OFF
SET ERR VAR dbcheck
SET VAR dbcheck TO -1
SET VAR choice TO 0
SET VAR done TO N
NEWPAGE
DISPLAY SCRNTEXT                 *(Displays Screen Block SCRNTEXT)
CHOOSE choice FROM MENU1 AT 10   *(Displays Menu Block MENU1)
IF choice EQ 0 THEN
  SET ERR MESS ON
  SET MESS ON
  QUIT
ENDIF
IF choice EQ 1 THEN
  NEWPAGE
  FILLIN dbname USING +
    "Enter database name or <Enter> to Quit: " AT 4 5
  IF dbname EXISTS THEN
    OPEN .dbname
    IF dbcheck NE 0 THEN
      BEEP
      WRITE +
        "Sorry, database doesn't exist, press any key to continue."
      PAUSE
      GOTO end
    ENDIF
    WHILE done EQ N THEN
      NEWPAGE
      CHOOSE choice1 FROM MENU2  *(Displays Menu Block MENU2)
      IF choice1 EQ 1 THEN
        NEWPAGE
        LIST ALL
        WRITE "Press any key to continue"
        PAUSE
      ENDIF
```

(continued)

```
      IF choice1 EQ 2 THEN
         NEWPAGE
         LIST TABLES
         FILLIN tblname USING +
           "Please select table or <Enter> to Quit: " AT 15 5
         NEWPAGE
         IF tblname EXISTS THEN
            CHOOSE choice2 FROM MENU3  *(Displays Menu Block MENU3)
            IF choice2 EQ 1 THEN
              LOAD .tblname WITH PROMPTS
            ENDIF
            IF choice2 EQ 2 THEN
              EDIT ALL FROM .tblname
            ENDIF
         ENDIF
       ENDIF
       FILLIN done USING "Are you done with this database? (Y/N)"
     ENDWHILE
   ENDIF
   LABEL end
ENDIF
IF choice EQ 2 THEN
   NEWPAGE
   FILLIN pathname USING "Enter Path or <Enter> to Quit: " AT 4 5
   IF pathname EXISTS THEN
     DIR .pathname
     WRITE "Press any key to continue"
     PAUSE
   ENDIF
ENDIF
RUN MAINPROC IN WORKMEN.PRC  *(Runs this same command block again)
$MENU
MENU1
COLUMN  Main Menu (Esc to Exit)
Select a Database
List Files
$MENU
MENU2
COLUMN Action Menu
List Tables and Columns
Work on the Database
$MENU
MENU3
COLUMN Work Menu
Add Records
Display/Edit/Delete Records
$SCREEN
SCRNTEXT
   This is the example procedure file in operation. The text
for this screen block is contained in the "$SCREEN" section of
the procedure file and is displayed with the command DISPLAY
scrntext. Pick a database to work on or get a directory listing
from the main menu.
```

The basic operation of this procedure file is simple. After you list the directory of a specified pathname or select a database to work on, the file lets you enter new data or edit existing data in a specified table. In the following discussion, not much time will be spent explaining the application of this procedure file. The objective here is to understand how the command, menu, and screen blocks work together and how they are executed. For further discussion of the actual functions of this file, see *CHOOSE* and *SET ERROR VARIABLE*. It is worth noting, however, that this file can be expanded into a useful utility.

The command block is called *MAINPROC*. There are three menu blocks—*MENU1*, *MENU2*, and *MENU3*—and one screen block, *SCRNTEXT*. Notice the comment in the third line of the file, which states that the file is to be compiled as a procedure file called *WORKMEN.PRC*. The procedure filename can be any name to a maximum of eight characters. However, in this example, the name of the procedure file is referenced in the last line of the command block (*RUN MAINPROC IN WORKMEN.PRC*). This line executes the main command block again to redisplay the main menu. Thus, the name you assign to the procedure file and the name you use in the RUN command must be the same.

To execute the procedure file from the R> prompt, type:

```
RUN MAINPROC IN WORKMEN.PRC
```

You can use the concept of subroutines in a procedure file by creating separate command blocks and using the RUN command to execute them from other command blocks. See *RUN* for a description of how to pass parameters between command blocks. Variables referenced in one command block can be referenced in another (see *Variables*).

As noted earlier, each menu block is called by a separate CHOOSE command. The screen block is called by the DISPLAY command.

The example procedure file displays the following screen:

```
This is the example procedure file in operation. The text for this
screen block is contained in the "$SCREEN" section of the procedure
file and is displayed with the command DISPLAY scrntext. Pick a
database to work on or get a directory listing from the main menu.




========================Main Menu (Esc to Exit)========================
                       (1)  Select a Database
                       (2)  List Files
```

■ **Comments**

Building procedure files usually consists of the following steps:

☐ First, create the main command file or files in ASCII format. Temporarily store the menu and screen text in individual text files. In the above example, create the following ASCII files: *WORKMEN.CMD* (the *MAINPROC* command block), *MENU1*, *MENU2*, *MENU3*, and *SCRNTEXT*. For the moment, use the CHOOSE and DISPLAY commands to call the files separately. Execute the application by typing: *RUN WORKMEN.CMD*. The contents of each of these files should look essentially the same as the above listing, except that the lines with the dollar sign and block name are omitted. Again, see *CHOOSE* and *DISPLAY* for more information about creating separate menu and screen text files.

☐ Once the above command file and associated menu and screen files work as intended, convert them into a procedure file. Use CodeLock to convert each file individually. You can use the individual block conversion options, or you can edit the existing files and combine them into one large file as shown in the above example. The above example is called an *ASCII application file* and can be converted using the appropriate option in CodeLock. See *CodeLock* for more information on converting blocks and application files.

You can use Application EXPRESS to do much of the work involved in creating procedures. Use it to design menus and help screens and then add your own command files using the *Custom* or *Macro* options. In many cases, this is a far easier approach than creating procedures from scratch.

See: *Application EXPRESS, CHOOSE, CodeLock, Command files, DISPLAY, Programming, RUN, and SET ERROR VARIABLE*

Programming

■ **Description**
You can issue R:BASE commands either one at a time at the R> prompt or as a *batch* of commands stored in a disk file. The term *batch file*, as used in MS-DOS and other operating systems, is derived from the concept of submitting a batch of commands for execution rather than issuing them one at a time. Although commands in a batch file are still executed one at a time, you need only issue one command to execute all the commands in the file.

In R:BASE, files based on this concept are called *command files*. A command file is a type of program. The R:BASE command RUN *cmdfile* executes the specified command file.

You can execute command files in ASCII format, or you can use CodeLock to translate them into binary format *procedure files*. Procedure files are similar to command files but are designed according to a special set of syntax rules and can only be executed in binary form. For more information see *Procedure files*.

Although you can accomplish much in R:BASE by issuing single commands from the R> prompt, you will find that some tasks are made easier or even require the use of command files. Some of these tasks are:

☐ Repetitively performing a sequence of commands

☐ Performing alternative sequences of commands, depending on specified conditions

☐ Performing operations that require variable values or table rows to be incremented

☐ Setting up applications that let you perform database operations from a menu or by responding to prompts

This book contains many examples of programs that perform these types of tasks. In particular, see the programs in *Application EXPRESS, Arithmetic and mathematical functions, CHANGE, CHOOSE, Financial functions, IF, Procedure files, SET POINTER,* and *WHILE.*

To create an R:BASE command file, use the R:BASE text editor, RBEDIT, or any other text editor. If you use a word-processing program, be sure you save the file as an unformatted ASCII file.

When we discuss programming in R:BASE, we refer to the set of R:BASE commands as the R:BASE programming language. Although you can execute virtually all R:BASE commands from the R> prompt, some of the commands are designed specifically for programming. For example, the WHILE or IF commands would not help you much if you tried to execute them from the R> prompt. These are examples of commands that perform looping and conditional operations typical of programming languages like BASIC or Pascal.

The main difference between R:BASE and conventional programming languages is that the R:BASE programming language is designed specifically for databases. Although you could develop a database application using BASIC or Pascal, it would take much more time and effort than if you used a database management system and programming language such as R:BASE.

The following paragraphs summarize the main features of the R:BASE programming language. See the referenced entries for detailed discussions and examples of these features.

■ **Variables**

Variables are used in programs to temporarily store data values or your responses. Variables are stored in memory until you exit R:BASE or use the CLEAR command to delete the variables from memory. Any command file, form, or report can access all variables defined in R:BASE System V because variables are independent of the currently open database.

Values can be passed to variables during command-file execution with the RUN command or any of the following: CHOOSE, COMPUTE, FILLIN, SET ERROR VARIABLE, SET POINTER, and SET VARIABLE.

Define variable data types explicitly with the SET VARIABLE command or implicitly by assigning a value to the variable.

For a complete discussion of variables, see *Variables*.

■ Control structures

A *control structure* (also called a decision structure) is a set of commands that creates a loop or causes alternative actions to take place based on specified responses or values. A loop is a series of commands that is repeated until the specified conditions change. Loops in R:BASE are created with the WHILE command. For example, commands in the following WHILE statement would execute as long as the variable *choice* is equal to *Y*:

```
WHILE choice = Y THEN
   list of commands
ENDWHILE
```

A control structure also causes alternative sets of commands to be executed depending on whether or not certain conditions are met. The IF command sets up this type of control structure. When the IF condition is met, commands within the IF statement are executed once. An optional *ELSE* clause allows alternative commands when the IF condition is not met. For example, the commands in the following IF statement are executed if the variable *choice* is equal to *Y*:

```
IF choice = Y THEN
   list of commands
ENDIF
```

Another possible control structure follows:

```
IF choice = Y THEN
   list of commands
ELSE
   list of commands
ENDIF
```

The GOTO command is often used with the IF statement to pass control to some other location in the command file, specified by the LABEL command.

The SET POINTER command is an extremely powerful command often used with IF or WHILE statements. Used together, these commands let you establish pointers for as many as three database tables and perform programming operations on a row-by-row basis.

■ **Input and output**

R:BASE provides many commands for entering data and sending information to the screen, a printer, or a disk file. The two main input commands are FILLIN and CHOOSE. Use the FILLIN command to store a value. The CHOOSE command accepts your selection from a menu. Enter data into a database with the LOAD and ENTER commands.

To display variables and text use the SHOW VARIABLE, WRITE, or DISPLAY commands. Use the OUTPUT command to direct the output of these commands to the screen, printer, a disk file, or a combination of the three. To print reports use the PRINT command.

■ **Subroutines**

An R:BASE program may be executed or *called* by another R:BASE program. A program that is called by another program is referred to as a *subroutine*. Subroutines are usually separate, smaller programs. R:BASE lets you use the RUN command to call subroutines from within command files. The RETURN command returns control from the subroutine to the calling program.

You also can use the RUN command to pass parameters from one command file to another command file. When you design an application with multiple command files, keep in mind that all R:BASE variables are independent and cannot be assigned to a specific command file.

■ **Comment lines**

It's always good practice to document your programs with *comment lines* that describe the purpose and function of the program. Use the *(comment)* structure to include comments (see *(comment)*).

■ **Debugging**

Program debugging is the process of finding and correcting errors in your programs. Always debug a command file before you add it to a larger application or before you encode it with CodeLock. The best way to find errors is to use the SET ECHO ON command to view each line of a command file as it is executed. You should also use SET ERROR MESSAGES ON and SET MESSAGES ON when you debug a command file. See *Error messages* and *SET ERROR VARIABLE* for further discussion of debugging.

Some common programming errors are listed below:

Incorrect variable data type: If you get unexpected results or error messages from expression definitions, define the variable data types explicitly at the beginning of the command file (see *Variables*).

Incomplete IF or WHILE statements: If your program aborts and the screen displays an I> prompt, an IF statement does not have a corresponding ENDIF. If your program aborts and the screen displays a W> prompt, a WHILE statement does not have a corresponding ENDWHILE.

Incomplete quotes: If your program aborts and the screen displays a +> prompt, a text message in the command file probably has a beginning quote but is missing the end-quote.

Incorrect use of QUIT: If your program aborts and the screen displays an R> prompt, you might have used a QUIT command in a loop or subroutine instead of a BREAK or RETURN command. QUIT terminates all command-file execution, as well as IF and WHILE statement execution (see *QUIT*).

Screen display errors: The screen coordinates specified in SHOW, WRITE, and DISPLAY commands must be within the numeric limits of the rows and columns of your monitor: 25,80, for example. If you are incrementing a row or column counter variable and using this variable as a screen coordinate, check to see if you have exceeded the screen coordinate limits.

■ Programming and Application EXPRESS

Application EXPRESS is an excellent vehicle for developing menu-driven applications. The *Custom* and *Macro* menu actions in EXPRESS let you integrate your own command files or other programs into a larger application developed with Application EXPRESS. In many cases, you can save much time and effort by starting an application with Application EXPRESS and then adding customized command files as needed.

■ Executing external MS-DOS files from within a program

The R:BASE ZIP command lets you execute external MS-DOS files that have the extensions *.EXE* and *.COM*. These files are executable programs in binary format. Like all R:BASE commands, ZIP can be executed at the R> prompt or from within a command file. Using the ZIP command, you can execute programs you have developed in other languages from within R:BASE programs.

■ Programming for multi-user applications

The multi-user environment in R:BASE is initiated with the SET MULTI command. Any program or application that works on a single-user system will also work on a multi-user system. However, consider the effects of multiple users simultaneously attempting to update the same data or simultaneously directing output to the same peripheral.

R:BASE prevents conflicts due to simultaneous data manipulation or peripheral access. Simultaneous access to databases and peripherals (called *resources*) is controlled by a resource waiting period. This places users in a queue when they simultaneously request access to a resource. After a set waiting period, the request is canceled and the executing command file or block terminates. The default waiting period is 4 seconds. Use the SET WAIT command to change the waiting period to a maximum of $4^1/_2$ hours.

R:BASE provides three types of controls with the resource waiting period:

Concurrency control: R:BASE checks to see if two or more people are using either the EDIT or ENTER commands to simultaneously update data in the same column. The first person is accepted, and the others are warned that the column has been changed. When the first person finishes, a second can access that column. In the meantime, other people can edit other columns or rows in the table.

Use the SET VERIFY ROW command to set the concurrency control for an entire row rather than a single column.

Table locking: Table locks prevent several people from simultaneously issuing commands that change the structure of the table or the data in the table. There is little difference between concurrency control and table locking. Concurrency control permits several people to be in the EDIT or ENTER modes but controls access to the data as described above. With table locks, only one user at a time can successfully enter the following commands:

APPEND
BUILD KEY
CHANGE
DELETE ROWS
EDIT ALL
ENTER *form* FROM *filespec*
FORMS
INTERSECT
JOIN
PROJECT
RENAME
REPORTS
SET LOCK ON
SUBTRACT
UNION
UNLOAD
VIEW

If one of the above commands is in operation, no one else can successfully issue any of these commands if it affects the locked table. They can, however, still read data from the locked table.

Use the SET LOCK command to set table locks for commands that are not in the above list.

188

Database locks: Database locks work on the same principle as table locks, but they control commands that affect the database structure. Only one user at a time can successfully enter the following commands:

BUILD KEY
DEFINE
EXPAND
FORMS
INTERSECT
JOIN
PROJECT
RENAME
RELOAD
REDEFINE
REMOVE
REMOVE COLUMN
REPORTS
SUBTRACT
UNION
UNLOAD
VIEW

Caution: Two or more people cannot work simultaneously on the same file in RBEDIT, Application EXPRESS, Definition EXPRESS, CodeLock, Forms EXPRESS, Reports EXPRESS, or FileGateway.

See: *Application EXPRESS, CHOOSE, CodeLock, Command files, DISPLAY, FILLIN, GOTO, IF, LABEL, NEXT, PAUSE, Procedure files, QUIT, RETURN, RUN, SET ERROR VARIABLE, SET LOCK, SET POINTER, SET VARIABLE, SHOW ERROR, SHOW VARIABLE, Variables, WHILE, WRITE,* and *ZIP*

PROJECT

- **Syntax**

- **Description**

Use the PROJECT command to create a new table from an existing table. PROJECT is the only relational command that works with a single table.

■ **Procedure**

The new table is *tblname2* and the existing table is *tblname1*. The *USING* clause must be specified. To create a duplicate table, specify *USING ALL*. You also can create a subset of the existing table by selecting individual columns to be included in the new table. The *SORTED BY* clause lets you create the new table in a sorted order; the *WHERE* clause lets you include only those rows that meet specific criteria.

The PROJECT command is one of the most useful R:BASE relational commands. Here are some of its many uses:

☐ Creating a duplicate table for testing computed columns, command files, or new forms and reports. Tables created with PROJECT do not contain keyed columns. Use the BUILD KEY command to create keys.

☐ Creating a sorted version of an existing table. After executing the PROJECT command, remove the old table and rename the new one to the original name.

☐ Creating a table with only specific items from the original table. For example, you could create a table of Boston clients from an existing table containing clients from all over the country.

☐ Creating a subset of an existing table by not including all the columns from the original table. From a general employee table, for example, you may want to create a smaller table containing only the employee's name and address.

Here are two examples of the use of PROJECT:

```
PROJECT NEWEMP FROM EMPLOYEE USING LNAME FNAME STREET +
   CITY STATE ZIP SORTED BY LNAME

PROJECT NEWCLI FROM CLIENT USING ALL SORTED BY EMPID WHERE +
   CITY EQ BOSTON
```

The syntax is straightforward. The first table in each command is the new table you wish to create (*NEWEMP* and *NEWCLI*). The second table in each command (*EMPLOYEE* and *CLIENT*) is the original table.

Cautions: Be sure that the new table name does not already exist in your database. If you intend to use the PROJECT command to create the same table repeatedly, first remove the existing version of the table. These steps can be included in a command file:

```
REMOVE NEWTABLE
PROJECT NEWTABLE FROM OLDTABLE USING ALL
```

Each time you execute these two commands, the old version of *NEWTABLE* is removed before the new one is created. Periodically use the PACK command to recover the unused disk space that results from the use of REMOVE.

If you use PROJECT with a view that contains a computed column, the computed column definition will be lost, but the value will be projected as a regular column.

See: *APPEND, INTERSECT, JOIN, Relational commands, SUBTRACT,* and *UNION*

- **R:BASE 5000 equivalent**
PROJECT

PROMPT

- **Syntax**

```
PROMPT ─┬─────────┬─
        └ cmdname ┘
```

- **Description**
The PROMPT command initiates the R:BASE on-line assistance mode, Prompt-By-Example. The Prompt-By-Example feature helps new users with the R:BASE command language and database environment by guiding them through a series of steps that create and execute the specified command.

- **Procedure**
You can execute PROMPT with or without a command name. If you use PROMPT without a command name, you are first prompted to open a database and then presented with the following screen:

```
┌──────────────────────────────────────────────────────────────────┐
│              Prompts are organized under these topics.             │
│      For a list of commands that have prompts, choose All commands.│
│                                                                    │
│         To leave PROMPTS for R:BASE command mode, press [ESC].     │
└──────────────────────────────────────────────────────────────────┘
┌─Data Manipulation──────Database Operations───────────Utilities─────┐
│ Look at data          Open a database        Application development│
│ Print data            Exit                   Database maintenance    │
│ Add data              Data Input             R:BASE environment       │
│ Edit data             Data Output            Edit an ASCII file       │
│ Import/export data    Create a database      DOS functions            │
│ Relational operations Modify a database      All commands             │
└────────────────────────────────────────────────────────────────────┘
```

After you select the action you want to perform, choose the appropriate command from the displayed list. If you select *Look at data*, for example, R:BASE displays the following screen, which explains the available command options:

```
┌──────────────────────────────────────────────────────────────────────┐
│ Several commands display data from a database.                         │
└──────────────────────────────────────────────────────────────────────┘

┌──────────────────────────────────────────────────────────────────────┐
│  SELECT    Displays data from a table in rows and columns.             │
│  BROWSE    Displays data while scrolling up, down, left and right in the│
│            rows and columns of a table.                                │
│  COMPUTE   Calculates the count, minimum, maximum, average, sum, number of│
│            rows, standard deviation, variance, or all of these for a column.│
│  TALLY     Displays unique values with number of occurrences in a column.│
│  CROSSTAB  Cross-tabulates values in two columns.                      │
│  LIST      Displays information about the structure of an open database or│
│            lists databases on the current directory.                   │
│  VIEW      Defines a view to look at data in multiple tables.          │
└──────────────────────────────────────────────────────────────────────┘
┌═══════════════════════════════Choose a command═══════════════════════┐
│ SELECT    BROWSE    COMPUTE   TALLY      CROSSTAB LIST       VIEW       │
└──────────────────────────────────────────────────────────────────────┘
```

If you choose SELECT as the command to execute, R:BASE prompts for a table to select from and then displays the following screen:

```
┌──────────────────────────────────────────────────────────────────────┐
│ SELECT ALL FROM CLIENT SORTED BY CLI-NUM CLINAME WHERE ...             │
└──────────────────────────────────────────────────────────────────────┘

┌═════════Select columns for conditions - Press [ESC] for none═════════┐
│ CLI-NUM  CLINAME  STREET   CITY     STATE    ZIP      PHONE            │
└──────────────────────────────────────────────────────────────────────┘
```

	Column	Operator	Value

From this screen you can construct a SELECT command that includes the appropriate columns and conditions.

If you execute PROMPT followed by a command name, you bypass the above screens and start working with the specific command. For example, if you type *PROMPT SELECT*, you go directly to the screens that work with SELECT. Note that for most commands you must open a database before you issue PROMPT followed by a command name.

■ **Comments**
You can begin Prompt-By-Example when you start R:BASE if you include a *-P* on the R:BASE command line in the *RBSYSTEM.ASC* file. Bypass Prompt-By-Example by removing the *-P* (see *RBSYSTEM*).

Most people will find that issuing R:BASE commands at the R> prompt is far more efficient and versatile than relying on Prompt-By-Example. However, the PROMPT command offers a good way to get started with R:BASE and to learn its command structure.

It's possible to modify or add prompts by editing the system files, *PROMPT1.ASC* and *PROMPT2.ASC*. However, to do this you must be careful to follow the procedure described in Chapter 10 of the R:BASE User's Manual. In most cases, however, you can accomplish the same objectives by writing your own command files and leaving the R:BASE prompt files alone.

■ **R:BASE 5000 equivalent**
PROMPT

The PROMPT feature in R:BASE 5000 is not as elaborate as the System V version, but it does guide you through the use of R:BASE commands.

QUIT

■ **Syntax**

```
QUIT ┬──────────────┬
     └ TO filespec ┘
```

■ **Description**
Use the QUIT command in command files to terminate execution of all open command files and IF and WHILE blocks.

■ **Procedure**
Unless you use the optional *TO filespec* clause, QUIT always returns R:BASE to the R> prompt. If you include the *TO filespec* clause, QUIT closes all current command-file operations and runs the specified command file.

Use QUIT only when you want to terminate an R:BASE program. Use the *TO filespec* clause only if you don't want to return control to the R> prompt. If you intend to return control from a subroutine to the command file which called the subroutine, use RUN and RETURN rather than QUIT TO *filespec*.

The following excerpt from *WORKMEN.CMD* (see *Procedure files*) terminates execution if the *choice* variable is set to zero (this occurs if you press ESC):

```
CHOOSE choice FROM MENU1 AT 10
IF choice EQ 0 THEN
  SET ERR MESS ON
  SET MESS ON
  QUIT
ENDIF
```

Alternatively, you can execute another command file when the user quits:

```
CHOOSE choice FROM MENU1 AT 10
IF choice EQ 0 THEN
  SET ERR MESS ON
  SET MESS ON
  QUIT TO EXIT.CMD
ENDIF
```

Caution: Never use QUIT in command files that will be accessed by an application developed in Application EXPRESS. QUIT terminates all command files including those created by Application EXPRESS.

See: *BREAK, Programming,* and *RETURN*

- **R:BASE 5000 equivalent**
  QUIT

RBASE

- **Syntax**
Select *R:BASE* from the RBSYSTEM menu or execute R:BASE from DOS:

```
RBASE  [ -R ] [ -P ] [ -Fn ] [ -Bn ] [ -Mn ] [ -Tn ] [ filespec ]
```

The *-R* option suppresses the display of the R logo. The *-P* option starts R:BASE in the Prompt-By-Example mode. The *-F* and *-B* options modify the foreground and background colors if you are using a color monitor. The *-M* and *-T* options modify other monitor characteristics. See the R:BASE System V installation guide for further information on monitor options.

- **Description**
The RBASE command starts R:BASE from the MS-DOS prompt.

The *filespec* option lets you specify a command file that will be executed when R:BASE is started. If you omit *filespec*, R:BASE uses the *RBASE.DAT* file if it exists in the current directory (see *Application EXPRESS* and *Command files*).

Caution: The following commands are available only if you start R:BASE from the RBSYSTEM menu; they are *not* available when you start R:BASE from MS-DOS: CODELOCK, EXPRESS, FORMS, GATEWAY, RBDEFINE, and REPORTS.

■ **R:BASE 5000 equivalent**
RBASE

R:BASE 5000 commands

■ **Description**
Some R:BASE 5000 commands are no longer formally documented in R:BASE System V. However, these commands still run in System V. The following R:BASE 5000 commands are undocumented in System V; they are listed with the System V commands that replaced them:

Undocumented R:BASE 5000 commands	Replacement in System V
ASSIGN	Included in CHANGE
CHANGE COLUMN	Renamed to REDEFINE
DRAW	EDIT USING or ENTER with variable forms designed in Forms EXPRESS
EDIT VARIABLE	EDIT USING with variable forms designed in Forms EXPRESS
ENTER VARIABLE	ENTER with variable forms designed in Forms EXPRESS
MOVE	Functionality replaced by the *SMOVE()* function (see *String manipulation functions*)

In general, the functionality of the undocumented commands is entirely replaced by the System V commands and functions. For example, the ASSIGN and CHANGE COLUMN commands have the identical syntax as the CHANGE and REDEFINE commands, respectively.

The DRAW, EDIT VARIABLE, and ENTER VARIABLE commands are used with R:BASE 5000 variable forms. You use variable forms in R:BASE 5000 to enter data into more than one table simultaneously. By using a variable form, you can enter values into the variables displayed on the form and then use the LOAD command to enter these variables into the appropriate tables.

The System V Forms EXPRESS module provides this same capability by allowing you to design a single form for multiple tables. In fact, variable forms are more cumbersome and much slower than System V forms. If you have applications in R:BASE 5000 that use variable forms, we recommend that you upgrade to System V and redesign the variable forms using Forms EXPRESS.

As of this writing, however, the functionality of Forms EXPRESS in System V does not *entirely* replace R:BASE 5000 variable forms.

For example, consider the Car Matching program in the *SET POINTER* entry. In the program, a variable form called *vcarform* (created with Forms EXPRESS) displays the client's name and salary. This form is shown in the following screen:

```
┌────────────────────────────────────────────────────────────────┐
│                                                                  │
│  Client Number: S     E  Client Name: S                     E    │
│                                                                  │
│             Annual Salary: S                     E               │
│                                                                  │
└────────────────────────────────────────────────────────────────┘
```

```
[ESC] Return  [F1] Insert  [F2] Delete  [F3] Review  [Shift-F10] More
Form: vcarform   Edit            Table:                Page 1  < 1, 1>
```

This variable form displays the variables *vclinum, vcliname,* and *vsalary.* (See the command file listing in *SET POINTER.*) The command file displays the form as shown in the following screen:

```
          CLIENT AND CAR MATCHING PROGRAM

          Enter Client Number to Match or <Enter> to Exit: 1
```

```
    Client Number: 1        Client Name: Harold Wilson

              Annual Salary: $27,500.00
```

```
    CARMAKE               MODEL               PRICE
    Renault               Alliance            $13,000.00
    Chevrolet             Citation            $12,000.00
    Toyota                Tercel              $8,000.00
    Nissan                Stanza              $7,000.00
```

```
    Press any key to continue
```

Unfortunately, in System V you must use the undocumented DRAW command to display the form and continue screen processing:

```
DRAW vcarform WITH ALL AT 4
```

If you use the System V equivalent, EDIT USING, R:BASE displays the form, but the command file pauses until you press ESC. In addition, you must first assign *vcarform* to a table if you want to use EDIT USING. The other alternative is to display the variables with the SHOW VARIABLE command rather than the variable form. However, this is a step backward and is far less convenient.

While this discussion might seem a little obscure unless you are an R:BASE 5000 programmer, the point is that the R:BASE 5000 DRAW command offers some functionality not provided by EDIT USING or ENTER in System V forms. If you want to display many variables on the screen without writing a lot of SHOW VARIABLE commands, create a variable form in Forms EXPRESS and locate the variables on the form. To display the form and continue processing, use the following command:

```
DRAW formname WITH ALL AT scrnrow
```

The final undocumented R:BASE 5000 command is MOVE. The syntax of the MOVE command is:

```
MOVE nchar FROM varname1 AT chrpos1 TO varname2 AT chrpos2
```

197

The syntax and description of the *SMOVE()* function are as follows:

```
SMOVE(text,pos1,nchar,string,pos2)
```

This moves *nchar* characters from the *text* value, starting at character position *pos1*, to *string*, starting at character position *pos2*. This function is indeed equivalent to the MOVE command.

See: *CHANGE, Conversion from different R:BASE versions, FORMS, REDEFINE, SET POINTER, and String manipulation functions*

RBDEFINE (Definition EXPRESS)

■ **Syntax**
Select Definition EXPRESS from the RBSYSTEM menu.

You also can execute RBDEFINE at the R> prompt if you entered R:BASE from the RBSYSTEM menu:

```
RBDEFINE ┬─────┬
         └ exec ┘
```

If you entered R:BASE from the MS-DOS prompt, you must exit R:BASE. You can then execute RBDEFINE from MS-DOS:

```
RBDEFINE ┬────┬ ┬────┬ ┬────┬ ┬────┬ ┬────┬ ┬─────┬
         └ -R ┘ └ -Fn ┘ └ -Bn ┘ └ -Mn ┘ └ -Tn ┘ └ exec ┘
```

The *-R* option suppresses display of the R logo. The *-F* and *-B* options modify the foreground and background colors if you are using a color monitor. The *-M* and *-T* options modify other monitor characteristics. (See the R:BASE System V Installation Guide for further information on monitor options.) The *exec* option lets you specify an *exec* file that runs when you start RBDEFINE from MS-DOS. (See *RECORD* and *PLAYBACK*.)

■ **Description**
The RBDEFINE command invokes Definition EXPRESS. Definition EXPRESS is fully described in its own entry.

■ **R:BASE 5000 equivalent**
Application EXPRESS

RBEDIT

■ **Syntax**

Select RBEDIT from the RBSYSTEM menu.

RBEDIT also can be started at the R> prompt:

```
RBEDIT ─┬─────────┬─
        └ filespec ┘
```

RBEDIT also can be started from MS-DOS:

```
RBEDIT ─┬────┬─┬─────┬─┬─────┬─┬─────┬─┬─────┬─┬──────────┬─
        └ -R ┘ └ -Fn ┘ └ -Bn ┘ └ -Mn ┘ └ -Tn ┘ └ filespec ┘
```

The *-R* option suppresses display of the R logo. The *-F* and *-B* options modify the foreground and background colors if you are using a color monitor. The *-M* and *-T* options modify other monitor characteristics. (See the R:BASE System V Installation Guide for further information on monitor options.) The *filespec* option lets you specify an existing file to be edited when RBEDIT starts. If the file does not exist, RBEDIT displays a blank screen that you can use to create a new file.

■ **Description**

The RBEDIT command invokes the R:BASE full-screen text editor, RBEDIT. You can use this text editor to prepare command and text files consisting of as many as 800 lines. Note, however, that you can use the ZIP command to invoke any text editor.

■ **Procedure**

When RBEDIT starts, you are prompted for a filename (unless you load RBEDIT from MS-DOS and specify a filename). When you enter an existing filename, RBEDIT loads the contents of the file and displays the first 23 lines. You then can edit the file. When you enter a new filename RBEDIT simply displays the edit screen. RBEDIT keeps track of the cursor position and displays the current line number and column coordinate in the upper right corner of the screen.

The maximum line width of RBEDIT files is 80 characters. Any characters that you enter beyond the 80-character limit are lost.

The following table lists the key functions in RBEDIT:

Keys	Function
Home	Displays the first screen (page) of the file and places the cursor at the leftmost character of the top line.
End	Displays the last line of the file on the first line of the screen.
PgUp/PgDn	Displays the previous or the next screen of text.
Up/Down arrow	Moves the cursor up or down one line.
Left/Right arrow	Moves the cursor one character to the left or right.
Ctrl-left/right arrow	Moves the cursor to the start or the end of the line.
F1	Inserts a line above the current line.
F2	Deletes the current line.
Ins	Inserts a blank character at the cursor position.
Del	Deletes the character at the cursor position.
F4	Toggles the repeat function on and off.
Alt and Numeric Keypad	Allow the use of the IBM extended character set.
Shift-F2	Deletes a marked text block.
Shift-F4	Copies a marked text block to the current cursor position.
Shift-F6	Marks the beginning and end of a text block.

Most of the above key functions are self-explanatory. However, the use of the F4 key and the keys for working with text blocks merit further discussion.

The F4 key toggles the repeat-character function on and off. When you turn on the repeat function and then type a character, RBEDIT repeats the character each time you move the cursor with an arrow key. Use the repeat function to create boxes or other repetitive patterns on the screen. Note that you can use the wide variety of IBM extended characters by holding down Alt and typing the character's ASCII code number on the numeric keypad. For a list of the extended character set ASCII codes see *Conversion functions.*

The Shift-F6 key sequence marks blocks of text in your text file for copying or deleting. Move the cursor to the beginning of the text you want to mark and press Shift-F6. Then move the cursor to the end of the text block and press Shift-F6 again. RBEDIT displays the screen coordinates of the beginning and the end of the block at the upper right corner of the screen.

Press Shift-F2 to delete the block. Be careful when you use this command: *You cannot recover deleted text blocks.* Shift-F4 copies the marked text block to the cursor position. The copied block of text *overwrites* any existing text at the cursor. Therefore, you must open enough space for the marked text by inserting blank lines with the F1 key before you copy a block of text.

■ **Comment**

In general, RBEDIT is convenient for quickly creating small files. The fact that you can load it from the R> prompt makes it ideal for editing a command file, running the file at the R> prompt, and then returning to RBEDIT to make additional changes. However, RBEDIT does not compare to some of the more powerful text editors available on the market.

The ZIP command lets you run most text editors from the R> prompt, provided there is enough memory available. However, using ZIP to switch back and forth between your own text editor and the R> prompt is much slower than loading RBEDIT.

■ **R:BASE 5000 equivalent**

RBEDIT

The R:BASE 5000 version does not include the text block marking, copying, and deleting functions.

RBSYSTEM

■ **Syntax**

`RBSYSTEM`

You can execute RBSYSTEM only at the MS-DOS prompt.

- **Description**

The RBSYSTEM command starts R:BASE System V and displays the System menu, which is shown in the following screen:

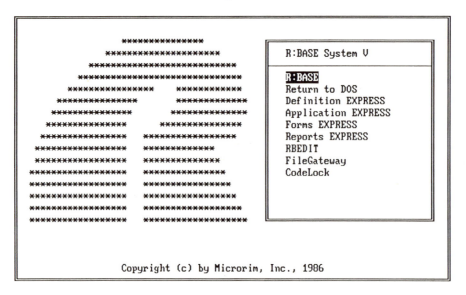

- **Procedure**

The System menu is controlled by the contents of the *RBSYSTEM.ASC* file, which is located in the same directory as the R:BASE executable files. The contents of the *RBSYSTEM.ASC* file that corresponds to the menu screen above are as follows:

```
SET COLOR FORE 7
SET COLOR BACK 0
5 R:BASE                "RBASE     -R -F7 -B0"
0 "Return to DOS"
1 "Definition EXPRESS"  "RBDEFINE -R -F7 -B0"
2 "Application EXPRESS" "EXPRESS  -R -F7 -B0"
3 "Forms EXPRESS"       "FORMS    -R -F7 -B0"
4 "Reports EXPRESS"     "REPORTS  -R -F7 -B0"
6 RBEDIT                "RBEDIT   -R -F7 -B0"
7 FileGateway           "GATEWAY  -R -F7 -B0"
8 CodeLock              "CODELOCK -R -F7 -B0"
```

If your System menu is different from the one above, notice that the lines numbered *5* and *0* in the above *RBSYSTEM.ASC* file are at the top of the command list. This demonstrates how you can customize the *RBSYSTEM.ASC* file. R:BASE is normally the fifth item in the System menu. You may find it tiresome having to move the highlight to the fifth row to start R:BASE or to the ninth row to select *Return to DOS*. You can eliminate this by placing these menu options at the top of the list as shown above. Simply use RBEDIT to change the locations of the lines in the file. Note, however, that the line numbers must remain the same. Always make a backup of the original *RBSYSTEM.ASC* file before you make any changes.

You also can modify the parameters appended to each command line. For example, *RBASE -R -F7 -B0* suppresses the R logo and sets the foreground and background characteristics when you load R:BASE from MS-DOS. A *-P* on this line will start R:BASE in the Prompt-By-Example mode. See Chapter 10 of the R:BASE User's Manual for further information about the codes and parameters that you can use whenever you modify command lines in the *RBSYSTEM.ASC* file.

You can add additional menu options to the *RBSYSTEM.ASC* file. To add a program or executable file to the System menu, start the line with three digits between 100 and 255; then type the menu text (enclose the text in quotes if it contains embedded blanks); finally, add the actual command. For example, to add the CLOUT module to the System menu, insert the following line in the *RBSYSTEM.ASC* file:

```
101  CLOUT      CLOUT
```

You also can add MS-DOS batch files as shown in the following example:

```
150 "My Batch File"    "COMMAND /C BATFILE"
```

When you add these two menu choices, the *RBSYSTEM.ASC* file looks like this:

```
SET COLOR FORE 7
SET COLOR BACK 0
5 R:BASE               "RBASE      -R -F7 -B0"
0 "Return to DOS"
1 "Definition EXPRESS"  "RBDEFINE -R -F7 -B0"
2 "Application EXPRESS" "EXPRESS  -R -F7 -B0"
3 "Forms EXPRESS"       "FORMS    -R -F7 -B0"
4 "Reports EXPRESS"     "REPORTS  -R -F7 -B0"
6 RBEDIT               "RBEDIT   -R -F7 -B0"
7 FileGateway          "GATEWAY  -R -F7 -B0"
8 CodeLock             "CODELOCK -R -F7 -B0"
101 CLOUT               CLOUT
150 "My Batch File"     "COMMAND /C BATFILE"
```

Note: These new lines can be placed anywhere in the file to change the order in which menu items appear in the System menu. Also, quotes are needed only for text or commands that contain embedded blanks.

■ **Comment**

In general, it's good practice to start all R:BASE modules from the System menu rather than directly from MS-DOS. When you execute RBSYSTEM from MS-DOS, you have access to all modules and commands. When you load individual modules from MS-DOS, you cannot switch to another module without first exiting the current module and then loading the next module.

- **R:BASE 5000 equivalent**

The *RB5000.DAT* file performs the same function in R:BASE 5000 as the *RBSYSTEM.ASC* does in System V. Simply type *RB5000* to load the R:BASE 5000 System menu.

RECORD

- **Syntax**

```
RECORD ─┬─ exec
        └─ OFF
```

You also can press Shift-F7 to run RECORD.

- **Description**

Use the RECORD command to store a series of commands in a disk file for replay with the PLAYBACK command.

- **Procedure**

The R:BASE documentation refers to recorded files as *exec* files. *Exec* files can have any valid MS-DOS filename. Record keystroke sequences in any R:BASE module by pressing Shift-F7, which performs the same function as RECORD.

The RECORD command is useful for storing often-used command sequences. To record to a file, press Shift-F7 and then enter the filename or type

```
RECORD filename
```

where *filename* is the name of the file in which recorded keystrokes are to be stored. After you enter all of the commands you want to store in the file, press Shift-F7 again or type

```
RECORD OFF
```

Use the PLAYBACK command (or press Shift-F8) to run the recorded *exec* file.

You can edit recorded *exec* files only with RBEDIT. Edit an *exec* file as you would any other command file—add new command lines, modify existing lines, add variables, and so on.

- **R:BASE 5000 equivalent**
None

REDEFINE

- **Syntax**

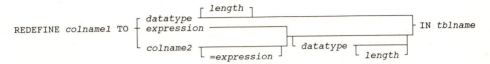

```
                        ┌ length ┐
                ┌ datatype          ┐
REDEFINE colname1 TO ┤ expression ─────────────────────────┤        IN tblname
                └ colname2 ┘        ┌ datatype ┐
                        └ =expression ┘        └ length ┘
```

- **Description**

Use the REDEFINE command to change any or all of the characteristics of an existing column. You can change the column name, the data type, the computed column expression, or a text column's character length.

- **Procedure**

The column change is limited to a single table. If multiple tables use the same column, you must use REDEFINE or RENAME to rename the column you are changing. Also, you cannot redefine columns that are part of a computed column expression. See *Columns* for a complete description of column data types and characteristics.

Redefining an existing column is much like defining a new one. However, you must always keep in mind how the change will affect existing data. For example, NOTE columns can be truncated when you change them to TEXT. R:BASE replaces incompatible data type values with NULL values. Although you can change a TEXT column to an INTEGER column, only column values containing numbers are retained; values containing alphabetic characters are changed to NULL values.

You can change numeric data types (INTEGER, REAL, DOUBLE, CURRENCY) with no difficulty. However, changing to INTEGER drops the digits after the decimal point.

Here are some examples using REDEFINE to change columns:

```
REDEFINE EMPID TO TEXT IN EMPLOYEE
REDEFINE YEARS TO ((.#DATE - HIREDATE)/365) IN EMPLOYEE
REDEFINE EMPID TO NEWID IN EMPLOYEE
REDEFINE LNAME TO TEXT 15 IN EMPLOYEE
REDEFINE YEARS TO NUMBER = ((.#DATE - HIREDATE)/365) IN EMPLOYEE
```

- **Comments**

The REDEFINE command creates a temporary table that is subsequently removed. Because removed tables create unusable disk space, we recommend that you execute the PACK command after you use the REDEFINE command several times.

See: *Columns, Data types, PACK,* and *RENAME*

■ **R:BASE 5000 equivalent**

CHANGE COLUMN

The CHANGE COLUMN command has the same syntax as the REDEFINE command.

Relational commands

■ **Description**

Relational commands let you combine, compare, and duplicate the tables in your database. These commands form the basis of the R:BASE approach to database design. To design efficient databases in R:BASE, you must understand the capabilities and uses of the relational commands.

The R:BASE relational commands are as follows:

Command	Description
APPEND	Appends rows from one table to another.
INTERSECT	Forms a new table from two existing tables using only those rows that have common column values.
JOIN	Compares similar data types in two tables and forms a new table based on the comparison.
PROJECT	Creates a duplicate of an existing table or a subset of an existing table.
SUBTRACT	Forms a new table from two existing tables using only those rows that do not have identical common column values (this is the opposite of INTERSECT).
UNION	Combines two tables with at least one common column to form a new table that uses all rows.
VIEW	Combines data from as many as five tables into a view (a table that can be used for display only).

This entry discusses the general concepts of relational operations.

For detailed descriptions and examples of the above commands, see the individual command entries. For detailed database design guidelines, see *Definition EXPRESS*.

■ **Comments**

It is often more efficient to break up data into logical groups and to store these groups in separate tables. You can avoid redundancy and maintenance problems by using this approach.

Although it might be efficient in the long run to store logical groups of data in separate tables, it is often necessary to temporarily combine columns from two or more tables to produce a report or to obtain the results of a query. For example, to produce an invoice report, you might combine information from the *INVOICE* and *CLIENT* tables. You would get the client name and address from the *CLIENT* table and the invoice number, date, amount, and description from the *INVOICE* table. Clearly, the two tables would require a common column (*CLINUM*, for example) in order to link the appropriate information together.

To generate such a report in earlier versions of R:BASE, you would use either the INTERSECT or UNION command to form a new table that contains the data needed for the invoice report. The UNION command would combine all rows from both tables, filling in null values where no data exists. The INTERSECT command would only combine those rows where the common column has identical values in each table.

The INTERSECT command would be more efficient because clients who have no invoices in the invoice table would be excluded. The UNION command would be useful because it also would include those clients who had no billings. In either case, you would then need to produce a report generated from the newly formed table. After printing the report, you would remove the new table and keep the report definition in the *REPORTS* table. The important point here is that the table formed by the UNION or INTERSECT commands is *not* updated when you update the *CLIENT* and *INVOICE* tables. You must create a new table each time you print the invoice report.

To see only the clients who had no billings, you would use the SUBTRACT command. SUBTRACT would create a table that includes only those clients without matching client numbers in the invoice table. Of course, there would not be much point in producing an invoice report from this table. But you could use the table for other purposes: for example, to prepare a report of clients who haven't purchased anything recently and therefore require more marketing attention.

In R:BASE System V, the most convenient way to produce the invoice report is to define a *view* with the VIEW command or with the *view* option in Definition EXPRESS. Although the R:BASE documentation does not include VIEW in its chapter on relational operations, VIEW is indeed a relational command. In fact, VIEW is one of the most useful relational commands.

A view is a combination of columns from a maximum of five tables. Each table must have a common column, and at least one other table must be included in the view. The view uses the same method of combining data as the

INTERSECT command. However, the view is not really a table because the data from the combined tables is not physically copied to the view. Because the data in a view can only be displayed and not altered, you can think of a view as a table *image* that displays data from multiple tables. A view works with all commands that display or query data. You can therefore produce a report from a view or use the SELECT command with a view.

Using a view to generate the invoice report offers two important advantages:

☐ Because it does not contain data, a view requires little storage space. A new table formed from an INTERSECT or UNION command actually contains the rows of data from the two source tables.

☐ A view does not have to be re-created or updated every time you display the view or print a report using the view. The view always uses the current data from the specified tables.

At this point, you might wonder why you would ever use INTERSECT or UNION when you have this wonderful VIEW command. There often might be situations in which you need to permanently reorganize your data. Or you might need to change your original database design and restructure your tables. The UNION, INTERSECT, and SUBTRACT commands actually alter the database, while a view only displays data.

The above commands form new tables or views from existing tables with common columns. The JOIN command differs in that it is generally applied to tables that do not have common columns. The JOIN command forms a new table from two existing tables based on a comparison of columns with the same *data types* and *length*. Because the JOIN command is one of the more difficult commands to understand, see *JOIN* for more information and a detailed example of command usage.

The PROJECT command creates a new table from an existing table or view. You can use it to create a duplicate table or to select individual columns and create a subset of the original table. The PROJECT command is useful for creating a sorted version of an existing table or for copying parts of a master table to a smaller table.

The APPEND command adds data from one table to the end of another table. Only data from common columns is appended. R:BASE inserts NULL values in the appended rows if no data exists for a column in the destination table. You also can append data from the same table to itself. This is useful for making a large table with which you can test performance.

The most useful application for the APPEND command is to append data from smaller tables to a master table. For example, a geothermal power company maintains separate tables for individual wells delivering steam. At the end of the month, the data from each well is appended to a master table to obtain overall performance data for the power plant.

See: *APPEND, DEFINE, Definition EXPRESS, INTERSECT, JOIN, PROJECT, SUBTRACT, UNION,* and *VIEW*

- **R:BASE 5000 equivalent**

R:BASE 5000 supports all of the above commands except VIEW.

RELOAD

- **Syntax**

```
RELOAD dbspec
```

- **Description**

The RELOAD command creates a copy of the currently open database using the path and filename specified with *dbspec*. In the process, any unusable disk space that exists in the original database is removed from the copy and the organization of rows and tables is optimized in the copy.

- **Procedure**

The DELETE ROWS, REMOVE, EXPAND, and REDEFINE commands create unusable disk space. In addition, extended use of the database disperses the data on disk, causing slower performance in large databases. The RELOAD command rectifies both of these problems. Although the PACK command eliminates unusable disk space, it does not reorganize the tables and rows.

The RELOAD command is useful either as a means of backing up the current database or for creating an optimized copy of the database. The following command sequence reloads the *CONSULT* database to a new database called *NEWCONS*, closes the database, renames *CONSULT* with a backup name, and then renames the optimized version as *CONSULT*:

```
OPEN C:\DATA\CONSULT
RELOAD C:\DATA\NEWCONS
CLOSE
RENAME C:\DATA\CONSULT?.RBF CONSBAK?.RBF
RENAME C:\DATA\NEWCONS?.RBF CONSULT?.RBF
OPEN C:\DATA\CONSULT
```

Note: You can use the wildcard character (?) in the command only if each database name is the same length.

- **Comment**

  You cannot use the RELOAD command to back up to multiple floppy disks. If the database to be reloaded is larger than the capacity of a floppy disk, either make additional space on the hard disk to accommodate the new copy or use BACKUP to back up to floppy disks.

  See: *BACKUP, COPY, PACK,* and *RENAME*

- **R:BASE 5000 equivalent**

  RELOAD

REMOVE

- **Syntax**

```
        ┌ COLUMN colname FROM tblname
        ├ FORM formname
REMOVE ─┼ REPORT rptname
        ├ RULE rulenum
        ├ TABLE tblname
        └ VIEW viewname
```

- **Description**

  The REMOVE command deletes specified columns, forms, reports, rules, tables, or views.

- **Procedure**

Command	Description
REMOVE COLUMN *colname* FROM *tblname*	Removes the specified column from the specified table. The column and its data are removed only from the specified table, even if the column exists in other tables.
REMOVE FORM *formname*	Removes the specified form.
REMOVE REPORT *rptname*	Removes the specified report.
REMOVE RULE *rulenum*	Removes the rule with the specified number. The number is located in the RULES table.
REMOVE TABLE *tblname*	Removes the specified table. The word TABLE is optional.
REMOVE VIEW *viewname*	Removes the specified view.

Here are some examples of the REMOVE command syntax:

```
REMOVE COLUMN YEARS FROM EMPLOYEE
REMOVE FORM DATAFORM
REMOVE RULE 1
```

Use the LIST command to review the names of columns, forms, reports, and so forth in your database. For example, the command LIST RULES displays all of the existing rule numbers and their descriptions.

■ **Comment**

It is good practice to pack the database after you use the REMOVE command because REMOVE creates unusable disk space.

Caution: Use REMOVE with care. You cannot recover data deleted with the REMOVE command.

See: *DELETE, PACK,* and *RELOAD*

■ **R:BASE 5000 equivalent**

R:BASE 5000 supports only REMOVE *tblname* and REMOVE COLUMN.

RENAME

■ **Syntax**

```
          ┌ COLUMN colname1 TO colname2 ┬─────────────┐
          │                             └ IN tblname ─┘
          │
          ├ FORM formname1 TO formname2
          ├ REPORT rptname1 TO rptname2
          ├ TABLE tblname1 TO tblname2
RENAME ───┤ VIEW viewname1 TO viewname2
          ├ OWNER password1 TO password2
          ├ MPW ┐
          │     ├─ TO password ┬─────────────┐
          └ RPW ┘              └ IN tblname ─┘
```

You also can enter RENAME in the form of the MS-DOS RENAME command:

```
RENAME filespec filename
```

■ **Description**

Use the RENAME command to give new names to specified items in the database or, in its MS-DOS command form, to rename existing MS-DOS files.

Database usage: The following names can be changed with the RENAME command: column names, form names, report names, table names, view names, the OWNER password, and MPW and RPW passwords.

Use the *IN tablename* clause to restrict the command to a single table. This is optional with the RENAME COLUMN and RENAME MPW/RPW commands. If you omit the table name, the specified column name or password name is renamed wherever it exists in the database. Below are some examples:

```
RENAME COLUMN EMPID TO NEWID IN EMPLOYEE
RENAME MPW TO JBC$6 IN EMPLOYEE
RENAME REPORT INVOICE TO NEWINV
```

MS-DOS usage: The R:BASE RENAME command functions exactly like the MS-DOS RENAME command. You can use wildcard characters when you change database names if the new name has the same number of characters as the old name. The following example renames the three *.RBF* files for the *CONSULT* database to *CONSBAK1.RBF*, *CONSBAK2.RBF*, and *CONSBAK3.RBF*:

```
RENAME CONSULT?.RBF CONSBAK?.RBF
```

If, however, you rename the *CONSULT* files to a name with a different number of characters using wildcard characters (? or *), the RENAME operation will not create the corresponding three files properly.

Of course, you can use RENAME to rename single files, as follows:

```
RENAME TEST.CMD NEWTEST.CMD
```

See: *COPY* and *DOS commands in R:BASE*

- **R:BASE 5000 equivalent**

R:BASE 5000 supports the MS-DOS version of RENAME as well as RENAME OWNER/TABLE/COLUMN. To rename forms and reports, use the CHANGE command (e.g., CHANGE *fname* TO *newname* IN FORMS WHERE *fname* EQ *oldname*). Use DEFINE to change MPW/RPW passwords.

REPORTS (Reports EXPRESS)

- **Syntax**

Select Reports EXPRESS from the RBSYSTEM menu.

You also can execute REPORTS at the R> prompt:

```
REPORTS ┌─────────┐┌─ tblname ─┐
        └ rptname ┘└─ viewname ─┘
```

Appending a report name and a table or view name only functions when executing REPORTS from the R> prompt with an open database.

REPORTS also can be executed from the MS-DOS prompt:

```
REPORTS ┌────┐ ┌─────┐ ┌─────┐ ┌─────┐ ┌─────┐
        └ -R ┘ └ -Fn ┘ └ -Bn ┘ └ -Mn ┘ └ -Tn ┘
```

212

The *-R* option suppresses the display of the R logo. The *-F* and *-B* options modify the foreground and background colors if you are using a color monitor. The *-M* and *-T* options modify monitor characteristics. See the R:BASE System V Installation Guide for further information on monitor options.

■ Description

Reports EXPRESS is a module in R:BASE System V for creating reports from tables in the database.

■ Procedure

Although you can generate simple reports in Application EXPRESS and simple lists with the SELECT command, this entry focuses on the advanced capabilities of Reports EXPRESS.

Report design considerations: Before you read the procedure for creating reports, familiarize yourself with the basic concepts of report design and the design options available in R:BASE System V.

Report formats. Reports can be designed for output to the screen, to the printer, or to both. Reports can have as many as 255 characters on each line if your printer can print that many characters.

Table access. In contrast to forms, reports are always associated with a single table or view. While you can use variables to look up data from other tables to include in your report, reports are usually generated faster if all data is contained in a single table or view. Often, you can use views to avoid using lookup variables.

Variables. The R:BASE system variables (*#DATE, #PAGE, #PI, #TIME*) can be used in reports. In addition, you can define a maximum of 40 of your own variable expressions. These can be very useful for table lookups, calculating totals and subtotals, and for concatenating text expressions. In general, follow the guidelines we listed for creating R:BASE expressions. However, the following guidelines apply specifically to the use of expressions in reports:

☐ Do *not* enclose *SUM OF* or lookup variable expressions in parentheses.

☐ Variable values are retained in memory after you exit or print a report. Therefore, if you print a report again during the same R:BASE session, the variables can yield inaccurate results. Use the CLEAR command to clear the appropriate variables before you reprint the report. You may want to use a short command file that first clears the variables and then prints the report.

Examples of these guidelines are given later in this entry.

Report sections. R:BASE reports are divided into sections that group and organize data. The following table describes the types of sections available:

Section	Description
Report header (RH)	Appears once at the beginning of the report.
Page header (PH)	Appears at the top of each page of the report.
Break header (H#)	Appears as the heading of a subgroup of data whenever the value of the specified break column or variable changes.
Detail lines (D)	Lines of data that form subgroups or comprise the body of the report.
Break footer (F#)	Footing for a corresponding break header (usually to calculate results from a subgroup).
Page footer (PF)	Appears at the end of each page of the report.
Report footer (RF)	Appears once at the end of the report.

It is not necessary to include all of the above sections in a report. Most reports include, as a minimum, a page header and detail lines. A mailing list, however, might only include detail lines. Other reports might include only break headers and footers that display subtotals.

Examples of the use of report sections are included later in this entry.

Designing a report: There are four main steps in designing and creating a report:

☐ Make a rough sketch of the report, identifying and locating the data values to be displayed.

☐ Define the variables and break points for the report, if necessary.

☐ Create the text and format of the report.

☐ Locate the columns and variables on the report.

To illustrate the creation of reports, the following example produces a report based on a view, called *INVFORM*, which combines data from the *INVOICE* and *CLIENT* tables. Here are the columns contained in this view:

```
Table: INVFORM        No lock(s)
Read Password: No
Modify Password: No

Column definitions
# Name      Type       Length         Key    Expression
1 CLINUM    INTEGER
2 INV-NUM   TEXT        8 characters
3 ENTRDATE  DATE                             .#DATE
4 DUE       CURRENCY
5 PREVBAL   CURRENCY
6 TOTAL     CURRENCY                         'PREVBAL'+'DUE'
7 CLINAME   TEXT       25 characters
```

CLINAME is the only column from the *CLIENT* table. However, it is more efficient to use a view rather than a lookup variable. The columns *DUE* and *PREVBAL* do not appear in the report but are part of the computed column expression for *TOTAL*.

The report summarizes the outstanding invoices and the amount owed by each client and reports the total amount owed by all clients. A sample of the completed report follows:

```
                    INVOICE SUMMARY REPORT


     Report Date:  12/04/86                        Page:        1

     Client Number:        1  Client Name: Johnson and Anderson Co.
     ===================================================================
          Inv. Num    Inv. Date    Amount      Total Due
          ========    =========    ======      =========
           001        10/22/86     3,000.00    $3,345.00
           002        10/22/86     7,898.00    $7,898.00
           003        10/22/86      $343.00     $943.00
           009        11/13/86      $500.00     $500.00
                      11/13/86                    $0.00
                                               ===========
                              Client Owes:    $12,686.00
                                               ===========

     Client Number:        2  Client Name: Cal Gas and Electric
     ===================================================================
          Inv. Num    Inv. Date    Amount      Total Due
          ========    =========    ======      =========
More output follows - press [ESC] to quit, any key to continue
```

```
                    INVOICE SUMMARY REPORT


     Report Date:  12/04/86                        Page:        4

     Client Number:       35  Client Name: Harbinger Supply Co
     ===================================================================
          Inv. Num    Inv. Date    Amount      Total Due
          ========    =========    ======      =========
           35-009     09/06/86     1,765.00    $2,065.00
                                               ===========
                              Client Owes:    $2,065.00
                                               ===========

                      Total for all Clients:  $33,212.00
                                               ===========

R>
```

215

Each client in the report represents a *break point*. The data is organized so that the invoices for each client are listed first, and then the total owed is computed for each client. A grand total is also computed and placed in a report footer at the end of the report.

The following screen shows the layout of the completed report:

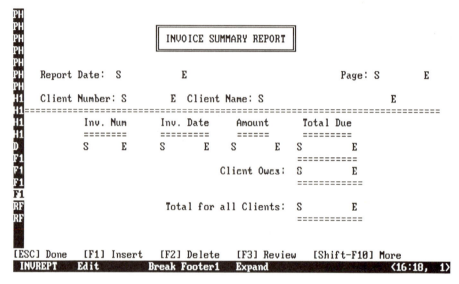

Note the column in the left margin that indicates the section definitions; this column is called the mark area. To identify each section of the report, refer to the table above that describes report sections.

Before you can create this report, you must define the necessary break columns, the variable that computes the subtotals, and the variable that computes the grand total. In this example, the primary break column is *CLINUM*. When the value of *CLINUM* changes, the next value of *CLINUM* is printed and all data for that client is summarized, and so on. Break columns are always printed in sorted order. Therefore we also specify *INV-NUM* as a secondary break column in order to print the invoice numbers in sorted order.

You also need two variables to compute the subtotals and the grand total. Each of these variables simply adds up the total due, which is represented by the *TOTAL* column. However, the variable that calculates subtotals must be reset to zero every time the client number changes. This type of variable is called a *break variable*. The variable for the grand total does not need to be reset since it maintains a running total for the entire list of clients.

Finally, you must define a variable to print the date and a variable to print the page numbers of the report. Set these variables equal to the system variables *#DATE* and *#PAGE*, respectively.

With this information, you are ready to create the report. Normally, at this point, you would have a sketch of the report and a list of the necessary variables and break columns.

Creating the report: As you design reports, you will frequently use the function keys to select various actions. The functions in Reports EXPRESS are listed in the following table:

Key	Description
F1	Inserts a line above the current line.
F2	Deletes the current line.
Shift-F2	Deletes the current field.
F3	Displays the defined variables and columns from the report's main table (or from other tables if you press F3 again). If the cursor is in a field, pressing F3 displays the field name and its data type.
F4	Toggles the repeat function on and off. The repeat function lets you repeat the last character you typed by pressing one of the arrow keys.
F5	Resets the values in the current field to their status before you modified them.
F6	Locates or relocates a field.
F7	Moves the cursor to the previous report section. If EXPAND (F9) is on and there is no previous section, F7 creates a new section.
F8	Moves the cursor to the next report section. If EXPAND (F9) is on and there is no next section, F8 creates a new section.
F9	Toggles the EXPAND mode on and off.
F10	Displays the context-sensitive help screen.
Shift-F10	Pages through function key descriptions.
Ins	Inserts a space at the cursor position.
Del	Deletes the character at the cursor position.

(continued)

Key	Description
Right/left arrow	Moves the cursor one character to the left or right.
Up/down arrow	Moves the cursor one character up or down.
Ctrl-left arrow	Moves the cursor to column 1.
Ctrl-right arrow	Moves the cursor to column 255.
Tab	Moves the cursor to the next tab setting in the work area. If the cursor is in the mark area, it is switched to the work area. Tabs are fixed at 10-column intervals to 250 and cannot be changed.
Shift-Tab	Moves the cursor to the previous tab setting unless the cursor is in column 1, in which case, the cursor is switched to the mark area.
Home	Moves the cursor to the top left corner of the report with EXPAND off or to the top left corner of the current section if EXPAND is on.
End	Moves the cursor to the bottom right corner of the report with EXPAND off or to the bottom right corner of the current section if EXPAND is on.
ESC	Exits from the current activity (mode) and displays the main REPORTS Definition menu.

When you start Reports EXPRESS from the R> prompt with an open database, the first menu you see is the Report Options menu. (Otherwise, R:BASE displays the Reports EXPRESS Main menu. From this menu, select a database, list, change directories, or exit from Reports EXPRESS.)

From the Report Options menu, you can duplicate, remove, list, edit, or create a report. The *Copy Reports* option is useful for making duplicates that let you test new modifications to a working report. The *Remove Report* option deletes the report from your database.

To edit or create a report, select *Edit/Create* from the Report Options menu. If the database contains existing reports, you can select one of these to edit or select a new report. For our example, select a new report and assign it the name *INVREPT*, which is associated with the view *INFVORM*.

Specify the report name and table to display the following screen:

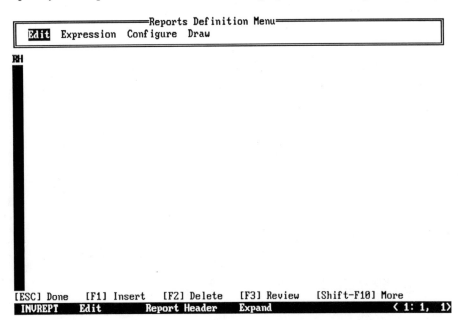

From this menu, you perform the main tasks of designing and creating your report. Select *Edit* to type in the text that will appear in your report and to locate the columns and variables in the report. If you want to draw lines or boxes, select *Draw* (if you are in the Edit mode, press ESC and then select the *Draw* option). *Expression* lets you define new variables and expressions and change or reorder existing expressions. Select *Configure* to specify break points, break variables, and report formatting characteristics such as the number of lines per page.

The bottom line of the Reports Definition menu screen lists the name of the report and the section of the report in which the cursor is currently located. With a new report, you always start in the Report Header section (RH). Move between sections with the F7 and F8 keys. When you start a report and move to the next section, you move from Report Header to Page Header to Detail Line to Page Footer and finally to Report Footer. You cannot move to a break header or footer section unless you have previously defined a break column or variable on the Configure screen.

To expand a section, move the cursor up or down with EXPAND on. The status of EXPAND is indicated on the bottom line of the screen, and the F9 key turns EXPAND on or off. With EXPAND off, the size of each section does not change as you move the cursor from one section to another. Delete or insert lines in the report with the F2 and F1 keys, respectively.

The next step in creating our report example is to define the break columns and break variable. First, define the break variable, because you'll need it when you specify the break column. Then select *Expression* from the Reports Definition menu. The break variable is called *vtotal*. The expression is *vtotal = SUM OF TOTAL*. We will return to the topic of defining variables after we specify the break column.

To define a break column, select *Configure* from the Reports Definition menu. R:BASE displays the following screen:

```
     Lines Per Page ................:     25
     Remove Initial Carriage Return..:   [NO ]
     Manual Break Reset .............:   [NO ]
     Page Footer Line Number.........:      0


            BREAKPOINTS             FORM FEEDS
         Break    Variable      Header          Footer
         Column   Reset      Before After    Before After
         -------- -------    ------ ------    ------ ------
    Report                   [NO ]  [NO ]     [NO ]  [NO ]
    Page              [NO ]
    Break1   CLINUM   [YES]   [NO ]
    Break2   INV-NUM  [NO ]   [NO ]
    Break3   [None]   [NO ]   [NO ]
    Break4   [None]   [NO ]   [NO ]
    Break5   [None]   [NO ]   [NO ]
    Break6   [None]   [NO ]   [NO ]
    Break7   [None]   [NO ]   [NO ]
    Break8   [None]   [NO ]   [NO ]
    Break9   [None]   [NO ]   [NO ]
    Break10  [None]   [NO ]   [NO ]

  [ESC] Done    [F2] Delete    [F3] Review   [↑] Up  [↓] Down   [Shift-F10] More
  INVREPT    Configure
```

Enter *CLINUM* and *INV-NUM* as break columns. Select *YES* to reset a variable for *Break1* (*CLINUM*). When you select *YES*, the following menu appears:

```
╔════════════════════Break Level 1 Variable Reset List═══════════════════╗
║  vtotal                                                                 ║
╚═════════════════════════════════════════════════════════════════════════╝
```

```
╔═════════════════════Choose variable to reset═══════════════════╗
║  vpage      vdate      vgrand    (RESET)                        ║
╚════════════════════════════════════════════════════════════════╝
```

Select *vtotal* as the break variable. Then return to the Edit menu.

There are two ways to define the necessary variables. You can either define them "on the fly" as you locate them on the report, or you can select *Expression* from the Reports Definition menu. *Expression* lets you view all of the defined variables as you proceed. Keep in mind that variables referenced by other expressions must already be defined or reordered so they precede the referencing expression. In our example, using the *Expression* option displays the following defined variables:

```
Define Expression:

   1: INTEGER :   vpage    =   .#PAGE
   2: DATE    :   vdate    =   .#DATE
   3: CURRENCY:   vtotal   =   SUM OF TOTAL
   4: CURRENCY:   vgrand   =   SUM OF TOTAL




[PgUp] Previous Page    [PgDn] Next Page    [ESC] Done    [F10] Help
   INVREPT      Expression
```

The variables *vpage* and *vdate* are set equal to the system variables *#PAGE* and *#DATE*, respectively. The variables *vtotal* and *vgrand* are set to the sum of the *TOTAL* column. Remember that this expression must be defined twice because we will use one variable as a break variable and the other variable to keep a running total.

Do not use parentheses around expressions involving *SUM OF*. The *SUM OF* operator is special to reports and does not follow the general guidelines for expressions. Note also that *vtotal* and *vgrand* are global variables that retain the last subtotal or total value after you finish printing the report. You must, therefore, clear the variables before you reprint the report.

The following screen shows how the date variable, *vdate*, is defined by the system or "on the fly":

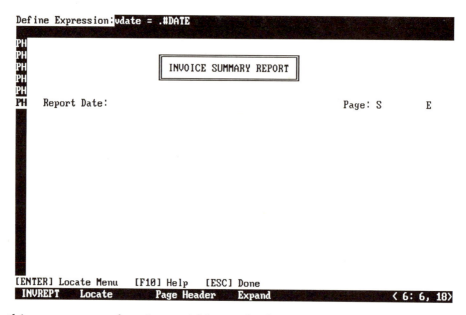

```
Define Expression:vdate = .#DATE

PH
PH
PH
PH
PH
PH    Report Date:                                    Page: S        E










[ENTER] Locate Menu    [F10] Help    [ESC] Done
INVREPT     Locate         Page Header      Expand           < 6: 6, 18>
```

In this case, you are locating variables and columns on the report screen in the Edit mode. Press F6 to locate a variable or column. If you specify a variable that has not been defined, R:BASE prompts you to supply an expression, as shown in the above screen. Press *S* and then *E* to locate the variable on the report. This process may be familiar to you if you have already created a data entry form using Forms EXPRESS. To modify an existing variable definition, use the *Expression* option.

At this point, return to the Edit mode to create the text and locate the columns and variables with the F6 key. You can press F3 at any time to review the defined variables and columns. Use the F7 and F8 keys to move between sections. Remember that the second break column, *INV-NUM*, can be located on a detail line because the break specifier sorts the invoice number.

When you complete the report design, return to the Configure screen to define the lines per page for printing, form feeds, and so on. This number might vary depending on your printer. See the section *Printing the report* later in this entry. For printing to the screen, specify 25 lines per page.

Additional comments on defining expressions: The above example demonstrates the main features of Reports EXPRESS. However, you can take advantage of R:BASE expressions to design more elaborate and complex reports. Here are a few examples of some of the capabilities of expressions:

Calculating averages. To calculate averages, define a variable that counts rows and then use that variable as the denominator of the average calculation. Do this by setting a variable equal to itself plus one. For example, suppose you want to calculate the average amount owed per invoice for each client. Add the following variables to the expression list:

```
vcount INTEGER
vcount = vcount + 1
vave = vtotal / vcount
```

Both these variables are specified as break variables like *vtotal*. Notice that *vcount* is explicitly set to the integer data type in the expression list.

Table lookup variables. Earlier in this entry, you used a view to combine the *CLINAME* column from the *CLIENT* table with the columns from the *INVOICE* table. You also could use the *INVOICE* table for the report and specify a lookup variable for *CLINAME* in the *CLIENT* table. The expression would look like this:

```
vcliname = CLINAME IN CLIENT WHERE CLINUM = CLINUM
```

Remember that *CLINUM* is the common column between the *INVOICE* and *CLIENT* tables. The lookup expression sets the variable *vcliname* equal to the value of *CLINAME* in the *CLIENT* table for the current client number (whichever row is currently displayed on the report). The *WHERE* clause must refer to a column in the lookup table. You can use other operands such as EQ, NE, GT, GE, LT, LE, CONTAINS, FAILS, and EXISTS (see *WHERE*).

Linking a series of text expressions. A common procedure is to link the text expressions for first and last names. The following expression does this:

```
vname = (FNAME & LNAME)
```

FNAME and *LNAME* are columns in the report table. You also could link two lookup variables that retrieve the first and last name from another table.

Printer control variables. You can define a variable that specifies printer control codes. Locate in your report the variable which will transmit print codes to the printer. For example, you may have a note column in a field of the report that you want to print in condensed print. To do this, locate a printer control variable immediately before the first line of the note field.

Printer variables have the following format:

```
printvar = <print code list>
```

The *print code list* must consist of the decimal ASCII values of the print codes for your printer. For example, to set condensed print on the IBM ProPrinter, locate the following variable in your report:

```
pcondens = <27 15>
```

Locate the place in your report at which the printer should return to normal print, and place the following variable at that position:

```
pnormal = <27 18>
```

Making changes to your report: You can change the text, the field locations, and the expression definitions in your report as needed. To delete a field, move the cursor to that field and press Shift-F2. To relocate a field, move the cursor to the field to be relocated and press F6. Select *Expression* from the Reports Definition menu to redefine or add expressions.

Changing report section lines from one type to another is a bit tricky. Shift-Tab moves the cursor into the highlighted column on the left margin (the mark area) that marks the sections. Before you press Shift-Tab, move the cursor to the appropriate line in the report as follows:

☐ If you want to change the line to the previous section, place the cursor at screen column 1 on the line immediately above the line you want to change.

☐ If you want to change the line to the next section, place the cursor at screen column 1 on the line immediately below the line you want to change.

Now, turn EXPAND on (the F9 key). Press Shift-Tab to move the cursor into the mark area. Press the up arrow key to change the line to the previous section. Use the down arrow key to change the line to the next section. When you are finished, press Tab to move back into the work area.

Printing the report: Use the PRINT command to print your report. Direct the output to the screen, the printer, or a disk file by issuing the OUTPUT command before you issue the PRINT command. Remember that the lines per page for a screen report will be different than for a report sent to the printer.

If you specify break columns in a report, you do not need to append the *SORTED BY* clause to the PRINT command unless there are additional columns to sort. If so, you must specify the report's break columns in the *SORTED BY* clause before specifying the additional columns. The best approach is to go back into the report and add the additional columns as break points.

See: *Expressions, OUTPUT, PRINT, Variables,* and *WHERE*

- **R:BASE 5000 equivalent**
REPORTS

R:BASE 5000 reports have essentially the same capabilities as in System V. The concepts of variable and break-point definitions are quite similar, although you cannot define complex expressions in R:BASE 5000. Most of the function key operations in System V reports are performed by menu selections in R:BASE 5000. R:BASE 5000 reports can be only 132 characters wide.

RESTORE

- **Syntax**

```
RESTORE filespec
```

- **Description**
The RESTORE command restores files created with the BACKUP command. See *BACKUP* for a complete description of the characteristics of files created by BACKUP.

- **Procedure**
To restore a file called *CONSULT.BAK*, at the R> prompt type:

```
RESTORE CONSULT.BAK
```

R:BASE then prompts you to enter the first disk to be restored. You must load multiple disks in their numbered sequence.

When restoring backup files, it is important to recognize that the backup files contain the database or table definition commands that initially defined the database or table. If the database or the table that is defined in the backup file already exists in the current directory, you will see error messages such as

Existing column cannot be redefined, even though the restore operation is successful. Note also that restored data does not overwrite but is appended to existing data. In any case, you should erase damaged databases or tables before you restore the backup version.

■ **Comment**

BACKUP and RESTORE perform the same function as UNLOAD and INPUT, except that BACKUP and RESTORE can back up and restore databases that require more than one floppy disk.

See: *Backing up data, BACKUP, INPUT,* and *UNLOAD*

■ **R:BASE 5000 equivalent**
None

RETURN

■ **Syntax**

RETURN

■ **Description**

Use the RETURN command in command files to return control to the calling command file. The RETURN command returns control to the line in the calling command file that follows the RUN or INPUT statement that called the command file containing the RETURN command. A RETURN in a command file executed from the R> prompt simply returns control to the R> prompt.

■ **Procedure**

The following command file excerpt shows the use of RETURN in an IF statement that checks if a valid client number has been entered. If the client number variable contains a NULL value (*vclinum*), the command file terminates and returns control to the calling program. The last command in the file is a RETURN command that returns control to the calling program when execution is completed.

```
WHILE vclinum EXISTS THEN
  SET VAR vrow TO 15
  WRITE "CLIENT AND CAR MATCHING PROGRAM" AT 1,15
  FILLIN vclinum USING "Enter Client Number to Match or <Enter> +
    to Exit: "  AT 3,15
  IF vclinum FAILS THEN  *(Check for valid CLIENT number)
    SET MESS ON
    SET ERR MESS ON
    RETURN
  ENDIF
```

(continued)

```
SET POINTER #1 p1 FOR CARCUST WHERE CLINUM EQ .vclinum
IF p1 EQ 0 THEN
  SET VAR vfname TO FRSTNAME IN #1
    .
    .
    .
  ENDIF
    .
    .
    .
ENDWHILE
RETURN
```

Let's say the above command file is named *CARMATCH.CMD* and is called by the following file:

```
*(Main command file)
RUN CARMATCH.CMD            *(calls CARMATCH.CMD)
CLS
    .
    .      *(list of commands)
    .
```

When the second command file is executed, the RUN command executes the *CARMATCH.CMD* command file. When RETURN is encountered in *CARMATCH.CMD*, control returns to the calling file at the CLS command line, which clears the screen.

■ **Comment**

In general, it's good practice to end all command files with the RETURN command. Although a command file may be stand-alone when you first develop it, you might want to add it to another application later. Any command file that you add to a procedure or Application EXPRESS application should include the RETURN command to ensure that control returns to the main application. See *Application EXPRESS* for additional information about adding command files to applications developed in Application EXPRESS.

See: *Application EXPRESS, BREAK, Procedure files, Programming, QUIT,* and *RUN*

■ **R:BASE 5000 equivalent**
RETURN

RMDIR

■ **Syntax**

RMDIR ⎯⎯⎯ *pathname*
      └ *d:* ┘

■ **Description**

The RMDIR command removes a directory from the specified drive. If you omit the drive designator, the directory is removed from the current drive.

The RMDIR command is virtually identical to the MS-DOS RMDIR command. Unlike the MS-DOS version, however, you must use a space between RMDIR and the leading backslash of the pathname.

■ **Procedure**

The following command removes the *\RBFILES\DATA* directory from the current drive:

```
RMDIR \RBFILES\DATA
```

Caution: The directory to be removed cannot contain any files or sub-directories. First, delete all files and subdirectories with the ERASE and RMDIR commands respectively. In addition, you cannot remove the root or the current directory. If you want to remove the current directory, use the CHDIR command to first change to another directory.

See: *CHDIR, DELETE, DIR, DOS commands in R:BASE, ERASE,* and *MKDIR*

■ **R:BASE 5000 equivalent**

RMDIR

Rows

■ **Description**

A row can be thought of as the horizontal dimension of a two-dimensional table. The vertical dimension consists of the table's columns. The rows in R:BASE tables are equivalent to *records* in the terminology of most relational databases. A row represents a single entity of related data in a single table. For example, the information relating to a specific employee ID number in an *EMPLOYEE* table is normally stored in a single row of columns.

A single row in an R:BASE table can contain a maximum of 4096 bytes of data. In other words, the sum of the column widths in a single row cannot exceed 4096 bytes. See *Columns* to determine how many bytes each R:BASE data type occupies. The number of columns in a single table (and therefore in a single row) cannot exceed 80, which is also the maximum number of columns allowed in a single database.

Rows are added to a table column by column using the LOAD or ENTER commands. They also can be appended from another table using the APPEND command. Delete rows with the DELETE ROWS command.

It's important to remember that an R:BASE table generates a row whenever an item of data is added to a column in the table. If no data is added to the other columns in the row, NULL values are assigned to them. A NULL value is, by default, represented by the -0- symbol. See *SET characters and keywords* for ways to change this symbol to a blank or some other character.

R:BASE internally numbers the rows in a table as they are entered. However, R:BASE does not automatically display row numbers. Use the COMPUTE ROWS command to count the number of rows in a table. You also can display rows according to row number or a range of row numbers by using the COUNT operator in a *WHERE* clause.

There is a large theoretical limit to the number of rows that can exist in a table. However, the practical limit is the storage capacity of your disk drives.

For example, let's say you have 10,000,000 bytes of available storage and a single database table that contains 500 bytes per row. 10,000,000 bytes divided by 500 yields a limit of 20,000 rows. The maximum number would actually be somewhat less because R:BASE requires storage space for the database definition file and the file that stores keys. As a general rule, estimate your required storage conservatively and allow room for unexpected expansion.

See: *Columns, COMPUTE, DEFINE, Definition EXPRESS, DELETE, Operators,* and *WHERE*

RULES

■ **Syntax**

Rules can be defined in Definition EXPRESS or in the DEFINE mode at the D> prompt by typing:

```
RULES
```

followed by one of the following syntax structures.

To compare a column to a constant value:

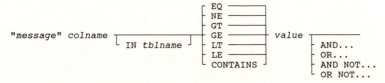

To compare a column to an existence condition:

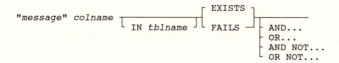

229

To compare a column value to another column value:

```
                                 ┌ EQA ┐
                                 ├ NEA ┤
"message" colname1 IN tblname1  ┤ GTA ├  colname2 IN tblname2 ─────────┐
                                 ├ GEA ┤                        ┌ AND...
                                 ├ LTA ┤                        ├ OR...
                                 └ LEA ┘                        ├ AND NOT...
                                                                └ OR NOT...
```

■ **Description**

Rules define conditions that must be met by the data that is entered into a specific column. Rules form the structure for data validation in R:BASE. You can enter into a column only data that meets the criteria of the rule associated with the column. If the data you enter does not meet the criteria, R:BASE displays the rule *message* and will not load the invalid data into the column. If you use a form to enter data into columns governed by rules, you must enter valid data before moving to the next field in the form or attempting to exit the form (see *FORMS*).

The rule criteria listed after the rule message specifies the conditions that the data must meet.

Types of rules: Before you read the methods for defining rules, familiarize yourself with the two types of rules that can be applied.

Each type of rule is characterized by a different group of operators. In both cases, the rule message cannot exceed 40 characters, and each rule can specify no more than 10 conditions using the AND, OR, AND NOT, or OR NOT operators.

Comparing a constant value or existence condition. You can require that the value to be entered into a column must match an arbitrary constant value or a range of constant values. To do this, use one of the following operators: EQ, NE, GT, GE, LT, LE, or CONTAINS (see *Operators*).

For example, the following rule specifies that the salary range must be between $15,000 and $60,000:

```
"Not a valid salary value" SALARY IN EMPLOYEE GE 15000 OR SALARY LE 60000
```

If you want this rule to apply to the *SALARY* column in all tables of the database, omit the *IN EMPLOYEE* clause.

Rules that compare input to an existence condition require either that the input contains data (*EXISTS*) or that the input has a NULL value (*FAILS*). If you press Enter when R:BASE prompts you to enter a value, the recorded column value is NULL (i.e., the column FAILS). For this reason, it is often desirable to require that a value be entered. For example:

```
"Invalid salary value" SALARY IN EMPLOYEE EXISTS AND SALARY NE 0
```

requires that a value other than NULL or zero be entered for the salary. Remember that NULL and 0 are not the same value.

Comparing column values. You can require that a column value match another column value or a range of column values, either in the same table or in another table. To do this, use one of the following operators: EQA, NEA, GTA, GEA, LTA, or LEA (see *Operators*). You must specify a table name with the *IN* clause when using these operators.

A typical application of this type prevents the user from entering duplicate values in the same column in the same table:

```
"Duplicate client number" CLINUM IN CLIENT NEA CLINUM IN CLIENT
```

This rule requires that the entered client number cannot duplicate an existing client number in the same table.

In another situation, you might want to ensure that client numbers entered in the *INVOICE* table match existing client numbers in the *CLIENT* table. To do this, enter the following:

```
"Not valid client number" CLINUM IN INVOICE EQA CLINUM IN CLIENT
```

You also can check values entered for one table against column values in another table. For example, you could create a small table (*JOBCODE*) that contains the valid job code numbers that can be entered in the *JOBS* table. Then, to validate the job code numbers, type:

```
"Not valid job code" JOBID IN JOBS EQA JOBCODE IN JOBCODE
```

Defining rules: Define rules in either the DEFINE mode or in Definition EXPRESS. In most cases, it is more convenient to use Definition EXPRESS.

The following command sequence uses DEFINE to define rules:

```
DEFINE CLIENT
RULES
"Client # does not exist in client table" CLINUM IN INVOICE +
 EQA CLINUM IN CLIENT
END
```

First, issue the DEFINE command followed by RULES. Enter a message surrounded by quotes, then enter the actual command criteria. The message can be a maximum of 40 characters. You can continue the command criteria on multiple lines by entering a plus sign (+) at the end of each line. You can enter multiple rules in a single DEFINE session. Type END to exit from the DEFINE mode.

In Definition EXPRESS, rules definition is one of the menu items for defining your database. As with other functions in Definition EXPRESS, you select menu items that guide you through the process of defining rules. The following screen shows a sample session in Definition EXPRESS:

```
Rule message:  Client does not exist in client table
```

	Column	Table	Operator	Value/Column	Table
	CLINUM	INVOICE	EQA	CLINUM	CLIENT

```
══════════════════════Choose column to validate══════════════════════
CLINUM  INV-NUM  ENTRDATE  DUE  PREVBAL  TOTAL  FORWHAT  PAID
```

```
[ENTER] Choose    [ESC] Done    [F3] Review    [F10] Help
Database CONSULT --- Table INVOICE --- Rule        1
```

See *Definition EXPRESS* for a further discussion of rules definition.

■ Comment

Even if you have defined rules, you can disable rules checking with the SET RULES and NOCHECK commands. It is often advisable to disable rules checking when you load data from an external file or when you test a database.

See: *DEFINE, Definition EXPRESS,* and *Operators*

■ R:BASE 5000 equivalent

RULES (available only in the DEFINE mode)

RUN

- **Syntax**

```
RUN cmdfile ┌──────────────┐ ┌──────────────────┐
            │ IN procfile  │ │ USING parmlist   │
            └──────────────┘ └──────────────────┘
```

- **Description**

The RUN command executes command files and procedure command blocks.

- **Procedure**

Like most R:BASE commands, RUN can be issued either from the R> prompt or from a command file. Use the *IN procfile* clause to run command blocks within binary procedure files. If you omit the *IN* clause, the command file must be an ASCII file. The *USING* clause allows you to pass a maximum of nine parameters (variable values) to the command file.

In its simplest form (*RUN cmdfile*), the RUN command is equivalent to the INPUT command.

To execute a stand-alone ASCII command file, type RUN followed by the filename:

```
RUN MYFILE.CMD
```

To execute a command block in a procedure file, type RUN, the name of the command block, the *IN* keyword, and the procedure filename. For example, to execute the command block *MAINPROC* in the procedure file *WORKMEN.PRC*, issue the following command:

```
RUN MAINPROC IN WORKMEN.PRC
```

To pass parameters with the RUN command, you must specifically design the command file to accept the parameters. The variables in the command file to which the parameters are passed must be named %1 through %9, and are assigned their values in the same sequence as the parameter list.

For example, the following command file produces a sorted text file from columns in the *EMPLOYEE* table and directs the output to a file that will be named when the text file is executed:

```
SET QUOTES=
OUTPUT .%1
UNLOAD DATA FOR EMPLOYEE USING FNAME LNAME STREET CITY ZIP +
   SORTED BY LNAME FNAME
OUTPUT SCREEN
```

Note that the *%1* variable in the first OUTPUT command line is preceded by a dot. The dot indicates the current value of the variable. The current value of *%1* is the value of the parameter that is issued with the RUN command.

If you name the command file *SORTLIST.CMD*, the following command directs the output to the file *B:SORTLIST.TXT*:

```
RUN SORTLIST.CMD USING B:SORTLIST.TXT
```

The filename *B:SORTLIST.TXT* is passed to the variable *%1* by the *USING* clause.

The *USING* clause can be used in either ASCII command files or in files encoded into binary procedure files (see *Procedure files*).

If you want to use RUN in a command file to execute another command file, see *RETURN* and *Programming* for discussions of subroutines and program control.

■ **Comment**

The RUN and INPUT commands are interchangeable for executing stand-alone ASCII command files or files generated by the UNLOAD command. However, you cannot use the INPUT command to pass parameters or to execute procedure blocks.

See: *Command files, INPUT, Procedure files, Programming, QUIT,* and *RETURN*

■ **R:BASE 5000 equivalent**
RUN

SELECT

■ **Syntax**

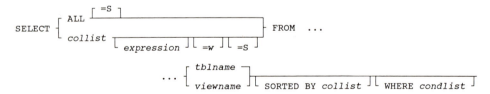

■ **Description**

The SELECT command displays selected rows of data from a table or view. SELECT is the primary R:BASE command for informal data inquiry. If you need only a quick listing of selected data on the screen or printer, SELECT is the appropriate command. If you need a more formal presentation of data, use REPORTS.

■ **Procedure**

Select a specific list of columns and computed column expressions, or use ALL to select all columns from a table or view. Display data in sorted order by appending the *SORTED BY* clause. The *WHERE* clause lets you specify conditions or criteria that the data must satisfy. The =*S* option computes a total for columns or expressions with numeric data types. The =*w* option specifies a display field width other than the default or defined column width.

By default, the SELECT command displays only 80 characters of data, regardless of the size of the table. However, you can issue the SET WIDTH 132 command to display more columns, to a width of 132 characters. You can use this display width when directing the output of SELECT to the printer. On a standard-width printer, use condensed mode to print 132 characters per line (see *OUTPUT*).

On the screen, the larger display width makes the data virtually unreadable, because each row wraps to the following line if a line exceeds 80 characters. An alternative to increasing display width is to use the =*w* option to narrow the width of individual columns. Columns wider than the specified width wrap to the next line, but they remain within the borders of the specified column width, as shown in the following example:

```
R>SELECT CLINUM=2 CLINAME=10 INV-NUM=4 ENTRDATE STREET=10 CITY=10 STATE FROM +
+>INVFORM WHERE LIMIT EQ 5
CL CLINAME    INV- ENTRDATE STREET     CITY       STATE
-- ---------- ---- -------- ---------- ---------- --------
 1 Johnson    001  10/22/86 101        San        CA
   and                      Howard     Francisco
   Anderson                 Street
   Co.
 2 Cal Gas    2-00 10/22/86 1000 Main  Oakland    CA
   and        3            Street
   Electric
35 Harbinger  35-0 09/06/86 400 Elm    San        CA
   Supply Co  09            St         Francisco
 1 Johnson    002  10/22/86 101        San        CA
   and                      Howard     Francisco
   Anderson                 Street
   Co.
 1 Johnson    003  10/22/86 101        San        CA
   and                      Howard     Francisco
   Anderson                 Street
   Co.
R>
```

Note that the column headings are truncated by the narrower column widths (the first column is *CLINUM*).

A powerful feature of the SELECT command is the ability to include computed column expressions in a selection. Expressions included in the SELECT command follow the same general rules as expressions. However, you cannot include columns from other tables in an expression in SELECT. Here is an example that uses expressions with the SELECT command:

```
R>SELECT CLINUM INV-NUM (.#DATE - ENTRDATE) TOTAL=S FROM INVFORM SORTED BY +
+>CLINUM WHERE TOTAL > 0
 CLINUM    INV-NUM  COMPUTED   TOTAL
 ---------- -------- ---------- ----------------
        1 001           49      $3,345.00
        1 009           27        $500.00
        1 003           49        $943.00
        1 002           49      $7,898.00
        2 2-003         49      $5,000.00
        2 2-004         49      $5,000.00
        8 8-001         48        $300.00
        8 8-004         48        $565.00
        8 8-008         48      $1,100.00
        8 8-002         48        $456.00
        8 8-005         48      $4,500.00
       10 10-001        48        $567.00
       10 10-002        48        $973.00
       35 35-009        95      $2,065.00
 ---------- -------- ---------- ----------------
                                $33,212.00
  R>
```

R:BASE always displays the computed expression under the *COMPUTED* heading. The system variable *#DATE* in this example is used to compute the elapsed days since the date the invoice was entered.

Notice that the =*S* option computes the total for the *TOTAL* column. The *SORTED BY* clause sorts the data according to client number, and the *WHERE* clause specifies that only clients whose *TOTAL* column is greater than zero be displayed.

Here is another example that shows two computed expressions (the $=S$ option computes the total for the second expression):

```
R>SELECT EMPID ((.#DATE - HIREDATE)/365) (0.02 * SALARY)=S FROM EMPLOYEE +
+>WHERE LIMIT EQ 15
  EMPID     COMPUTED COMPUTED
---------- -------- ----------------
         1 3.323288          $500.00
         2 4.873972          $500.00
         3 1.405479          $360.00
         4 5.356164          $640.00
         5 4.575343          $750.00
         6 2.693151          $900.00
         7 2.693151          $900.00
         8 4.071233          $700.00
         9 5.156164          $900.00
        10 0.654795          $460.00
        11 3.323288          $600.00
        12 4.789041          $700.00
        13 1.068493          $720.00
        14 5.690411          $600.00
        15 3.989041        $1,000.00
---------- -------- ----------------
                           $10,230.00
R>
```

The *WHERE LIMIT* clause specifies that only the first 15 rows of the table be included in the selection.

For a detailed discussion of the types of conditions that can be applied, see *WHERE* and *Operators*.

■ **Comment**

If you use a particular SELECT command often, record it as an *exec* file so you do not have to retype it each time you use it (see *RECORD*).

If you frequently use SELECT to calculate the same computed expression, it might be more convenient to add this expression as a computed column in the table (see *EXPAND*).

See: *Expressions, Operators, OUTPUT, SORTED BY,* and *WHERE*

■ **R:BASE 5000 equivalent**

SELECT

SELECT is essentially identical in R:BASE 5000 except that computed expressions are not supported.

237

SET characters and keywords

- **Syntax**

```
SET

SET keyword value

SET chrname=value
```

- **Description**

Use the SET command with one of the following special characters or keywords to define specific settings for the currently open database.

Special characters

BLANK

DELIMIT

PLUS

QUOTES

SEMI

Keywords

AUTOSKIP	MULTI
BELL	NULL
CASE	REVERSE
CLEAR	RULES
COLOR	SCRATCH
CURRENCY	TIME
DATE	TOLERANCE
ECHO	USER
ERROR MESSAGES	VERIFY
ESCAPE	WAIT
LINES	WIDTH
MESSAGES	ZERO

The following keywords apply only to a multi-user environment: MULTI, VERIFY, and WAIT. See *Programming* and *SET LOCK* for further discussion of multi-user settings.

■ **Procedure**

The following settings are saved when you exit a database:

☐ Special Character settings

☐ AUTOSKIP, BELL, CASE, CURRENCY, DATE, NULL, QUOTES, REVERSE, TIME, TOLERANCE, and ZERO

You can modify other settings temporarily, but they are reset to the default settings when you exit R:BASE. However, you can permanantly change the R:BASE default settings by modifying the R:BASE system file called *DEFAULT.ASC*. The procedure for altering this file is explained in Chapter 10 of the R:BASE User's Manual.

To temporarily change default settings, enter the SET command, the character or keyword, and the new value. Note the difference in syntax when you specify special characters and keywords: You must use an equal sign to set a special character (SET DELIMIT = " ", for example); you do not need to use an equal sign to set a keyword (SET ECHO ON, for example).

Alternatively, you can issue the SET command by itself, in which case the following *SET entry screen* is displayed:

```
Type in the new character or value, press [ESC] when done

┌─────────────────┬──────────────────────────────────┬─────────────────────┐
│   Characters    │ User set values                  │ Currency            │
│                 │                                  │                     │
│ BLANK     ■     │ DATE format      MM/DD/YY        │ SYMBOL        $     │
│ DELIMIT   ,     │ DATE sequence    MMDDYY          │ LOCATION     PREF   │
│ SEMI      ;     │ TIME format      HH:MM:SS        │ DIGITS        2     │
│ QUOTES    "     │ TIME sequence    HHMMSS          │ CONVENTION B        │
│ PLUS      +     │ LINES per page      20           │                     │
│                 │ WIDTH per line      79           │                     │
│                 │ TOLERANCE               0.       │                     │
│                 │ NULL symbol        -0-           │                     │
│                 │ Lock WAIT time       4           │                     │
├─────────────────┴──────────────────────────────────┴─────────────────────┤
│ Toggle switches for the environment                                       │
│                                                                           │
│ (AUTOSKIP ) OFF AUTOmatically SKIP to the next field when editing         │
│ (BELL     ) OFF Sound the BELL on an error                                │
│ (CASE     ) OFF Distinguish between UPPER and lower CASE                   │
│ (CLEAR    ) ON  CLEAR data buffers after modifications                    │
│ (ECHO     ) OFF ECHO input from command files                             │
│ (ERROR    ) ON  Display ERROR messages during processing                  │
│ (ESCAPE   ) ON  ESCAPE allowed to abort processing                        │
│ (MESSAGES ) ON  Display informational MESSAGES during processing          │
└───────────────────────────────────────────────────────────────────────────┘
```

Scroll through this screen and set values as desired.

You also can use the SHOW command to display the current values of the above settings.

The various settings are described below. Settings that require frequent changes are discussed in greater detail.

SET special characters: Special characters are used to separate or *delimit* data fields and to interpret data input. Normally, the default values for the special characters need to be changed only when you use external data formats.

For example, to output an R:BASE table in ASCII format with the UNLOAD command, surround the text fields with double quotation marks ("), which is the default character for QUOTES. You can set the quotes character to a blank if you do not want quotes to appear in the ASCII output. To set quotes to a blank character, issue the command SET QUOTES = " ". For an example of a typical ASCII delimited file, see *FileGateway*.

It is good practice to set QUOTES (and other special characters) back to the default value after you perform the operation that required the change. The double quote symbol (") is *not* interpreted as the QUOTES symbol when QUOTES is set to some other value. Similarly, you can set BLANKS to another character. Again, be aware that you will have to enter this character instead of a blank when you type R:BASE commands. For example, consider the following sequence:

```
SET BLANK=#
SELECT#ALL#FROM#EMPLOYEE
```

Because you set the # symbol as the blank character in the above example, you must use it to separate commands in the command line.

The delimiter between data fields is normally a comma. You can set DELIMIT to another character if exported or imported data files require it.

The SEMI character is normally a semicolon and is used to separate commands on the same command line. The PLUS character is normally the plus symbol and is used to indicate that a command continues on the next line. You can change these characters if you want (see *Command structure*).

Caution: Do not define the same character symbol for more than one special character. R:BASE will have problems interpreting command syntax and the results will be unpredictable.

SET keywords: Setting keywords affects the database operating environment. The operating environment controls how R:BASE formats and manipulates the database input and output. This general concept becomes clearer when we look at the features controlled by SET *keyword*. Each keyword is described below, and its default value given in parentheses:

AUTOSKIP (OFF). With *AUTOSKIP OFF*, you must press Enter to move the cursor to the next column or data entry field. *AUTOSKIP ON* moves the cursor to the next field when all of the spaces in the current column or field are filled. With *AUTOSKIP ON*, you don't have the opportunity to correct errors before you move to the next field.

BELL (ON). With *BELL ON*, the computer's speaker beeps when an error occurs. It is sometimes desirable to use the SET BELL OFF command in command files or applications, particularly when you reload a backup file and you expect trivial errors. The beep can be annoying in these circumstances. On the other hand, the bell can be an important signal that something is wrong (see *INPUT* and *Error messages*).

CASE (OFF). With *CASE OFF*, R:BASE makes no distinction between uppercase and lowercase text values when it makes comparisons based on RULES and conditional statements such as *WHERE*, IF, and WHILE. With *CASE ON*, R:BASE does not match text values if they are not in the same case.

CLEAR (ON). With *CLEAR ON*, R:BASE writes data to the disk each time you modify data. With *CLEAR OFF*, R:BASE fills a memory buffer before it writes to disk. *CLEAR OFF* can improve performance, but if the computer malfunctions, you risk losing more data.

COLOR (the default value depends on the type of display adapter you use). For *COLOR* specifications, see the R:BASE Single User or Multi-User installation guides and the User's Manual.

CURRENCY ($ PREF 2 B). The *CURRENCY* default values are set for standard U.S. currency, with the $ symbol as the prefix and 2 decimal places specified. The default convention for displaying thousands places a comma after each three digits of a number.

With the SET CURRENCY command you can change the currency symbol (a maximum of four characters), prefix and suffix status, and the decimal and thousands conventions. See the R:BASE User's Manual for further details.

DATE (FOR = MM/DD/YY, SEQ = MMDDYY). SET DATE FOR sets the date output format. The default format is MM/DD/YY. This format displays Christmas Day, 1986, as 12/25/86. The SET DATE FOR MM/DD/YYYY command changes the display to 12/25/1986. The SET DATE FOR "WWW + , MMM + DD, YYYY" command changes the display to Thursday, December 25, 1986. Note that you must use quotes because the definition includes embedded blanks. If you omit the plus symbols after WWW and MMM, R:BASE displays only the first three letters of the week and month (Thu, Dec 25, 1986).

The SET DATE SEQ command specifies the sequence in which you must enter the month, day, and year. For example, SET DATE SEQ DDMMYY sets the sequence to day, month, and year, which is the format in many countries. In this case, you enter Christmas Day, 1986, as 25/12/86.

If you omit *SEQ* and *FOR* from the SET DATE command, you can use the following syntax to set both the format and sequence:

```
SET DATE "MM-DD-YY"
```

For a complete description of the available date formats, see the R:BASE User's Manual.

Cautions: If you need to enter data involving other centuries, use YYYY as the year format. Also, pay particular attention to date formats when you transfer data to or from external data files. Be sure that the selected R:BASE date format is compatible with the date format in the external file. It's best to import or export a few rows of data as a test and then display it with the YYYY format to ensure that the year is correct (see *FileGateway* and *UNLOAD*).

ECHO (OFF). With *ECHO OFF*, R:BASE displays only the results or the output of commands on the output device. With *ECHO ON*, the command is also repeated ("echoed") on the output device. *ECHO ON* is useful as a debugging tool when you test the operation of command files. In finished programs or applications, however, you normally set *ECHO OFF* (see *Programming*).

ERROR MESSAGES (ON). With *ERROR MESSAGES ON*, R:BASE displays an error message and sounds the bell whenever an error occurs. *ERROR MESSAGES OFF* suppresses error messages and disables the bell. See *Error messages* for further discussion of this option.

Note: Rules messages are displayed no matter what the status of the error messages (see *SET RULES* later in this entry). See *SET ERROR VARIABLE* for a discussion of error-trapping variables.

ESCAPE (ON). *ESCAPE OFF* disables ESC as a means of exiting or aborting the processing of command files or applications. This feature is helpful for controlling the activity of other people who work with your programmed applications.

LINES (20). The *LINES* option lets you change the number of lines of data to be displayed on the output device. This option does not affect the output of reports because REPORTS provides its own line-setting option.

MESSAGES (ON). This controls the output of diagnostic messages (e.g., *Database exists* after opening a database). It is often useful to set *MESSAGES* to *OFF* in command files and applications. See *Error messages* for more information about diagnostic messages.

MULTI (OFF). With *MULTI OFF*, R:BASE is set to the single-user mode. *MULTI ON* activates the settings necessary for controlling multi-user data access. The SET MULTI command does not affect the currently open database until it is closed and reopened. Remember that the SET MULTI status is not saved with the database and is reset to *OFF* when you exit R:BASE. See the R:BASE Multi-User Installation Guide for further information.

NULL value indicator (-0-). Columns or variables that contain no data are set to NULL and assigned the NULL value indicator. *No data* is not equivalent to zero or blank. NULL means exactly that—nothing. To suppress the display of NULL values, set NULL to a blank character:

```
SET NULL " "
```

Note that NULL values can be counted as zero if you set *ZERO ON* (see below). The NULL value indicator can have a maximum of four characters.

Caution: Set NULL to its default value when you use BACKUP or UNLOAD.

REVERSE (ON). With *REVERSE ON*, R:BASE displays data-entry fields and prompts in reverse video. *REVERSE OFF* disables this feature.

RULES (ON). With *RULES ON*, R:BASE checks data input against existing rules. *RULES OFF* causes R:BASE to ignore existing rules. If an owner password is defined for the current database, R:BASE will not accept the SET RULES OFF command until you enter the password. See *RULES*.

SCRATCH (ON). With *SCRATCH ON*, the temporary scratch files used by R:BASE are stored in the same directory and drive as the database. *SCRATCH OFF* causes R:BASE to store these files in the current directory and the default drive. This feature is helpful if you are using a database that is stored on a floppy disk.

TIME (HH:MM:SS). The SET TIME FOR command sets the time output. The default format is HH:MM:SS. To suppress the display of seconds, set the format to *HH:MM* (SET TIME FOR HH:MM). You can display AM and PM as follows: SET TIME FOR "HH:MM AP". Again, note that you must use quotes because the setting has an embedded blank.

The SET TIME SEQ command specifies an input sequence of hour, minute, and second. If you omit *SEQ* and *FOR* from the SET TIME command, you can use the following syntax to set both the format and sequence:

```
SET TIME "HH:MM AP"
```

Caution: Pay particular attention to time formats when you transfer data to or from external data files. Be sure that the selected R:BASE time format is compatible with the time format in the external file.

TOLERANCE (0.00000). The default *TOLERANCE* setting requires that REAL or DOUBLE data types must match exactly to six digits when used in comparisons. For example, the *WHERE REALNUM EQ 58* clause requires that *REALNUM* be equal to 58.0000. You can adjust the tolerance to another value with SET TOLERANCE. If you set tolerance to 0.05, *REALNUM* in the above example could range from 57.95 to 58.05 and still satisfy the *WHERE* condition.

USER (none). The SET USER command is identical to the USER command and lets you enter a password. SET USER is actually the R:BASE 5000 equivalent of USER and is still available in System V. See *Data security, OWNER,* and *PASSWORDS* for more information.

VERIFY (COLUMN). The SET VERIFY command is a multi-user setting that prevents the simultaneous entry of columns or rows by two or more users. This function is called concurrency control and is fully described in *Programming.* The default setting (SET VERIFY COLUMN) prevents simultaneous data entry of a single column. SET VERIFY ROW prevents concurrent modification of an entire row.

WAIT (4). *WAIT* is a multi-user setting that defines the *resource waiting period.* This waiting period manages access to databases and peripherals (called *resources*). R:BASE places users in a queue when they simultaneously request access to a resource. After a specified waiting period, the request is cancelled, and the currently executing command file or block terminates.

The default waiting period is four seconds. This period might be too short for access to a busy printer, for example. Use the SET WAIT command to set the waiting period to a maximum of 4.5 hours (16,200 seconds). For example, SET WAIT 1200 sets the resource waiting period to 20 minutes. You can include this command in a command file when you direct output to the printer:

```
WRITE "Report in queue; max wait period set to 20 minutes" +
   AT 4,5
OUTPUT PRINTER
SET WAIT 1200
PRINT MYREPT
SET WAIT 4
OUTPUT SCREEN
```

WIDTH (79). The SET WIDTH command specifies the number of characters that R:BASE displays on a line. On a normal monitor, the display width is 80 characters. If *WIDTH* is set to a number greater than this width, data wraps onto the next line, usually making the screen difficult to read. Therefore, SET WIDTH is primarily used to set the line width on a printer.

WIDTH must be set to a number between 40 and 256. The maximum display width with the SELECT command is 132. A standard-sized dot matrix printer can print 132 characters per line in condensed mode. A wide carriage printer usually can print the maximum width of 256 in condensed mode.

The SET WIDTH command does not affect reports because REPORTS has its own functions for setting width and controlling the printer.

ZERO (OFF). With *ZERO OFF*, R:BASE ignores numeric columns or variables that contain NULL values in computations such as totals or averages. Also, calculations involving NULL values will not successfully execute. With SET ZERO ON, NULL values in numeric columns or variables are treated as zero in calculations. For an example of SET ZERO ON, see the program example in *Financial functions*.

- **R:BASE 5000 equivalent**
SET

R:BASE 5000 supports most of the special characters and keywords in System V, with the following exceptions: *CURRENCY, TOLERANCE, ZERO, MULTI, VERIFY*, and *WAIT*.

SET ERROR VARIABLE

- **Syntax**

```
SET ERROR VARIABLE ⌐ varname
                   ⌐ OFF
```

- **Description**
Use the SET ERROR VARIABLE command in command files to trap R:BASE error codes in the specified variable when errors occur during the execution of the file or application. You then can check the value of the error variable in an IF or WHILE statement.

- **Procedure**
When a valid command is executed, the value of the error variable is set to zero. If an error occurs, the value of the variable is set to the error code that corresponds to the error. The complete set of R:BASE error codes is listed in

the *ERRVAL.DOC* file on the R:BASE System V Utilities 2 diskette, and a partial list is included in the R:BASE Error Messages booklet. R:BASE resets the error variable value after it executes each command in the command file.

To disable the error-trapping function, issue the SET ERROR VARIABLE OFF command. You can specify only one error variable with the SET ERROR VARIABLE command. This means that only the most recently defined error variable will trap error codes.

The most important characteristic of the error variable is that it is reset after each command is executed. This means that you must check the value of the variable immediately after the command line that you wish to test for an error. One option is to save the value of the error variable in another variable. Consider the following command file excerpt:

```
SET MESS OFF
SET ERR MESS OFF
SET ERR VAR dbcheck              *(Define the error variable "dbcheck")
FILLIN dbname USING "Enter database name or <Enter> to Quit: " +
  AT 4,5
IF dbname EXISTS THEN
  OPEN .dbname
  SET VAR errvar TO .dbcheck    *(Save error value in variable "errvar")
  WRITE "The error variable value is: " AT 6,5
  SHOW VAR errvar AT 6,34       *(Display error code)
  IF errvar NE 0 THEN
    BEEP
    SHOW ERR errvar AT 9,5      *(Display error code message)
    PAUSE
    GOTO end
  ENDIF
ENDIF
LABEL end
RETURN
```

The objective of this block of commands is to determine if you have entered a valid or existing database name. In this example, the error variable is defined as *dbcheck*. The command immediately following OPEN *.dbname* saves the value of the error variable in the variable *errvar*. To demonstrate how error variables work, display the value of the error variable. (You normally would not display the error code in a real application.)

If *errvar* is not equal to zero, an invalid database name has been entered and the commands within the second IF statement are executed. Here is what happens in this case:

```
R>RUN ERROR.CMD


    Enter database name or <Enter> to Quit: WRONG

    The error variable value is:            7


    -ERROR- Unable to open database
```

The error code for an invalid database is 7, as shown in the above screen. When the SHOW ERR command is executed, R:BASE displays the message *Unable to open database*. This is the error message corresponding to error code 7.

Here is what happens if you enter a valid database name:

```
R>RUN ERROR.CMD

    Enter database name or <Enter> to Quit: CONSULT

    The error variable value is:        0
```

R:BASE sets the error variable to 0 and skips the second IF statement block. With a more complete command file, normal processing would then continue. In this excerpt, the database is opened and control returns to the R> prompt. See *Procedure files* for a complete command file that uses the SET ERROR VARIABLE command.

- **Comment**

Since R:BASE resets the error variable to zero as soon as it encounters another valid command, the technique of saving the error variable in a separate variable (as shown above) is often more useful than checking the error variable value directly. Using this technique, you can work with the error variable later in the command file rather than immediately after the error occurs. You also can store error codes in different variables as execution progresses, thus compiling a history of errors that you can refer to for debugging.

Note that you can use the WRITE command to create your own error message and that you can display this message instead of the error code message supplied by the SHOW ERR command (see the example in *Procedure files*).

In most applications, turn off error messages (SET ERROR MESSAGES OFF) when you use the SET ERROR VARIABLE command.

Note: You can use a special error variable with the SET POINTER command to check for rows that meet the SET POINTER condition.

- **R:BASE 5000 equivalent**

SET ERROR VARIABLE

See: *Command files, Error messages, IF, Procedure files, Programming, SET characters and keywords, SET POINTER, SHOW ERROR,* and *WHILE*

SET LOCK

■ **Syntax**

```
SET LOCK tbllist ─┬─ ON
                  └─ OFF
```

■ **Description**

Before you use the SET LOCK command, we recommend that you read the discussion of multi-user applications in *Programming*, where the concepts of database locking, table locking, and concurrency control are discussed.

Use the SET LOCK command to prevent simultaneous data modification or updating to tables in multi-user applications. Although R:BASE provides table locking and concurrency control for most commands, some commands and operations are not automatically controlled. The SET LOCK command lets you explicitly set table locks for a table or list of tables. (R:BASE's automatic table locking is unaffected by the SET LOCK command.)

■ **Procedure**

Remove explicit table locks with the SET LOCK OFF command. One SET LOCK OFF command must be issued for each SET LOCK ON command.

SET LOCK is most commonly used in command files that include the SET POINTER command. The SET POINTER command is not governed by automatic concurrency control or table locking.

The following excerpt from the Car Matching program presented in the *SET POINTER* entry shows the use of SET LOCK:

```
*(CARMATCH.CMD)
    .
    .        *(list of commands)
    .
SET VAR vclinum TO 0
*(Main body of program)
WHILE vclinum EXISTS THEN
    .
    .        *(list of commands)
    .
   SET LOCK CARCUST CARLIST ON      *(Set table locks ON)
   SET POINTER #1 p1 FOR CARCUST WHERE CLINUM EQ .vclinum
   IF p1 EQ 0 THEN
     .
     .        *(list of commands)
     .
    SET POINTER #2 p2 FOR CARLIST WHERE PRICE LE .vsal50%
   ELSE
     WRITE "NOT ENOUGH INFORMATION, PRESS ANY KEY TO CONTINUE" +
       AT 5,15
     PAUSE
     GOTO restart
   ENDIF
```

(continued)

248

```
WRITE "CARMAKE          MODEL            PRICE" AT .vrow,1
WHILE p2 EQ 0 THEN
   .
   .      *(list of commands)
   .
   NEXT #2 p2
ENDWHILE
.
.        *(list of commands)
.
ENDWHILE
SET LOCK CARCUST CARLIST OFF       *(Set table locks OFF)
RETURN
```

Before the program issues the first SET POINTER command, it sets locks for both tables that are accessed by the pointers (*CARCUST* and *CARLIST*). While locks are in effect, no one else on the system can update or modify data in these two tables. After processing, the locks are set to off for both tables.

■ **Comment**

Although other users can still display data from a locked table, they cannot update or modify data.

Caution: It is extremely important to set locks to OFF after you work with a table. If you don't, you can inadvertently lock out other users. You must issue one SET LOCK OFF command for each SET LOCK ON command.

See: *Programming, SET characters and keywords,* and *SET POINTER*

SET POINTER

■ **Syntax**

```
SET POINTER #n ┬─────────┬ FOR tblname ┬───────────────────┬┬─────────────────┬
               │         │             └─ SORTED BY collist ┘└ WHERE condlist ─┘
               ├ varname ┤
               └ OFF ────┘
```

■ **Description**

The SET POINTER command creates a pointer that moves through a table row by row. The main purpose of SET POINTER is to allow you to extract or change values in an R:BASE table on a row-by-row basis. Although comprehensive changes and data selection are possible with one-line commands such as CHANGE or SELECT, many situations require you to use variable values to make changes or extract data one row at a time.

For example, you might want to store a column value in a variable, perform some operations on the variable, move to the next row in the table, store the next column value in the variable, perform the same operations, and so on, until you have operated on every row in the table. SET POINTER lets you perform this type of operation.

■ **Procedure**

Three pointers can be active at one time in an R:BASE session. Pointers are designated by *route numbers*, which are labeled *#1, #2,* and *#3* (*#n* in the syntax structure). The route numbers apply to the table for which the pointer is defined. A pointer accesses rows in the order you specify with the optional *SORTED BY* clause and points only to rows that meet the optional *WHERE* clause conditions. The NEXT command moves the pointer to the next row.

The optional variable (*varname*) is an error-trapping variable that is set to zero until the pointer encounters the end of the file or cannot find any more rows that satisfy the conditions specified in the SET POINTER command. Although use of the variable is optional, most practical applications require it.

The *OFF* option disables the pointer and clears the memory buffer used by the specified route number. Although this option is rarely required, you might need it in applications that use many variables and multiple pointers.

The following commands are frequently used with SET POINTER: CHANGE, SET VARIABLE, and DELETE. The syntax of each of these commands provides an option to access a route number rather than a table name. For example, CHANGE *columnname TO value IN #1* changes the column in the table pointed to by route *#1*.

■ **Example 1**

The following example demonstrates the use of the CHANGE command with SET POINTER (see *CHANGE*). The objective is to extract the first and last initials from the *FRSTNAME* and *LASTNAME* columns of the *EMPLOYEE* table and to insert them in the *INITIALS* column:

```
SET POINTER #1 p1 FOR EMPLOYEE
WHILE p1 = 0 THEN
  SET VAR initvar TO " . "
  SET VAR fname TO FRSTNAME IN #1
  SET VAR lname TO LASTNAME IN #1
  SET VAR initvar = (SMOVE(.fname,1,1,.initvar,1))
  SET VAR initvar = (SMOVE(.lname,1,1,.initvar,3))
  CHANGE INITIALS TO .initvar IN #1
  NEXT #1 p1
ENDWHILE
*(Result of the CHANGE command)

SELECT FRSTNAME LASTNAME INITIALS FROM EMPLOYEE WHERE LIMIT EQ 5
```

FRSTNAME	LASTNAME	INITIALS
Harold	Wilson	H.W
Marjorie	Lawrence	M.L
Barbara	Graham	B.G
Paula	Stanton	P.S
Franklin	Johnson	F.J

The pointer is set to route *#1*, which is defined as the *EMPLOYEE* table. Note that you can limit the rows accessed by the route number by using a *WHERE* clause (for example, *WHERE HIREDATE LT 1/1/76*). If you specify a *WHERE* clause, the pointer accesses only those rows that satisfy the *WHERE* clause. The SET VARIABLE (SET VAR) commands extract the first and last initials and store them in the variable *initvar*. The CHANGE command moves the current value of *initvar* into the *INITIALS* column. The SELECT command at the end displays the result of the operation.

The variable *p1* checks for the end-of-data. The NEXT command moves the pointer to the next row and updates the value of *p1*. Each time NEXT finds another row, *p1* is set to zero. When the pointer reaches the end of the table, NEXT does not find a row and sets the variable *p1* to the End-of-data error code (error code 2046). For more information, see *SET ERROR VARIABLE*.

The error variable in a SET POINTER command is assigned one of the following codes:

Code	Description
0	Found another row
56, 137, 2137	No rows satisfy the *WHERE* clause
493	Invalid route number or route does not exist
2406	End-of-data encountered

See *SET ERROR VARIABLE* and *SHOW ERROR* for further discussions of error codes.

In the above example, the commands in the WHILE loop execute until *p1* is set to one of the above non-zero error codes.

■ **Example 2**

Here is a more complicated example of the use of SET POINTER. This example (from *JOIN*) matches clients with cars based on the condition that the car cannot cost more than 50% of the client's salary. The SET POINTER command offers a more elegant way to obtain this information than the JOIN command. Here are the tables involved:

```
Table: CARCUST          No lock(s)
Read Password: No
Modify Password: No

Column definitions
# Name      Type     Length       Key    Expression
1 CLINUM    INTEGER
2 FRSTNAME  TEXT     15 characters
3 LASTNAME  TEXT     15 characters
4 SALARY    CURRENCY
5 SAL50%    CURRENCY                      .50 * 'salary'
6 HIREDATE  DATE
7 SEX       TEXT      1 characters
8 INITIALS  TEXT      3 characters

Current number of rows:      9
```

(continued)

```
Table: CARLIST           No lock(s)
Read Password: No
Modify Password: No

Column definitions
# Name      Type      Length          Key    Expression
1 MAKE      TEXT          15 characters
2 MODEL     TEXT           8 characters
3 PRICE     CURRENCY

Current number of rows:       22


    Form        Table
    --------    --------
    VCARFORM
```

This application also uses a variable form called *vcarform,* which displays some of the variables in the command file.

The following command file matches clients and cars:

```
*(Command file to match clients and affordable cars)
SET MESSAGES OFF
SET ERROR MESSAGES OFF
OPEN NEWTEST
NEWPAGE
*(Declare variables)
SET VAR vclinum TO 0
*(Main body of program)
WHILE vclinum EXISTS THEN
   SET VAR vrow TO 15
   WRITE "CLIENT AND CAR MATCHING PROGRAM" AT 1,15
   FILLIN vclinum USING +
     "Enter Client Number to Match or <Enter> to Exit: " AT 3,15
   IF vclinum FAILS THEN
      SET MESS ON
      SET ERR MESS ON
      BREAK
   ENDIF
   SET POINTER #1 p1 FOR CARCUST WHERE CLINUM EQ .vclinum
   IF p1 EQ 0 THEN
      SET VAR vfname TO FRSTNAME IN #1
      SET VAR vlname TO LASTNAME IN #1
      SET VAR vcliname = (.vfname & .vlname)
      SET VAR vsalary TO SALARY IN #1
      SET VAR vsal50% TO SAL50% IN #1
      DRAW vcarform WITH ALL AT 4
      SET POINTER #2 p2 FOR CARLIST WHERE PRICE LE .vsal50%
   ELSE
      WRITE "NOT ENOUGH INFORMATION, PRESS ANY KEY TO CONTINUE" +
        AT 5,15
      PAUSE
      GOTO restart
   ENDIF
   WRITE "CARMAKE                        MODEL +
                  PRICE" AT .vrow,1
   WHILE p2 EQ 0 THEN
      SET VAR vrow TO .vrow + 1
        IF vrow GE 20 THEN
          SET VAR vrow TO .vrow + 2
          WRITE "Press any key to continue" at .vrow,1
          PAUSE
          CLS
          WRITE "CARMAKE                       MODEL +
                    PRICE" AT 1,1
          SET VAR vrow TO 3
        ENDIF
```

(continued)

```
        SET VAR vmake TO MAKE IN #2
        SET VAR vmodel TO MODEL IN #2
        SET VAR vprice TO PRICE IN #2
        SHOW VAR vmake AT .vrow,1
        SHOW VAR vmodel AT .vrow,30
        SHOW VAR vprice AT .vrow,40
        NEXT #2 p2
      ENDWHILE
      SET VAR vrow TO .vrow + 2
      WRITE "Press any Key to Continue" AT .vrow,1
      PAUSE
      LABEL restart
      NEWPAGE
    ENDWHILE
    RETURN
```

Executing the command file for a sample client displays the following screen:

```
    CLIENT AND CAR MATCHING PROGRAM

    Enter Client Number to Match or <Enter> to Exit: 1
```

```
  ┌─────────────────────────────────────────────────┐
  │                                                   │
  │   Client Number: 1      Client Name: Harold Wilson│
  │                                                   │
  │          Annual Salary: $27,500.00                │
  │                                                   │
  └─────────────────────────────────────────────────┘
```

CARMAKE	MODEL	PRICE
Renault	Alliance	$13,000.00
Chevrolet	Citation	$12,000.00
Toyota	Tercel	$8,000.00
Nissan	Stanza	$7,000.00

```
    Press any key to continue
```

We will limit our discussion to the use of SET POINTER in the above command file. For discussions of other aspects of the command file, see *SET VARIABLE, SHOW VARIABLE, WHILE,* and *WRITE.*

The first pointer (*#1*) defines the *CARCUST* table and points to the row in the *CARCUST* table where *CLINUM* is equal to the value of *vclinum*, which is entered by the user. Notice that if you enter a non-existent client number, *p1* is not equal to zero, and control passes to the *ELSE* clause, which prints the *NOT ENOUGH INFORMATION...* message and passes control to the bottom of the main WHILE loop. The main WHILE loop repeats as long as you enter a value for *vclinum* (WHILE *vclinum* EXISTS).

The NEXT command is not used with pointer #1. Pointer #1 looks only for the row containing the value of *vclinum*. If the pointer finds a row, the SET VARIABLE commands within the IF statement (IF *p1* EQ 0) extract various information from the row, such as the client's first and last name, salary, and half-salary (*SAL50%*).

The second pointer (#2) is defined within this first IF statement. There is no point in establishing a second pointer if the first pointer fails. Pointer *#2* finds every row in the *CARLIST* table that satisfies the *WHERE* condition (*WHERE PRICE LE SAL50%*). Note that NEXT moves the pointer to the next row. When all of the cars and clients are matched, the program displays data on the screen, as shown above.

Note that the variable form *vcarform* displays the client's name and salary. The DRAW command that we use to display the form is, as of this writing, an undocumented command that works in R:BASE System V. However, it is officially supported only in R:BASE 5000 (see *R:BASE 5000 commands*).

See: *IF, NEXT, Programming, SET ERROR VARIABLE, SHOW VARIABLE, WHERE,* and *WHILE*

- **R:BASE 5000 equivalent**
  SET POINTER

SET VARIABLE

- **Syntax**

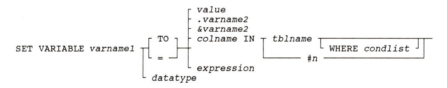

- **Description**
  Use the SET VARIABLE command, at the R> prompt or in command files, to assign values or explicit data types to variables. For a complete discussion of variables, see *Variables*.

■ **Procedure**

The SET VARIABLE command allows three basic types of variable assignments:

Assignment	Command
Data Type Assignment:	SET VARIABLE *varname data_type*
Value Assignment:	SET VARIABLE *varname* TO *value*
	SET VARIABLE *varname* TO *.varname*
	SET VARIABLE *varname* = *expression*
Column Value Assigment:	SET VARIABLE *varname* TO *colname* IN *tablename* WHERE ...
	SET VARIABLE *varname* TO *colname* IN *#n*

Data type assignment: You can explicitly assign the following data types to a variable: CURRENCY, DATE, DOUBLE, INTEGER, NOTE, REAL, TEXT, or TIME. See *Data types* for further discussion of data types. When you explicitly set a variable to a data type, only data values compatible with that data type can be assigned to the variable. For example, the following command sequence shows what happens when you assign a text value to a variable defined as an integer:

```
R>SET VAR vtest INTEGER
R>SET VAR vtest = "How do you do?"
-ERROR- Your value does not have the same type as your variable
```

Be sure to follow the command syntax when you assign a data type. The data type follows the variable name.

We strongly recommend that you explicitly assign data types to variables that are to be assigned the value of an expression. Expression values are sometimes incorrectly interpreted if the variable is not assigned a data type.

Value assignment: The values you assign to variables can be constants, the values of other variables, or string and arithmetic expressions. If the data type is not explicitly defined, the variable assumes the data type of the assigned value.

To assign a constant value to a variable, simply define the value to be assigned, as in the following examples:

```
SET VAR vname = "SMITH"
SET VAR vamount = 100.98
```

To assign the values of other variables, precede the variable holding the value to be assigned with a dot (.). For example:

```
SET VAR newname = .vname
```

assigns the value of *vname* to *newname*.

Precede a variable with an ampersand (&) only if the contents of a variable are to be used in a command line. For example,

```
SET VAR vlist = "CLINUM CLINAME FROM CLIENT"
SELECT &vlist
```

executes the following command:

```
SELECT CLINUM CLINAME FROM CLIENT
```

Do not assign values to an ampersand variable (e.g., *SET VAR &varname1 = varname2*). The stored value will be inaccurate. See *Variables* for further discussion of ampersand variables.

String expressions must always be enclosed in parentheses. For example, the following string expression links the series of text values of the variables *vfname* and *vlname*:

```
SET VAR vname = (.vfname & .vlname)
```

Here, the ampersand links (concatenates) the two text values and inserts a space between them. Use the plus symbol (+) to link two text values without a separating space (see *Operators*).

Although arithmetic expressions do not require parentheses, in some cases expressions might not be correctly parsed without parentheses. Here are some examples of arithmetic expressions:

```
SET VAR vsqrt = SQRT (ABS(AVE(.num1,.num2)))
SET VAR vmod = MOD(.num1,.num2)
SET VAR varea = .#PI * (.vrad ** 2)
```

See *Expressions* for further examples of arithmetic expressions.

Column value assignment: Variables can be set to the value of a column in a table or in a route number. For example,

```
SET VAR vfname TO FRSTNAME IN #1
```

assigns the value of *FRSTNAME*, in the row pointed to by route #1, to *vfname*.

See *SET POINTER* for several examples of setting variables equal to column values in route numbers. Note that you cannot include a *WHERE* clause in the SET VARIABLE command when you access a column in a route. This is because the columns are qualified by the *WHERE* clause in the SET POINTER command itself.

You also can set a variable equal to the value of a column in a table that is not specified in a route. If you omit the *WHERE* clause, the first row in the table will be used to assign the value. Here is an example that uses *WHERE*:

```
SET VAR vname TO NAME IN EMPLOYEE WHERE EMPID = 103
```

■ **Comment**

The command file listings in this book contain many examples of the use of SET VARIABLE. In particular, see *SET POINTER, Arithmetic and mathematical functions, Financial functions,* and *Procedure files.*

The CLEAR command clears all or selected variables from memory.

Caution: Most errors involving variables are caused by incompatible data types. It is good practice to define variable data types explicitly to avoid errors.

See: *CHOOSE, COMPUTE, FILLIN, SET ERROR VARIABLE,* and *SET POINTER*

See also: *Programming* and *Variables*

■ **R:BASE 5000 equivalent**

SET VARIABLE

R:BASE 5000 does not support ampersand (&) variables, and expressions can contain only one operator.

SHOW

■ **Syntax**

```
         ┌ CHARACTERS
SHOW ─┤ keyword
         │ ─────────────
         └ RULES ┌─┐
                  │ n │
                  └─┘
```

■ **Description**

The SHOW command displays the current values of R:BASE special characters, keywords, and the database's defined rules. For more details, see *SET characters and keywords* and *RULES.*

■ **Procedure**

If you enter the SHOW command with no options, R:BASE displays all special character and keyword values. You can add an optional rule number to the *RULES* clause to display a specific rule.

Here are a few examples of the SHOW command:

```
R>SHOW RULES
(RULES    ) ON  Check data validation RULES
RULE 1          CLINUM IN INVOICE EQA CLINUM IN CLIENT
     Message:Invalid Client Number


R>SHOW
BLANK
DELIMIT      ,
SEMI         ;
QUOTES       "
PLUS         +

DATE format      MM/DD/YY
DATE sequence    MMDDYY
TIME format      HH:MM:SS
TIME sequence    HHMMSS
LINES per page   20
WIDTH per line   79
TOLERANCE                0.
WIDTH per line   79
TOLERANCE                0.
NULL symbol      -0-
Lock WAIT time       4
EDIT verification level COLUMN
CURRENCY SYMBOL      "$"
CURRENCY LOCATION    PREF
CURRENCY DIGITS      2
CURRENCY CONVENTION B

(AUTOSKIP ) OFF AUTOmatically SKIP to the next field when editing
(BELL     ) ON  Sound the BELL on an error
(CASE     ) OFF Distinguish between UPPER and lower CASE
(CLEAR    ) ON  CLEAR data buffers after modifications
(ECHO     ) OFF ECHO input from command files
(ERROR    ) ON  Display ERROR messages during processing
(ESCAPE   ) ON  ESCAPE allowed to abort processing
(MESSAGES ) ON  Display informational MESSAGES during processing
(MULTI    ) ON  MULTI-user database access capability.
(REVERSE  ) ON  REVERSE video highlighting on data entry/edit
(RULES    ) ON  Check data validation RULES
(SCRATCH  ) ON  SCRATCH files on same drive as the database
R>
```

See: *RULES, SET characters and keywords, SHOW ERROR,* and *SHOW VARIABLE*

■ **R:BASE 5000 equivalent**
SHOW

SHOW ERROR

■ **Syntax**

```
SHOW ERROR varname ┌─────────────────────┐
                   └ AT scrnrow scrncol ┘
```

■ **Description**

The SHOW ERROR command displays the error message that corresponds to the error code stored in the specified error variable. The variable can be a defined error variable or a separate variable to which the value of the defined error variable is copied.

The entire list of R:BASE error codes is contained in the file *ERRVAL.DOC* on the R:BASE System V *Utilities* 2 disk. The Error Messages booklet contains a partial list.

Note: Before you use SHOW ERROR, see *SET ERROR VARIABLE*.

■ **Procedure**

For an example of the SHOW ERROR command, assume that the variable *errvar* contains the error code *2046*. The following command displays (at row 5, column 5) the message that corresponds to error code 2046:

```
SHOW ERROR errvar AT 5,5
```

If you receive the following message,

```
-ERROR- Column is not in the table
```

you know that an attempt to access an invalid column name caused the error.

See: *SET ERROR VARIABLE*

■ **R:BASE 5000 equivalent**
SHOW ERROR

SHOW VARIABLE

■ **Syntax**

```
SHOW VARIABLE ┌──────────────────────────────────────┐
              └ varname ┌────┐┌──────────────────────┐┘
                        └ =w ┘└ AT scrnrow scrncol ┘
```

■ **Description**

The SHOW VARIABLE command displays the value of a specified variable or, if no variable name is specified, the values of all variables.

■ **Procedure**

You can add the $=w$ clause to the specified variable name to control the display width of the variable value. The *AT* clause lets you display the variable value at the specified screen row and column. Note that the row and column coordinates apply only to the screen display and will not work with a printer or other output devices. The row coordinates you specify must be in the range of 1 to 24; the column coordinates must be in the range of 1 to 80.

You can issue the SHOW VARIABLE command at the R> prompt or from a command file. To display all the variables in memory, simply type the command without specifying a variable. If you type SHOW VARIABLE after you set up the Car Matching program example in the SET POINTER entry, R:BASE displays the following screen:

```
R>SHO VAR
Variable = Value                                    Type
-------    -------------------------------          --------
#DATE    = 12/13/86                                 DATE
#TIME    = 13:26:07                                 TIME
#PI      = 3.14159265358979                         DOUBLE
vclinum  = -0-                                      INTEGER
vrow     = 15                                       INTEGER
p1       = 0                                        INTEGER
vfname   = Harold                                   TEXT
vlname   = Wilson                                   TEXT
vcliname = Harold Wilson                            TEXT
vsalary  = $27,500.00                               CURRENCY
vsal50%  = $13,750.00                               CURRENCY
p2       = 406                                       INTEGER
vmake    = Chevrolet                                TEXT
vmodel   = Nova                                     TEXT
vprice   = $10,000.00                               CURRENCY
R>
```

Note: SHO VAR is a valid command abbreviation for SHOW VARIABLE (see Command structure).

To display individual variables, include the variable name in the command. For example, if you use the COMPUTE command to compute a value and store it in a variable, you could use the SHOW VARIABLE command to display the value:

```
R>COMPUTE vavecost AS AVE PRICE FROM CARLIST
R>SHOW VAR vavecost
            $16,409.09
R>
```

SHOW VARIABLE is also used in command files to display variables on the screen. For example, the Car Matching program in the SET POINTER entry uses SHOW VARIABLE to display the list of affordable cars. The following excerpt from that command file demonstrates how to use SHOW VARIABLE with a variable row counter:

```
SET VAR vrow TO 15
  .
  .
  .
WRITE "CARMAKE                        MODEL +
                  PRICE" AT .vrow,1
WHILE p2 EQ 0 THEN
  SET VAR vrow TO .vrow + 1
    IF vrow GE 20 THEN
      SET VAR vrow TO .vrow + 2
      WRITE "Press any key to continue" at .vrow,1
      PAUSE
      CLS
      WRITE "CARMAKE                      MODEL +
                PRICE" AT 1,1
      SET VAR vrow TO 3
    ENDIF
  SET VAR vmake TO MAKE IN #2
  SET VAR vmodel TO MODEL IN #2
  SET VAR vprice TO PRICE IN #2
  SHOW VAR vmake AT .vrow,1
  SHOW VAR vmodel AT .vrow,30
  SHOW VAR vprice AT .vrow,40
  NEXT #2 p2
ENDWHILE
SET VAR vrow TO .vrow + 2
WRITE "Press any key to continue" AT .vrow,1
```

The following screen shows the output from the Car Matching program:

```
          CLIENT AND CAR MATCHING PROGRAM

       Enter Client Number to Match or <Enter> to Exit: 1




   ┌─────────────────────────────────────────────────────────┐
   │                                                           │
   │  Client Number: 1        Client Name: Harold Wilson      │
   │                                                           │
   │        Annual Salary: $27,500.00                         │
   │                                                           │
   └─────────────────────────────────────────────────────────┘


   CARMAKE                  MODEL                PRICE
   Renault                  Alliance          $13,000.00
   Chevrolet                Citation          $12,000.00
   Toyota                   Tercel             $8,000.00
   Nissan                   Stanza             $7,000.00


   Press any key to continue
```

Any row and column coordinates that you specify *must* be in the range of 1 to 24 and 1 to 80 respectively. Specifying coordinates outside this range generates a syntax error. If you study the block of commands above, you'll notice that many of the commands limit the screen coordinate variables (particularly, *vrow*) so that the values are always within the screen boundaries.

If the number of cars to be displayed exceeds the number of rows available in the first screen (*vrow GE 20*), the program clears the screen, displays the screen heading again, and sets *vrow* to row number three. The second screen appears as follows:

```
CARMAKE                 MODEL                 PRICE

Volkswagen              Bus                   $10,000.00
AMC                     Jeep                   $9,500.00
Alfa Romeo              Firenze               $13,400.00
Fiat                    124                    $8,800.00
Renault                 Le Car                 $6,500.00
Honda                   Accord                 $9,800.00
Chevrolet               Nova                  $10,000.00

Press any key to continue
```

A final example illustrates the use of the =*w* option to control the display width. If you refer to the command file example in the *Date and time functions* entry, you will notice that the integer and date values are all right-justified, which leaves blanks between the text and the displayed variable values. Although you can avoid this problem by using the *CTXT()* conversion function, you also can use the =*w* option. The following command file (from the *Date and time functions* entry) specifies the display widths:

```
SET ECHO OFF
SET VAR vdate TO .#DATE
WHILE vdate EXISTS THEN
  NEWPAGE
  FILLIN vdate USING +
    "PLEASE ENTER A DATE (mm/dd/yy): " AT 5,5
  IF vdate FAILS THEN
    BREAK
  ENDIF
  SET VAR vjdate = (JDATE(.vdate))
  SET VAR vday = (IDAY(.vdate))
  SET VAR vmon = (IMON(.vdate))
  SET VAR vyr = (IYR(.vdate))
  SET VAR vweek = (TDWK(.vdate))
  SET VAR vmonth = (TMON(.vdate))
  SET VAR vweeknum = (IDWK(.vdate))
  SET VAR daymonth = (.vweek + "," & .vmonth)
  WRITE "This date is " AT 7,5
  SHOW VAR daymonth AT 7,18
  SHOW VAR vday=2 AT 7,36
  WRITE "," AT 7,38
  SHOW VAR vyr=4 AT 7,40
  WRITE "In Julian format, this date is: " AT 9,5
  SHOW VAR vjdate=5 AT 9,37
  WRITE "It is month number " AT 11,5
  SHOW VAR vmon=2 AT 11,24
  WRITE "The day of the week is number" AT 13,5
  SHOW VAR vweeknum=1 AT 13,35
  WRITE "Press any key to continue" AT 15,3
  PAUSE
ENDWHILE
```

The $=w$ option displays the variables *vday, vyr, vjdate, vmon,* and *vweeknum* as follows:

```
PLEASE ENTER A DATE (mm/dd/yy): 12/12/86

This date is Friday, December  12, 1986

In Julian format, this date is: 86346

It is month number 12

The day of the week is number 5

Press any key to continue
```

To see the effect of the $=w$ option, compare this screen with the one in *Date and time functions.*

■ **Comment**

You cannot specify coordinates when you use the SHOW VARIABLE command to display variables on a printer. This can be a problem if you want to print the screen output from a command file. Using the Shift-PrtSc key combination is not a good alternative because you would need to print each screen manually. You also could rewrite your command file using WRITE commands to format the display output for the printer, but that can be a tedious process.

Perhaps the most convenient method, however, is to store the values of the variables in a small table and to design a report that prints the table values. If you want to print the variables values only once, use a report directly. However, the example Car Matching program generates a list of cars, and the variable values change each time the loop is executed. The trick, then, is to store the variable values in a row in the special table each time the loop is executed. Print the report when the loop is completed. After the report is printed, remove the rows from the special table so that it will be empty for the next batch of data.

The Car Matching program requires one column in the table for each variable that the SHOW VARIABLE command displays. Use the LOAD command to load the variable values into the table. Then, design and print a report that displays the data in the same format as it is on the screen.

See: *Programming, SET POINTER,* and *SET VARIABLE*

■ **R:BASE 5000 equivalent**

SHOW VARIABLE

SORTED BY

■ **Syntax**

```
... SORTED BY colname1 ┌─────┐ ┌ colname2 ─────┐     ┌ colname10 ─────┐ ...
                       │ =A  │ └         │ =A  │└     │          │ =A  │└
                       │ =D  │           │ =D  │                │ =D  │
```

■ **Description**

The *SORTED BY* clause lets you access and display columns in sorted order.

■ **Procedure**

The following commands can include a *SORTED BY* clause: BACKUP, BROWSE, EDIT, PRINT, PROJECT, SELECT, SET POINTER, and UNLOAD. You can specify a maximum of 10 columns in a single *SORTED BY* clause. The first column you specify is the primary sort column.

You can sort rows in either ascending or descending order. Ascending order starts with the letter *A*, the symbol #, the oldest date, the earliest time, or the smallest number and ends with the letter *Z*, the most recent date, the latest time, or the largest number. Descending order is exactly the opposite. The default sort order is ascending.

To sort a column in descending order, append the *=D* option to the column name. You can also specify both ascending and descending sorts in a single *SORTED BY* clause.

Some examples of the use of the *SORTED BY* clause follow:

```
PRINT MYREPT SORTED BY LASTNAME FIRSTNAME
PROJECT NEWTABL FROM CLIENT SORTED BY CLINUM=D CLINAME
EDIT ALL FROM EMPLOYEE SORTED BY LASTNAME FIRSTNAME
```

The PROJECT command in the second example creates a duplicate table in sorted order.

Caution: Be careful when you use the *SORTED BY* clause with the PRINT command. If your report contains breakpoints (see *REPORTS*), the report will be sorted according to the breakpoint columns. If you want to sort by additional columns in the report, be sure that the breakpoint columns in the report are the first columns you specify in the *SORTED BY* clause.

See: *BACKUP, BROWSE, EDIT, PRINT, PROJECT, SELECT, SET POINTER,* and *UNLOAD*

■ **R:BASE 5000 equivalent**

SORTED BY

String manipulation functions

Use the string manipulation functions to perform operations on text values.

For a general description of available functions in R:BASE System V see *Functions*. If you need more information about a function, consult the other function entries, because some categories overlap.

■ **Description**

You can convert, modify, and reformat text strings using the string manipulation functions. R:BASE provides the following functions:

Function	Description
SFIL(*chr,nchar*)	Returns a text string of *nchar* characters using the specified character, *chr*.
SGET(*text,nchar,loc*)	Returns a text string *nchar* characters long from *text* starting at the character position specified by *loc*.
SLEN(*text*)	Returns the length of the *text*.
SLOC(*text,string*)	Searches *text* for the specified *string*. If *string* is found, SLOC() returns the first character position of the string. If the string is not found, SLOC() returns a zero.
SMOVE(*text,pos1,nchar,string,pos2*)	Moves *nchar* characters starting at character position *pos1* from *text*, to *string* starting at character position *pos2*.
SPUT(*text,string,loc*)	Moves *string* into *text*, starting at the character position specified by *loc*.
STRIM(*text*)	Removes trailing blanks from *text*.
ULC(*text*)	Converts *text* from uppercase to lowercase.
LUC(*text*)	Converts *text* from lowercase to uppercase.
ICAP1(*text*)	Capitalizes the first letter of the first word in *text*.

(continued)

Function	Description
ICAP2(*text*)	Capitalizes the first letter of each word in *text*.
CTR(*text,width*)	Centers *text* within the specified *width*.
LJS(*text,width*)	Left-justifies *text* within the specified *width*.
RJS(*text,width*)	Right-justifies *text* within the specified *width*.

■ **Procedure**

String manipulation functions are particularly useful for changing the text in existing data. Use the SET POINTER command with the string functions to perform operations row by row.

The following example extracts the first and last initials from the *FRSTNAME* and *LASTNAME* columns of the *EMPLOYEE* table and inserts them in the *INITIALS* column:

```
SET POINTER #1 p1 FOR EMPLOYEE
WHILE p1 = 0 THEN
  SET VAR initvar TO " . "
  SET VAR vfname TO FRSTNAME IN #1
  SET VAR vlname TO LASTNAME IN #1
  SET VAR initvar = (SMOVE(.vfname,1,1,.initvar,1))
  SET VAR initvar = (SMOVE(.vlname,1,1,.initvar,3))
  CHANGE INITIALS TO .initvar IN #1
  NEXT #1 p1
ENDWHILE
*(Display result of the CHANGE command)

SELECT FRSTNAME LASTNAME INITIALS FROM EMPLOYEE WHERE LIMIT EQ 5

FRSTNAME         LASTNAME         INITIALS
---------------- ---------------- --------
Harold           Wilson           H.W
Marjorie         Lawrence         M.L
Barbara          Graham           B.G
Paula            Stanton          P.S
Franklin         Johnson          F.J
```

The program sets the variables *vfname* and *vlname* to the values of the *FRSTNAME* and the *LASTNAME* columns. Then, the function *SMOVE()* moves the first letter from each of these variables into the variable *initvar*.

Note: Expressions involving text strings must be enclosed in parentheses.

Because the *initvar* variable is defined as a three-character field with a period as the second character, *SMOVE()* moves the initials into the first and third positions of *initvar*. The sample output above shows the result.

You can use a similar command file with many of the other string manipulation functions. For example, the following command file converts all of a column's text values to uppercase:

```
SET POINTER #1 p1 FOR EMPLOYEE
WHILE p1 = 0 THEN
   SET VAR textvar TEXT
   SET VAR vfname TO FRSTNAME IN #1
   SET VAR textvar = (LUC(.vfname))
   CHANGE FRSTNAME TO .textvar IN #1
   NEXT #1 p1
ENDWHILE
```

The *LUC()* function sets the variable *textvar* to the uppercase value of *vfname*. (You can use the *ULC()* function to convert *textvar* back to lowercase.)

The *SGET()* and *SPUT()* functions extract and insert text strings respectively. They each perform part of the function of *SMOVE()*, which moves text from one string to another. Let's say you want to display the first three letters of *FRSTNAME*. Use the *vfname* variable shown in the above command files (currently equal to *HAROLD*), to set a variable equal to *SGET(.vfname,3,1)*:

```
R>SET VAR frsthree = (SGET(.vfname,3,1))
R>SHOW VAR frsthree
HAR
R>
```

Then, insert the value of *frsthree* in the fourth character position of *vfname*:

```
R>SET VAR vfunny = (SPUT(.vfname,.FRSTHREE,4))
R>SHOW VAR vfunny
HARHAR
R>
```

The *SLEN()* function returns the number of characters in the specified string:

```
R>SET VAR vlength = (SLEN(.vfunny))
R>SHOW VAR vlength
        6
R>
```

Use the *SLOC()* function to locate the starting character position of the specified string (remember that *vfname* = *HAROLD*):

```
R>SET VAR vwhere = (SLOC(.vfname,"OLD"))
R>SHOW VAR vwhere
        4
R>
```

Most of the other string manipulation functions are useful for formatting data to be displayed in command file output, forms, or reports. For example, suppose you repeatedly need to display 25 asterisks in a form or report. Rather than typing them every time and having to count as you type, you can use the *SFIL()* function to store the asterisks in a variable:

```
R>SET VAR startext = (SFIL("*",25))
R>SHOW VAR startext
***************************
R>
```

The *SFIL()* function is also useful in conjunction with the WRITE command.

The *STRIM()* function removes trailing blanks from the specified text field. For example, *STRIM("Smith   ")* returns the value *"Smith."* The *LJS()* and *RJS()* functions left- and right-justify text within the specified field width. These functions are useful for displaying data in columnar format. For example, *RJS("Smith",10)* returns a value of " *Smith*". The *CTR()* function centers the text within the specified field width (e.g., " *Smith* ").

SUBTRACT

■ **Syntax**

```
SUBTRACT tblname1 FROM tblname2 FORMING tblname3 ┌─────────────────┐
                                                  └ USING collist ┘
```

■ **Description**

The SUBTRACT command forms a new table from two tables that have one or more common columns. The new table (*tblname3*) consists only of rows that exist in *tblname2* but not in *tblname1*. The primary purpose of the SUBTRACT command is to compare data from two tables by removing data common to both tables.

■ **Procedure**

The following command sequence demonstrates the use of the SUBTRACT command:

```
R>SELECT CLINUM LOAN-NUM FROM LOAN
   CLINUM     LOAN-NUM
   ----------  ----------
          1          1
          2          2
         67          3

R>SELECT CLINUM CLINAME FROM NEWCLI
   CLINUM     CLINAME
   ----------  -------------------------
        1 Johnson and Anderson Co.
        2 Cal Gas and Electric
        3 Power Research Associates
        4 Stone Construction Co.
        5 Ohio Electric Power Co.

R>SUBTRACT NEWCLI FROM LOAN FORMING CHECK USING CLINUM LOAN-NUM
   Successful subtract operation, 1 rows generated

R>SELECT ALL FROM CHECK
   CLINUM     LOAN-NUM
   ----------  ----------
         67          3
```

The *LOAN* table has a client number (*67*) that does not exist in the *NEWCLI* table. When you subtract *NEWCLI* from *LOAN*, only the row containing client 67 is included in the new table. When you subtract *LOAN* from *NEWCLI*, however, only clients 3, 4, and 5 are included.

Note: The *USING* clause can contain only columns from the second table and must specify at least one common column. If you omit the *USING* clause, R:BASE uses all columns in the second table to form the new table.

The table formed by the SUBTRACT command must be a new table. If you want to use an existing table name, you must first remove or rename the existing table. See *Relational commands* for a general discussion of relational commands.

The INTERSECT command performs the opposite function of the SUBTRACT command. In the above example, it uses only the rows containing clients *1* and *2*.

■ **Comment**

The following guidelines will help you use the SUBTRACT command most efficiently:

☐ Performance of the SUBTRACT command is greatly improved if you key the common column in the second table (*tblname2*). In the above example, you would key *CLINUM* in the *LOAN* table. For more information, see *Keys* and *BUILD KEY*.

☐ If one table is much larger than the other, make the smaller table the second table in the SUBTRACT command and do not use keys.

☐ If both tables are large, specify the table with the shorter row length first, and use a key in the common column of the second table.

See: *APPEND, BUILD KEY, INTERSECT, JOIN, Keys, PROJECT, Relational commands, UNION, and VIEW*

■ **R:BASE 5000 equivalent**

SUBTRACT

Tables and TABLES

■ **Tables**

A database table consists of rows and columns. An R:BASE database may contain a maximum of 80 tables and 800 columns. A table can contain as many as 398 columns. Table names cannot be more than eight characters long. For guidelines for designing R:BASE tables, see *Definition EXPRESS* and *Relational commands*. For specific information on defining columns, see *Columns*.

You can define tables in Definition EXPRESS or in the DEFINE mode using the TABLES command. You also can use relational commands to form tables from existing tables.

Definition EXPRESS provides the easiest method for defining tables. In Definition EXPRESS, you define or modify existing tables by using a convenient full-screen display of the columns and their data types. You can invoke Definition EXPRESS from the RBSYSTEM menu or from within R:BASE with the RBDEFINE command.

- **TABLES command**

The following command sequence demonstrates the use of the TABLES command:

```
R>DEFINE CHARGES
 Begin R:BASE Database Definition
D>COLUMNS
D>CLI-NUM INTEGER KEY
D>ID-NUM INTEGER
D>HR-RATE CURRENCY
D>HOURS REAL
D>MULTIPLE REAL
D>CHARGE = ('HR-RATE' * HOURS * MULTIPLE)
D>COMMENT TEXT 30
D>TABLES
D>BILLING WITH CLI-NUM ID-NUM HR-RATE HOURS MULTIPLE CHARGE +
+>COMMENT
D>END
 End R:BASE Database Definition
R>
```

This sequence first defines a database called *CHARGES*, and then the COLUMNS and TABLES commands define the columns and the database table, respectively. R:BASE treats each line that follows the COLUMNS command as a column definition until it encounters another valid command (in this case, the TABLES command).

The TABLES command is followed on the next line by the table name (*BILLING*) and then by the *WITH* clause, which lists the column names to be included in the table. Notice that you can continue the table definition on a second line by ending the first line with a plus symbol (+).

Define multiple tables by starting a new line and following the next table name with a *WITH* clause. All columns must be associated with a table definition. Any columns that you do not specify in a table definition are lost when you use the END command to exit from the DEFINE mode.

The TABLES command is valid only in DEFINE mode (at the D> prompt). Except for defining small tables, you gain no advantage using the DEFINE command instead of Definition EXPRESS. In fact, the DEFINE command is more difficult to use and more susceptible to data entry errors.

Display the names and structures of existing tables with the LIST command. Notice that R:BASE creates its own tables when you define forms, reports, rules, and views. R:BASE always names these tables as follows: *FORMS*, *REPORTS*, *RULES*, *VIEW*, and *VIEWCOND*.

Although you can display and manipulate the data in these tables like any other R:BASE table, you should do so cautiously so as not to corrupt the definitions contained in the tables.

You can delete tables, as well as individual columns in tables, with the REMOVE command. Add columns to a table by using the EXPAND command or by using the menus in Definition EXPRESS. Use the relational commands to combine tables with other tables.

Always remember that you can restrict access to your tables by defining passwords with the OWNER and PASSWORDS commands. You also can define passwords in Definition EXPRESS.

See: *Columns, DEFINE, Definition EXPRESS, LIST, Relational commands, REMOVE, and Rows*

■ **R:BASE 5000 equivalent**
TABLES

TALLY

■ **Syntax**

```
                               ┌─  tblname  ─┐
TALLY colname FROM  ┤            ├┌─────────────────────┐
                               └─ viewname ─┘└ WHERE condlist ┘
```

■ **Description**

The TALLY command counts the number of occurrences of identical values in a column. The TALLY command displays a list of column values that includes the number of occurrences of each value.

■ **Procedure**

Use the optional *WHERE* clause to specify the conditions that the column values must meet to be included in the TALLY command.

The TALLY command is used primarily for obtaining a quick count of the occurrences of a particular quantity in a column. For example, if you want a tally of the employees with salaries over $25,000, type:

```
TALLY SALARY FROM EMPLOYEE WHERE SALARY GT 25000
```

to display the following:

```
SALARY                    Number of Occurrences
-----------------------   ---------------------
      $25,300.00                1
      $27,500.00                6
      $29,700.00                3
      $30,800.00                3
      $33,000.00                4
      $35,200.00                2
      $36,300.00                1
      $38,500.00                4
```

Omit the *WHERE* clause in the above example to tally all salaries.

■ **Comment**

Use TALLY for ad hoc data inquiry. If you want a more formal output of tally results, use REPORTS or write your own command file.

In most cases, the CROSSTAB command is more useful than TALLY because it lets you cross-tabulate between two columns in a table. For a discussion of tabulating matching occurrences in more than one column, see *CROSSTAB*.

■ **R:BASE 5000 equivalent**

TALLY

Trigonometric functions

■ **Description**

R:BASE System V provides the basic trigonometric functions: *sine, cosine,* and *tangent* as well as their inverse functions: *arcsine, arccosine,* and *arctangent*. R:BASE also provides the hyperbolic functions: *sinh, cosh,* and *tanh*. For a general description of all available functions, see *Functions*.

In the following descriptions and examples, note that R:BASE always computes angles in *radians* rather than degrees. There are 2π (2pi) radians in 360 degrees. To calculate the angle in degrees, multiply the angle given in radians by 360 and divide it by 2π.

The following table lists the trigonometric and hyperbolic functions available in R:BASE System V:

Function	Description
ACOS(*arg*)	Computes the arccosine of the value specified in *arg*, a real number between and including -1 and 1 ($-1 <= \text{arg} <= 1$).
ASIN(*arg*)	Computes the arcsine of the value specified in *arg*, a real number between and including -1 and 1 ($-1 <= \text{arg} <= 1$).
ATAN(*arg*)	Computes the arctangent of the value specified in *arg*, a real number between and including -1 and 1 ($-1 <= \text{arg} <= 1$).
COS(*angle*)	Computes the cosine of the *angle*.
SIN(*angle*)	Computes the sine of the *angle*.

(continued)

273

Function	Description
TAN(angle)	Computes the tangent of the angle.
COSH(angle)	Computes the hyperbolic cosine of the angle.
SINH(angle)	Computes the hyperbolic sine of the angle.
TANH(angle)	Computes the hyperbolic tangent of the angle.

■ Trigonometric Functions

Consider the right triangle shown in Figure 1. Side c is the hypotenuse. The acute angles are X and Y. The side adjacent to angle X is side b. The side opposite angle X is side a. The values of the trigonometric functions in terms of the X angle are as follows:

sine X = a/c
cosine X = b/c
tangent = a/b.
arcsine (a/c) = X
arccosine(b/c) = X
arctangent(a/b) = X

The inverse functions are often denoted with an exponent of negative one (e.g., arcsine = sine^{-1}).

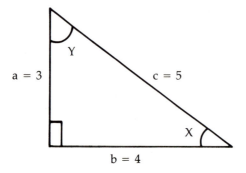

a = 3
c = 5
b = 4

Figure 1. *A right triangle*

For example, assume the above right triangle is a *3-4-5* triangle ($a = 3$, $b = 4$, $c = 5$). Using the R:BASE System V trigonometric functions, we can make the following computations:

```
R>SET VAR vyangle REAL
R>SET VAR vxangle REAL
R>SET VAR vxangle = ASIN(3/5)
R>SHOW VAR vxangle
     0.643501
R>SET VAR vyangle = ACOS(3/5)
R>SHOW VAR vyangle
     0.927295
R>SET VAR vtotal = ANINT((.vyangle + .vxangle) * 360 / (2 * .#PI))
R>SHOW VAR vtotal
     90.
R>SET VAR vytan = TAN(.vyangle)
R>SHOW VAR vytan
        1.33333330548801
```

The variables *vxangle* and *vyangle* hold results in radians. To confirm their accuracy, the formula computes the sum of the two angles multiplied by $360/2\pi$ and assigns the result to the variable *vtotal*. Note that the *ANINT()* function rounds off the result to 90 degrees. The variable *vytan* is assigned the tangent of the Y angle, which is 1.333 or ($^4/_3$).

Following is an example of a database table that you can use to enter the two legs of a right triangle to obtain the hypotenuse and angles:

```
LIST RT-TRI

    Table: RT-TRI          No lock(s)
    Read Password: No
    Modify Password: No

    Column definitions
    # Name      Type      Length        Key    Expression
    1 SIDE1     REAL
    2 SIDE2     REAL
    3 HYPOT     REAL                           (SQRT(('SIDE1')**2
                                               + ('SIDE2')**2))

    4 ANGLE1    REAL                           (ASIN
                                               ('SIDE1' / 'HYPOT') /
                                               (2 * .#PI) * 360)

    5 ANGLE2    REAL                           (ACOS
                                               ('SIDE1' / 'HYPOT') /
                                               (2 * .#PI) * 360)

    Current number of rows:      23

SELECT ALL FROM RT-TRI
    SIDE1    SIDE2    HYPOT     ANGLE1    ANGLE2
    -------- -------- --------  --------  --------
         8.      11.  13.60147  36.02737  53.97263
         1.       6.  6.082763  9.462322  80.53768
         9.       4.  9.848858  66.03751  23.96249
        16.       8.  17.88854  63.43495  26.56505
        10.       6.  11.6619   59.03625  30.96375
```

HYPOT, *ANGLE1*, and *ANGLE2* are computed columns. Therefore, you can enter values only for *SIDE1* and *SIDE2*. A data entry form for this table is shown in the *FORMS* entry.

- **Hyperbolic functions**

The hyperbolic functions are combinations of the exponentials e^x and e^{-x}:

SINH $x = (e^x + e^{-x}) / 2$
COSH $x = (e^x - e^{-x}) / 2$
TANH x = SINH x / COSH x

The following table computes the above hyperbolic functions for the entered value:

```
LIST HYPER
    Table: HYPER               No lock(s)
    Read Password: No
    Modify Password: No

    Column definitions
    # Name      Type      Length       Key    Expression
    1 VAL       REAL
    2 VALSINH   REAL                          SINH('VAL')
    3 VALCOSH   REAL                          COSH('VAL')
    4 VALTANH   REAL                          TANH('VAL')
    Current number of rows:       20

SELECT ALL FROM HYPER
VAL       VALSINH  VALCOSH  VALTANH
--------  -------- -------- --------
       1. 1.175201 1.543081 0.761594
       2.  3.62686 3.762196 0.964028
       3. 10.01787 10.06766 0.995055
       4. 27.28992 27.30823 0.999329
       5. 74.20321 74.20995 0.999909
      -1.  -1.1752 1.543081 -0.76159
      -2. -3.62686 3.762196 -0.96403
      -3. -10.0179 10.06766 -0.99505
      -4. -27.2899 27.30823 -0.99933
      -5. -74.2032 74.20995 -0.99991
```

The following figures (generated in Lotus 1-2-3) show the graphs of the equations $y = \sinh x$ (2a), $y = \cosh x$ (2b), and $y = \tanh x$ (2c). To generate these graphs, use FileGateway to export the *HYPER* table to the 1-2-3 format, and then use the Lotus graphics function.

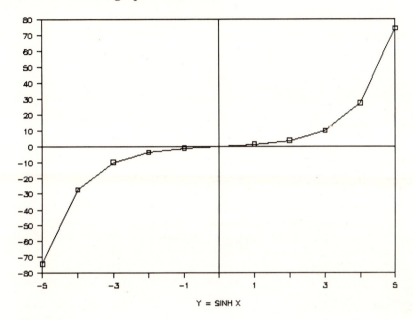

Figure 2a

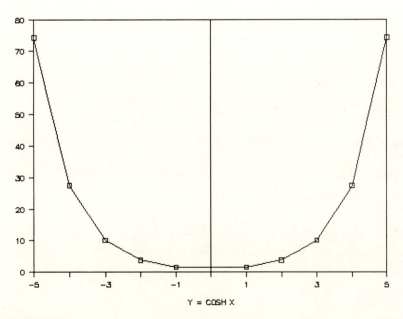

Figure 2b

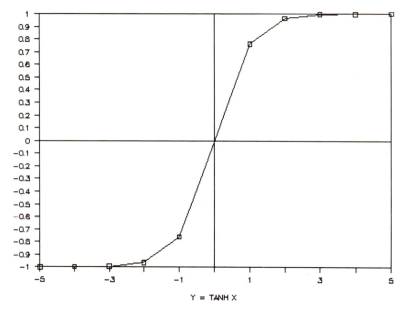

Figure 2c

- **R:BASE 5000 equivalent**
None

TYPE

- **Syntax**

```
TYPE filespec
```

- **Description**
The TYPE command displays the specified file on an output device such as the screen or a printer. The command is similar to the MS-DOS TYPE command and can be used to display any ASCII text file. The R:BASE version of TYPE is more convenient than the MS-DOS version because it pauses at the end of each screenful of text.

- **Procedure**
The TYPE command provides a convenient method to review or print a file quickly. For example, to obtain a printout of the command file, *TESTING.CMD*, type the following commands:

```
OUTPUT PRINTER
TYPE TESTING.CMD
OUTPUT SCREEN
```

■ **R:BASE 5000 equivalent**

TYPE

UNION

■ **Syntax**

UNION *tblname1* WITH *tblname2* FORMING *tblname3* ⌐ USING *collist* ⌐

■ **Description**

The UNION command is a relational command that forms a new table from two existing tables that have one or more common columns. Rows from the source tables in which the common column values are identical are combined into single rows in the new table. Rows in the source tables without matching column values are also included in the new table, but R:BASE inserts NULL values into them. This characteristic of the UNION command distinguishes it from the INTERSECT command, which combines only rows that have identical values in the common columns.

For a general discussion of UNION, see *Relational commands*.

■ **Procedure**

Users of R:BASE 5000 often use UNION to combine two tables into a temporary table from which they generate a report. This function is largely superseded by the VIEW feature in R:BASE System V, which provides a much more convenient method to generate temporary tables for purposes such as printing reports (see *Relational commands*, *REPORTS*, and *VIEW*).

We used the *LOAN* and *NEWCLI* tables in the examples in the INTERSECT and SUBTRACT entries. Compare those examples with the following sequence of commands, which uses UNION to combine the two tables:

```
SELECT CLINUM LOAN-NUM AMTOWED FROM LOAN

CLINUM      LOAN-NUM    AMTOWED
----------  ----------  ----------------
         1           1        $4,604.51
         2           2        $6,501.50
        67           3        $4,408.99

SELECT CLINUM CLINAME FROM NEWCLI

CLINUM      CLINAME
----------  ------------------------
         1  Johnson and Anderson Co.
         2  Cal Gas and Electric
         3  Power Research Associates
         4  Stone Construction Co.
         5  Ohio Electric Power Co.
```

(continued)

279

```
UNION LOAN WITH NEWCLI FORMING NEWLOAN USING CLINUM CLINAME +
LOAN-NUM AMTOWED

 Successful union operation, 6 rows generated

SELECT ALL FROM NEWLOAN

    CLINUM    CLINAME                          LOAN-NUM   AMTOWED
    --------- ------------------------------   --------   --------------

           1 Johnson and Anderson Co.              1       $4,604.51
           2 Cal Gas and Electric                  2       $6,501.50
          67 -0-                                    3       $4,408.99
           3 Power Research Associates -0-         -0-
           4 Stone Construction Co.     -0-        -0-
           5 Ohio Electric Power Co.    -0-        -0-
```

In contrast to the INTERSECT command, UNION combines all rows regardless of whether or not the common column values are identical. R:BASE inserts NULL values in columns that do not match. If you omit the *USING* clause, UNION combines all columns from both tables. The *USING* clause lets you specify a list of columns (*collist*) from either table.

Note: The order of columns in the new table is based on the order of columns in the first table (tblname1). Columns in the second table (tblname2) that are not common columns are then added to the new table.

The table to be formed cannot already exist in the database. If you want to form a new version of an existing table, you must first delete the old table with the REMOVE command.

Caution: If the tables to be combined include computed columns, be sure you include the columns that are part of the computed column expression in the *USING* clause. Otherwise, R:BASE displays an error message similar to the following:

```
R>UNION INVOICE WITH CLIENT FORMING NEWTEMP USING TOTAL CLINUM CLINAME INV-NUM
-ERROR- Expression for column total contains column prevbal which
        is not in table newtemp.
        Column total in table newtemp is no longer a computed column.
        You should rename total in table newtemp.
 Successful union operation, 22 rows generated
```

Note that the UNION command executes successfully. Although the *TOTAL* column is no longer a computed column expression in the new *NEWTEMP* table, it is still a computed column in the *INVOICE* table. Therefore, you now have two column definitions for the same column name, and that can wreak havoc in the database. You must either rename the *TOTAL* column in the new table or execute the UNION command again and include the columns of the computed column expression in the *USING* clause.

- **Comment**

    Following are some guidelines for improving the performance of the UNION command:

    ☐ You can greatly improve the performance of the UNION command by keying the common column in the second table (*tblname2*). In the above example, key the *CLINUM* column in the *NEWCLI* table.

    ☐ If one table is much larger than the other, make the smaller table the second table in the UNION command and do not use keys.

    ☐ If both tables are large, specify the table with the shorter row length first and use a key in the common column of the second table.

    See: *APPEND, BUILD KEY, INTERSECT, JOIN, Keys, PROJECT, Relational commands, SUB-TRACT,* and *VIEW*

- **R:BASE 5000 equivalent**

    UNION

UNLOAD

- **Syntax**

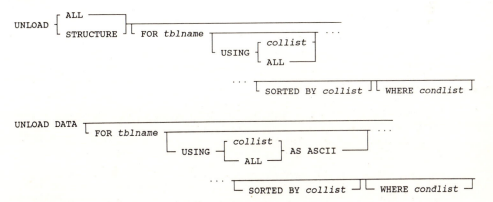

- **Description**

    The UNLOAD command backs up the database structure, the data, or both to a disk file. To recover files backed up with the UNLOAD command, use the INPUT or RUN commands. The UNLOAD command is similar to the BACKUP command except that UNLOAD cannot back up to multiple floppy disks. For files smaller than the capacity of a floppy disk, you can use the UNLOAD and BACKUP commands interchangeably.

■ **Procedure**

Use the *FOR* clause to back up a specific table; use the *USING* clause to back up specific columns in a table. You also can sort the data to be backed up by including a *SORTED BY* clause, and select specific rows to be backed up by including a *WHERE* clause. You must use a *FOR* clause with the *USING*, *SORTED BY*, and *WHERE* clauses. If you omit the *FOR* clause, UNLOAD backs up the entire database.

The UNLOAD command backs up the database in ASCII format. The database structure is backed up as a series of R:BASE commands that define the database. When you use the INPUT or RUN command to restore your backup file, the database is redefined. If you restore a database or table that already exists, the backup file commands produce a series of error messages, but the restore operation still completes successfully (see *Error messages*). If the database already exists, UNLOAD appends the backed-up data to the existing tables. The *AS ASCII* option can be used with UNLOAD DATA to leave the R:BASE commands out of the backup file. With this option, only the table data is unloaded. This feature is useful for unloading data to be used with other programs.

Before you use the UNLOAD command, you must issue an OUTPUT command to specify a destination file for the backup. For example, if you want to back up the *PROPOSAL* table of the *CONSULT* database to a file called *B:PROPOSAL.BK*, issue the following commands:

```
OPEN CONSULT
OUTPUT B:PROPOSAL.BK
UNLOAD DATA FOR PROPOSAL
OUTPUT SCREEN
```

The output of the UNLOAD command is directed to *B:PROPOSAL.BK*. The second OUTPUT command resets the output device to the screen. A listing of the *PROPOSAL.BK* file follows:

```
SET DELIMIT=NULL
SET DELIMIT=,
SET SEMI=NULL
SET SEMI=;
SET QUOTES=NULL
SET QUOTES="
SET PLUS=NULL
SET PLUS=+
SET CASE OFF
SET AUTOSKIP OFF
SET REVERSE ON
SET BELL OFF
SET TOLERANCE 0.
SET NULL -0-
SET DATE SEQUENCE MMDDYYYY
SET TIME SEQUENCE HHMMSS
SET CURRENCY "$" PREFIX 2 B
```

(continued)

```
USER   NONE
LOAD   PROPOSAL
1,"Building Analysis",30000.00,0.8,1,-0-
2,"Database Development",50000.00,0.4,2,-0-
4,"Stress Calculations",80000.00,0.9,3,-0-
5,"Seismic Eval. Report",150000.00,0.5,4,-0-
END
USER   none
SET DATE FORMAT "MM/DD/YY"
SET TIME FORMAT "HH:MM:SS"
SET DATE SEQUENCE MMDDYY
SET TIME SEQUENCE HHMMSS
```

Notice that the backup file is essentially a command file that you can use to restore the data. Some special character and keyword settings also are saved in the backup file (see *SET characters and keywords*). The UNLOAD ALL command creates a similar, but more extensive, file that contains all the data in the database plus the commands for defining the tables, forms, and reports.

You can use the output files generated by the UNLOAD command to change the name of the database or table that you send the recovered files to. For example, in the *PROPOSAL.BK* listing, you could use a text editor like RBEDIT to change the line *LOAD PROPOSAL* to *LOAD NEWTABLE*. Similarly, you can change the database name in the output from an UNLOAD STRUCTURE or UNLOAD ALL command. In that case, you would change the *DEFINE* line to include the name of the new database. This is one way to copy data from one database to another.

To back up the database structure for a database called *CONSULT*, use the following commands:

```
OPEN CONSULT
OUTPUT B:CONSULT.STR
UNLOAD STRUCTURE
OUTPUT SCREEN
```

To selectively back up data, use a *WHERE* clause in the UNLOAD command. For example, you might want to back up only rows that have a certain date. To do this with a table called *PURCHASE* that contains a date column called *PDATE*, type:

```
UNLOAD DATA FOR PURCHASE WHERE PDATE EQ 01/05/87
```

You also can unload data from a reports table as you would from any other table. Therefore, you can move a report definition from one database to another. Of course, you must be sure that the column and table definitions are compatible or the report will not run in the other database. The target database must have a defined *REPORTS* table. If it doesn't, you can easily create one by making a small dummy report (see *Tables and TABLES*).

To copy a report called *TESTRPT* from the *TEST* database to the *REALDAT* database, execute the following sequence of commands:

```
OPEN TEST
OUTPUT REPORT.FIL
UNLOAD DATA FOR REPORTS WHERE RNAME EQ TESTRPT
OUTPUT SCREEN
OPEN REALDAT
INPUT REPORT.FIL
```

Note that the *WHERE* clause unloads only the data for the report named *TESTRPT*. If you omit the *WHERE* clause, all report definitions from the *TEST* database are unloaded.

■ Comments

Usually, the best approach to backing up a database is to back up the database structure separately from the data. Unless you change the database structure, there is no point to repeatedly backing it up. On the other hand, the data in the database constantly changes and you should back it up regularly. Once you begin to use a database regularly, you might want to back up the structure and keep it on a separate floppy disk. Then, all you must do is periodically back up the data (see *Backing up data*).

Cautions: Before you issue the UNLOAD command, be sure the NULL value is set to the default value (-0-). When you recover data from a backup copy, set NULL to its default value in the database and also check the input file for the correct SET NULL value. Also, to properly save the backed-up data, always enter the OUTPUT SCREEN command immediately after you execute the UNLOAD command.

See: *BACKUP, FileGateway, INPUT, RESTORE,* and *RUN*

■ R:BASE 5000 equivalent
UNLOAD

USER

■ Syntax

USER ⌐ *password* ⌐

■ Description

The USER command enters a password to permit access to the database. The types of passwords that you can define are discussed in *Data security, OWNER,* and *PASSWORDS*.

■ **Procedure**

To enter a password at the R> prompt, type

```
USER password
```

where *password* is the defined password. The password must be eight characters or less. The USER command does not control or define passwords; you use it only to enter a password.

If you attempt to perform an operation that is subject to password control (for example, modifying the database structure) without first entering the password, R:BASE notifies you that a password is required. You then can use the USER command to enter the password.

■ **R:BASE 5000 equivalent**

SET USER (See *SET characters and keywords.*)

Variables

■ **Description**

Variables store temporary values in memory during an R:BASE session. When you exit R:BASE, the defined variables are erased from memory. You will find many examples of the use of variables throughout this book. This discussion offers a general description of variables, guidelines for their use, and cross references to relevant entries.

R:BASE variables are either *global variables* or *error variables*. Global variables store temporary values used in command files, forms or reports. They can be accessed from any operation in R:BASE and are independent of the currently open database. In contrast to some other database and programming languages, R:BASE does not employ local variables.

Error variables trap error codes during the execution of a command file or application. For a detailed discussion of error variables, see *SET ERROR VARIABLE* and *SET POINTER*.

A variable name can be a maximum of eight characters and cannot include any of the R:BASE operator symbols such as +, ?, %, and so on (see *Operators*). You also cannot use R:BASE reserved words as variable names (see Tables *1-8* and *1-9* in the R:BASE User's Manual). In addition to the variables that you create, R:BASE defines four *system variables* that you can use during an R:BASE session. These are #DATE, #TIME, #PAGE, and #PI. The contents of these variables are the current date, the current time, the current report page (if any), and the value of π (pi), respectively.

R:BASE provides the following commands for working with variables:

Command	Description
COMPUTE	Computes a value from a column or expression and stores it in a variable.
CHOOSE	Passes the keyboard entry of a menu choice to a variable.
FILLIN	Passes the keyboard entry of a value to a variable.
SET ERROR VARIABLE	Defines a variable as an error variable.
SET POINTER	Defines a variable as a special error variable for evaluating the status of a pointer.
SET VARIABLE *value*	Assigns a value or expression to a variable.
SET VARIABLE *datatype*	Assigns a data type to a variable.

All variables are assigned an R:BASE data type (see *Data types*). You can assign the data type explicitly by declaring the data type with the SET VARIABLE *datatype* command, or you can implicitly assign the data type by setting the variable equal to an initial value. R:BASE then assigns the data type that corresponds to the initial value.

The SET VARIABLE command is the only command with which you can explicitly define the variable data type. Although explicit data typing is not always necessary, we strongly recommend it if you intend to use the variable in an expression. R:BASE often misinterprets implicitly defined variables in expressions, especially expressions that perform arithmetic operations. This misinterpretation can cause an error or produce an erroneous result.

For example, you might initially assign an integer value to a variable (implicit data typing) and then later set this variable equal to an arithmetic expression that yields a real number. Only the integer portion of this result, however, is stored in the variable. If the result is less than 1, the variable is set to zero.

Delete defined variables with the CLEAR command. You can reset the variable data type by issuing another SET VARIABLE *datatype* command.

Precede a variable name with a dot (*.varname*) to use the *current value* of the variable in a command or expression. It is not always evident when you should use a dotted variable name. The basic rule is: Use a dotted variable when you substitute a variable for an arbitrary value. For example, *WHERE SALARY EQ 20000* compares the column *SALARY* to the arbitrary value *20000*. Use the following clause to substitute the value of a variable for the arbitrary value: *WHERE SALARY EQ .vamount*.

The IF and WHILE commands compare variables against specific values in order to select the appropriate course of action. The variable that is used to compare or check the value should *not* be preceded with a dot. However, when you compare the variable against the value of another variable, the same basic rule as above applies: precede the variable that you compare against with a dot (e.g., *IF vsalary GT .vamount THEN . . .*).

Generally, you display variables with the SHOW VARIABLE command. When you display a variable with SHOW VARIABLE, do not use a dotted variable. You also can use the WRITE command to display variables. However, since WRITE displays values rather than variables, you must use a dotted variable with it.

An ampersand variable stores portions of a command. By including a variable preceded by an ampersand (&) in your command, you can execute the contents of the variable as part of the command. For example:

```
SET VAR CMDLIST = "SALARY FROM EMPLOYEE WHERE EMPID EQ 3"
SELECT &CMDLIST
```

is equivalent to:

```
SELECT SALARY FROM EMPLOYEE WHERE EMPID EQ 3
```

Use the RUN command and the special % variables to pass variable values from one command file to another during file execution (see *RUN*).

Following are some general guidelines for using variables:

☐ Use meaningful variable names that describe the function or purpose of the variable. It's good practice to use the letter *v* as the first letter of a variable name to distinguish it from a column name. Precede report variables with *rv* and form variables with *fv*.

☐ Explicitly define the data types of variables used in expressions.

☐ Precede a variable name with a dot when the variable is used in place of an arbitrary value.

□ Do not use the CLEAR ALL VARIABLES command in command files that are incorporated into an Application EXPRESS application. Use the CLEAR command with an individual list of variables.

□ If you access variables in either a form or a report, be sure to define the variables before you enter the form or print the report.

□ Use ampersand variables only as part of command lines.

See: *Application EXPRESS, CHOOSE, CLEAR, Command files, COMPUTE, FILLIN, FORMS, Procedure files, Programming, REPORTS, RUN, SET ERROR VARIABLE, SET POINTER,* and *SET VARIABLE*

VIEW

■ **Syntax**

```
VIEW viewname WITH collist FROM tbllist ┌──────────────────┐
                                        └ WHERE condlist ┘
```

■ **Description**

Use the VIEW command (or Definition EXPRESS) to define a view. A view is a table image, or pseudo table, that combines columns from as many as five different tables. The main reason to define a view is to display data from multiple tables simultaneously.

A view is called a pseudo table because it does not physically store the data from the combined tables. A view is a definition stored in the database structure, which, when accessed, combines the current data from the specified tables. R:BASE always creates a *VIEWS* table to maintain the view definitions in the database. A secondary table, called *VIEWCOND*, stores the *WHERE* conditions that you specify for the view.

■ **Procedure**

Each table specified in the view must have a common column with at least one other table. VIEW combines tables in the same way as the INTERSECT command. Append a *WHERE* clause to specify the conditions that the rows must meet to be included in the view.

You cannot redefine an existing view. From within R:BASE, you first must remove the existing view and then issue a new VIEW command. You can, however, modify views in Definition EXPRESS.

Typically you use a view to combine two or more tables to produce a report. There are two advantages to using a view rather than the relational commands.

☐ A view does not have to be updated. It always displays the current data in the combined tables. A combined table created with the relational commands must be redefined every time the data in the source tables changes.

☐ A view requires little storage space because it does not physically store the data from the source tables. Relational commands create new tables that physically store the data. In addition, when you redefine an updated table, you must remove the old table.

The following example uses VIEW to combine columns from the *INVOICE* and *CLIENT* tables. After you create the view, the LIST command is used to list the contents of the view:

```
LIST INVOICE

    Table: INVOICE         No lock(s)
    Read Password: No
    Modify Password: No

    Column definitions
    # Name     Type       Length        Key   Expression
    1 CLINUM   INTEGER                  yes
    2 INV-NUM  TEXT        8 characters
    3 ENTRDATE DATE                           .#DATE
    4 DUE      CURRENCY
    5 PREVBAL  CURRENCY
    6 TOTAL    CURRENCY                       'PREVBAL'+'DUE'
    7 FORWHAT  TEXT       50 characters
    8 PAID     TEXT        1 characters

    Current number of rows:    17

  LIST CLIENT

    Table: CLIENT          No lock(s)
    Read Password: Yes
    Modify Password: Yes

    Column definitions
    # Name     Type       Length        Key   Expression
    1 CLINUM   INTEGER
    2 CLINAME  TEXT       25 characters
    3 STREET   TEXT       25 characters
    4 CITY     TEXT       20 characters
    5 STATE    TEXT        2 characters
    6 ZIP      TEXT        5 characters
    7 PHONE    TEXT       12 characters

    Current number of rows:    11
```

(continued)

```
VIEW INVREPT WITH CLINUM CLINAME TOTAL PAID ENTRDATE FROM +
INVOICE CLIENT

LIST INVREPT

    Table: INVREPT          No lock(s)
    Read Password: Yes
    Modify Password: Yes

    Column definitions
    # Name       Type        Length          Key    Expression
    1 CLINUM     INTEGER
    2 CLINAME    TEXT        25 characters
    3 TOTAL      CURRENCY                            'PREVBAL'+'DUE'
    4 PAID       TEXT        1 characters
    5 ENTRDATE   DATE                               .#DATE

    Current number of rows:    N/A
```

The current number of rows is given as *N/A*. Since views do not actually store any data, the number of rows is not applicable to a view.

In the above example of VIEW, you can add a *WHERE* clause to restrict the range of clients or invoice dates to be included in the view, as follows:

```
VIEW INVREPT WITH CLINUM CLINAME TOTAL PAID ENTRDATE FROM +
 INVOICE CLIENT WHERE ENTRDATE GE 1/1/85
```

■ **Comments**

If you assigned passwords to the tables in the view, the view assumes the passwords of the first table that you specify in the table list (*tbllist*). A view also can have separate passwords (see *Data security*).

A view constructed from more than one table can be used only for data inquiry, but a single-table view can be edited, although rows may not be deleted or added.

Specify a *WHERE* clause with a single-table view to access only a subset of the source table. For example, if you have a personnel table that includes confidential salary information, you can create a view that excludes this information but allows you access to other columns of the table. See *Definition EXPRESS* for an alternate method of defining views.

Cautions: You cannot use the following commands in a view: ENTER, DELETE ROW, INTERSECT, JOIN, LOAD, REDEFINE, REMOVE COLUMN, SET POINTER, SUBTRACT, and UNION. You can use the commands BROWSE, CHANGE, and EDIT only with single-table views.

Do not use the PROJECT command with a view that contains computed columns: The computed column expression will not be transferred to the new table. The column in the projected table will be assigned the data type of the computed column expression, but it will no longer contain the expression it-self. This creates two definitions in your database for the same column, which can wreak havoc in your database.

See: *Definition EXPRESS, LIST, Relational commands, REMOVE, REPORTS,* and *SELECT*

- **R:BASE 5000 equivalent**

None

WHERE

- **Syntax**

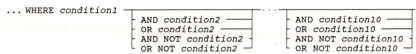

```
... WHERE condition1        AND condition2          · · ·        AND condition10
                            OR condition2                        OR condition10
                            AND NOT condition2                   AND NOT condition10
                            OR NOT condition2                    OR NOT condition10
```

- **Description**

Use the *WHERE* clause with many commands to specify conditional criteria that must be met by the columns or variables specified in the command. The *WHERE* clause lets you limit or restrict the rows that you include in a command.

- **Procedure**

Use the *WHERE* clause with the following commands:

> APPEND
> BACKUP
> BROWSE
> CHANGE
> COMPUTE
> CROSSTAB
> DELETE ROWS
> EDIT
> EDIT USING
> JOIN (for a special usage of *WHERE*, see *JOIN*)
> PRINT
> PROJECT
> SELECT
> SET POINTER
> SET VARIABLE
> UNLOAD
> VIEW

You can use any of the following operators with the *WHERE* clause:

Operators	Meaning
Value operators:	
EQ or $=$	equal
NE or $<>$	not equal
GT or $>$	greater than
GE or $>=$	greater than or equal to
LT or $<$	less than
LE or $<=$	less than or equal to
CONTAINS	contains a text string
EXISTS	contains data (value other than NULL)
FAILS	contains a NULL value (-0-)
Column value operators:	
EQA	equal
NEA	not equal
GTA	greater than
GEA	greater than or equal to
LTA	less than
LEA	less than or equal to
Row count operators:	
COUNT	finds a specified row
LIMIT	limits the number of rows affected by a command
Boolean operators:	
AND	Both conditions separated by AND must be true.
OR	One of the two conditions separated by OR must be true.
AND NOT	The first condition must be true and the second condition must be false.
OR NOT	Either the first condition must be true or the second condition must be false.

For detailed information about the above operators, see *Operators*.

You can specify as many as ten conditions in a single *WHERE* clause. You can find many examples of the use of the *WHERE* clause in this book. In particular, see *CHANGE, Operators, SELECT,* and *SET POINTER.*

Following are some typical commands that use the *WHERE* clause:

```
SELECT ALL FROM EMPLOYEE WHERE ZIP CONTAINS "94"
SELECT ALL FROM EMPLOYEE WHERE ZIP = 94*
SELECT LNAME FNAME FROM NAMES WHERE SALARY GT 20000 AND SALARY LT 50000
PRINT MYREPT WHERE ENTRDATE GT 1/1/86
DELETE ROWS FROM EMPLOYEE WHERE EMPID FAILS
DELETE ROWS FROM NAMES WHERE LNAME EXISTS
SET POINTER #1 P1 FOR EMPLOYEE WHERE EMPID EQ .vempid
```

■ **Comment**

You can improve the performance of commands that use a *WHERE* clause by making the last column in the condition list a key column. Key processing is most efficient when an EQ or = operand follows the key column. If there are multiple conditions, key processing is most effective when the AND operator precedes the last condition (see *Keys* and *BUILD KEY*).

See: *Operators* and *SELECT*

■ **R:BASE 5000 equivalent**

WHERE

WHILE

■ **Syntax**

```
WHILE condlist THEN
    while-block
ENDWHILE
```

■ **Description**

Use the WHILE command in command files to establish a loop in which a block of commands is repeated while the specified conditions are true. When the conditions in the WHILE statement are false, control passes to the command immediately following the ENDWHILE command.

■ **Procedure**

A *condition* is a combination of variables and operators that together form a logical statement. A logical statement also can include functions and expressions. The *condlist* can consist of a single logical statement or as many as ten statements connected by the operators AND, OR, AND NOT, or OR NOT. You also can use the following conditional operators in a logical statement:

EXISTS, FAILS, CONTAINS
EQ (=), NE (<>), GT (>), GE (>=), LT (<), LE (<=)

For further information, see *Operators*.

WHILE loops can be nested inside other WHILE loops. R:BASE lets you use as many as nine levels of nested WHILE loops. You also can use the BREAK command with an IF statement to prematurely exit a WHILE loop in progress.

Because WHILE loops repeatedly execute a set of commands, values or variables are normally changed or incremented after each cycle of the loop so that they can be tested against the *conditionlist* of the WHILE command. For example, the following program uses WHILE with SET POINTER to update the rows of a table until the WHILE condition is no longer true:

```
SET POINTER #1 p1 FOR EMPLOYEE
WHILE p1 = 0 THEN
  SET VAR initvar TO " . "
  SET VAR fname TO FRSTNAME IN #1
  SET VAR lname TO LASTNAME IN #1
  SET VAR initvar = (SMOVE(.fname,1,1,.initvar,1))
  SET VAR initvar = (SMOVE(.lname,1,1,.initvar,3))
  CHANGE INITIALS TO .initvar IN #1
  NEXT #1 p1
ENDWHILE
```

The status variable *p1* remains zero until no further rows are encountered. Therefore, the statements within the WHILE loop are executed until the status variable is set to a non-zero value. See *SET POINTER* for more information about the SET POINTER command.

The WHILE command also is commonly used to continue executing a command file until a NULL value (to quit) is entered:

```
WHILE vloan# EXISTS THEN
  CLS
  WRITE "Loan Update Program" AT 1,10
  FILLIN vloan# USING "Enter Loan Number to Update or <ENTER> +
    TO QUIT: " at 3,10
  IF vloan# FAILS THEN
    SET MESS ON
    SET ERR MESS ON
    BREAK
  ENDIF
*(list of commands)
ENDWHILE
RETURN
```

In this example, processing continues as long as you enter a loan number (*vloan# EXISTS*). When you press Enter without entering a value at the FILLIN prompt, the variable *vloan#* is set to NULL (*FAILS*) and causes the commands in the IF statement to be executed. The BREAK command in the IF statement transfers control from the WHILE loop to the command line immediately after ENDWHILE.

This book contains many examples that demonstrate the use of the WHILE command. In particular, see *Procedure files* and *SET POINTER*.

- **Comment**

  If you execute a command file and the screen suddenly displays a *W>* prompt, R:BASE is warning you either that a WHILE command has not ended with a corresponding ENDWHILE or that you pressed ESC to abnormally exit the WHILE loop. Type ENDWHILE to return to the R> prompt, then check the command file for missing ENDWHILE or BREAK commands.

  Caution: Avoid creating an endless loop. Be sure the command file contains a method to set the WHILE condition to *false*. For example, the following is an endless loop:

  ```
  SET VAR varnum = 1
  WHILE varnum GT 0 THEN
    SET VAR varnum EQ .varnum + 1
  ENDWHILE
  ```

  This WHILE loop executes until your computer reaches its integer-processing limit or until you press ESC.

  See: *BREAK, Expressions, GOTO, IF, Operators, QUIT, RETURN,* and *SET POINTER*

- **R:BASE 5000 equivalent**

  WHILE

WRITE

- **Syntax**

```
WRITE "message"
                  └─ AT scrnrow scrncol ─┘
```

- **Description**

  Use the WRITE command in command files to display a message on the current output device.

- **Procedure**

  You can substitute the value of a variable for *message*. The optional *AT scrnrow scrncol* clause specifies the screen coordinates at which R:BASE displays the message. Note that these coordinates apply only to the screen and are not valid for specifying printer coordinates. If you omit the *AT* clause, R:BASE displays the message or variable value on the line below the current cursor position. Therefore, successive WRITE commands will not overwrite the output of previous WRITE commands.

The WRITE command is most frequently used to display a message on the screen during command file execution. For example, it's often necessary to display the prompt, *Press any key to continue*, when you use the PAUSE command. You can do this easily with WRITE, as seen in the following command sequence from the *LOAN* update program in *Financial functions*:

```
WRITE "Loan number not found, press any key to continue" at 7,10
PAUSE
```

You also can use the WRITE command to send messages and values to a printer. Because you cannot use screen coordinates to control the printer, you must use successive WRITE or SHOW VARIABLE commands to move the page to the desired position. Unfortunately, this is a cumbersome exercise that involves much trial and error. Whenever possible, use REPORTS to create printer output. For suggestions about using reports for displaying variables, see *SHOW VARIABLE*.

The *SFIL()* function is useful for storing text strings that you can then display with the WRITE command (see *String manipulation functions*). For example, if you want to print a line of hyphens, store the hyphens in a variable and then display them as needed with the WRITE command:

```
SET VAR vhyphens = (SFIL("-",80))
OUTPUT PRINTER
WRITE .vhyphens
```

You can use a similar command sequence to display a line of blanks:

```
SET VAR blanktxt = " "
SET VAR vblanks = (SFIL(.blanktxt,80))
WRITE .vblanks
```

Note that the *SFIL()* function will not accept the argument " ". You must assign the " " value to an intermediate variable (*blanktxt*) because *SFIL()* interprets " " as a NULL value when it is used directly.

See: *FILLIN, SHOW VARIABLE,* and *String manipulation functions*

■ **R:BASE 5000 equivalent**
WRITE

ZIP

■ **Syntax**

```
ZIP ┌─────────┐ progname
    └ ROLLOUT ┘
```

■ **Description**

The ZIP command executes external programs from within R:BASE.

■ **Procedure**

If the memory required by an external program is less than the system's un-used memory, you can execute the external program directly by issuing ZIP followed by the program name. In this case, R:BASE remains loaded in memory while the external program executes. If, however, the external program requires more memory than is available with R:BASE loaded, you must use the *ROLLOUT* option to run the external program. In this case, R:BASE is temporarily exited and its current settings are saved in the *RBSYSTEM.DAT* file. When the external program ends, R:BASE is then reloaded.

If your system has 640 kilobytes (KB) of memory, you generally can run small external programs that require less than approximately 80 KB of memory. Programs such as the MS-DOS FORMAT program or a simple text editor can be executed directly. Larger programs, such as Microsoft Word or Lotus 1-2-3, require the use of the *ROLLOUT* option.

Here are some examples of the ZIP command:

```
ZIP COMMAND /C BATNAME
```

This command executes the MS-DOS command processor, COMMAND.COM, which in turn runs the batch file that is called *BATNAME.BAT*. Note that COMMAND.COM is executed with the /C parameter, which instructs the command processor to return to R:BASE when the batch file ends.

The following command formats the disk in drive B:

```
ZIP FORMAT B:
```

The *ROLLOUT* option is used to execute larger programs:

```
ZIP ROLLOUT WORD DOCFILE.DOC
```

This command executes Microsoft Word with the file *DOCFILE.DOC*. Note that you can specify an R:BASE variable value (*.varname*) in place of *DOCFILE.DOC* in the above example.

■ **Comment**
The ZIP command is convenient for running small external programs directly. However, the ZIP ROLLOUT command is not much faster than exiting R:BASE manually and starting your other program.

■ **R:BASE 5000 equivalent**
None

Appendix

R:BASE Graphics

■ Description

The R:BASE Graphics program is a separate product from Microrim for creating graphs from R:BASE databases and specially formatted ASCII data files. Graphs provide an effective means of visually presenting and interpreting data. Although a lengthy report full of numbers can contain the required information, it is often easier to analyze or interpret graphic representations of large quantities of data.

R:BASE Graphics provides a menu-driven interface similar to the R:BASE EXPRESS modules such as Application EXPRESS. By selecting a series of menu options, you can create eight types of graphs. The data for the graphs can come from a table in an R:BASE database or from a specially formatted ASCII data file. The package also contains options for creating a split screen to display multiple graphs and for creating slide-show presentations.

Some of the most impressive features of R:BASE Graphics are its data reduction capabilities, which let you take raw data from a database and reduce it to a smaller set of statistical information that can be easily graphed. For example, you might have 1000 rows of data from which you want to produce a graph. Clearly, it is not practical to plot 1000 points on a graph. R:BASE Graphics provides methods to reduce this set of data to a smaller, more manageable data set.

R:BASE Graphics lets you reduce and manipulate the data that you intend to graph with options for grouping and sorting the data, calculating statistics, and defining variables. With the exception of the string manipulation and logical functions, you can use all R:BASE System V functions in R:BASE Graphics (see *Functions*).

R:BASE Graphics includes editing functions for editing data sets and graph formats (Data Set Editor and Graph Format Editor, respectively).

The following table describes the key functions in R:BASE Graphics. Note that some key functions apply only to specific activities, which are given in parentheses.

Key	Function
F1	Inserts a cell (Data Set Editor); splits a window (Split Screen).
Shift-F1	Inserts a column (Data Set Editor).
F2	Deletes a column (Data Set Editor).
F3	Brings up the Display menu from which you can display the database structure, current table or graph data, display and print graphs (most areas); merges windows (Split Screen).
F4	Selects a graph for a split-screen window (Split Screen).
F6	Clears the data from the data set worksheet (Data Set Editor).
F7	Saves a data set file (Data Set Editor).
F8	Retrieves a data set file (Data Set Editor).
F9	Duplicates a column (Data Set Editor).
Shift-F9	Rotates the columns on the data set worksheet (Data Set Editor).
F10	Provides help information on the current menu.
Shift-F10	Pages through the function key descriptions.
ESC	Returns to the previous action or menu.
Tab	Moves the cursor to the next column (Data Set Editor).
Shift-Tab	Moves the cursor to the previous column (Data Set Editor).
Ctrl-right arrow	Moves the cursor one page to the right (Data Set Editor).
Ctrl-left arrow	Moves the cursor one page to the left (Data Set Editor).
Up/down arrow	Moves the cursor up or down one line (Data Set and Graph Format Editors).

(continued)

Key	Function
Left/right arrow	Moves the cursor left or right one character (Data Set and Graph Format Editors).
Enter	Selects the highlighted option or moves the cursor to the next row or column.
Home	Moves the cursor to the first column in the upper left corner of the screen (Data Set and Graph Format Editors); moves the cursor up one row and left one column (Freetext entry).
End	Moves the cursor to the last column in the bottom right corner of the screen (Data Set and Graph Format editors); moves the cursor down one row and left one column (Freetext entry).
PgUp	Moves the cursor to the previous page (Data Set and Graph Format editors); moves the cursor up one row and right one column (Freetext entry).
PgDn	Moves the cursor to the next page (Data Set and Graph Format editors); moves the cursor down one row and right one column (Freetext entry).
Ins	Inserts a space at the cursor (Data Set and Graph Format editors); alternates between the Expand/Contract modes (Split Screen); alternates between large and small cursor movement (Freetext entry).
Del	Deletes the character at the cursor (Data Set and Graph Format editors).
[−] numeric key pad	Clears a current cell in the data set worksheet (Data Set Editor).

F3 is an important function key because it brings up the Display menu. The Display menu provides selections for reviewing a database or a graph data set and also provides options for displaying or printing the current graph.

The R:BASE Graphics Main menu: The following screen shows the Main menu of R:BASE Graphics:

```
═══════════════════════════════R:BASE Graphics Main Menu═══════════
        ⟨1⟩ Create a new graph
        (2) Modify a graph
        (3) Graph utilities
        (4) Output utilities
        (5) Dos functions
        (6) Exit from R:BASE Graphics
```

Use the *Create* option to create new graphs. The *Modify* option lets you retrieve and modify existing graphs. Use the *Graph Utilities* option to copy, rename, delete, save, or retrieve an existing graph definition. The Graph Utilities *Copy* option lets you copy a graph definition present in memory so that you can create a new graph based on an existing definition. Use the Graph Utilities *Save* option periodically to save the graph that you are working on and to protect your graph from a computer malfunction. (The *Exit* option also saves your graphs.) The Graph Utilities *Retrieve* option lets you load an existing graph into R:BASE Graphics. With the *Output Utilities* option, you can send a graph to a printer or plotter, create a split-screen graphic, or produce a computer-screen slide show. These options are discussed later in this entry. The *DOS Functions* option lets you access MS-DOS file maintenance commands (see *DOS commands in R:BASE*). Use the *Exit* option to exit R:BASE Graphics; R:BASE Graphics prompts you to save unsaved graphs.

Creating a graph: The following example creates a simple graph derived from a table called *EMPLOYEE* in the *PERSONL* database:

```
Table: EMPLOYEE          No lock(s)
Read Password: No
Modify Password: No

Column definitions
# Name      Type       Length      Key   Expression
1 EMPID     INTEGER                 yes
2 FRSTNAME  TEXT       15 characters
3 LASTNAME  TEXT       15 characters
4 DEPT      TEXT        5 characters
5 SALARY    CURRENCY
6 HIREDATE  DATE
7 SEX       TEXT        1 characters
8 ENTRDATE  DATE                          .#DATE
9 YEARS     INTEGER                       (NINT((.#DATE -
                                          'HIREDATE') / 365))

Current number of rows:     39
```

This example uses the data in the *EMPLOYEE* table to graph average salary against the number of years of employment. The data for the graph is derived from the *SALARY* and *YEARS* columns.

Start by selecting the *Create a new graph* option from the Main menu. Answer the prompt for a graph name (the name can be a maximum of eight characters), then select a database or a data file as the graph's data source. You can use an R:BASE database or a specially formatted ASCII file (discussed later in this entry) as the data source. In this example, select the *Database* option and then the *PERSONL* database as the data source.

R:BASE Graphics then presents the list of the available tables in the selected database. You can press the F3 key at any time to display the structure of the database or of a particular table. In this case, select the *EMPLOYEE* table. Note that you cannot create graphs from views (see *VIEW*). If you want to graph data from a view, you must first create an equivalent table using the INTERSECT or UNION command (see *Relational commands*).

After you select the data source, R:BASE Graphics prompts you to define the type of data (column or variable) to be used for the horizontal axis of the graph, as shown in the following screen:

```
╔══════════════════════════Select type of horizontal data set═══════════════════╗
║ Column  Variable  (CLEAR)                                                       ║
╚═════════════════════════════════════════════════════════════════════════════════╝




   Horizontal (X-axis):

   Vertical (Y-axis):


   Sorted by:

   Conditions:


    [ESC] Done [F3] Display [F10] Help
   GRAPH NAME: NEWTEST
```

You can select a column or a variable as the data type for the horizontal axis. In many cases, you might want to define a variable as the horizontal data type in order to use an R:BASE function or to define an expression (see *Expressions*).

For example, to plot the months from the *HIREDATE* column along the horizontal axis, you would define a variable that uses the *IMON()* function to extract the integer value of the month (e.g., *vmon = IMON(HIREDATE)*). Another common use of variables is to convert integer values, such as ID numbers, to text values so that they are evenly spaced on the X-axis (e.g., *vtextid = CTXT(IDNUM)*).

In this example, select *Column* as the horizontal data type and the *YEARS* column as the horizontal data set. This will display the number of years of employment on the X-axis. Select the *(Done)* option after you have defined the horizontal axis.

Next, select the data type for the vertical axis. This is where you can take advantage of the data reduction capabilities of R:BASE Graphics. As shown in the following screen, one of the options in the vertical data set menu establishes a grouping:

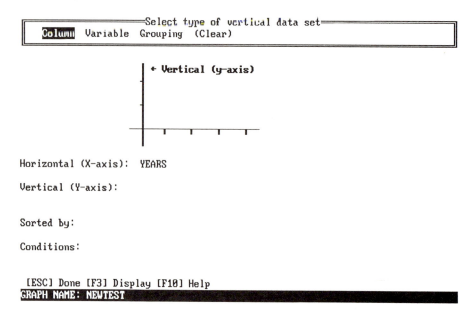

A *grouping* represents data on the vertical axis that is grouped as a function of the horizontal data. In this example, we want to group the average salary as a function of years of employment. The horizontal data type is essentially equivalent to a break point in an R:BASE report. For each value of *YEARS* on the horizontal axis, R:BASE Graphics computes the average salary of the employees with the corresponding number of years of employment.

After you select the *Grouping* option, you must assign a name to the grouping. The grouping name represents a variable that calculates the grouping values. In this example, name the grouping *vavesal*. Next, R:BASE Graphics displays the following menu:

```
                     ══════Select grouping function══════
   ┌──────────────────────────────────────────────────────────────┐
   │ SUM OF  AVERAGE OF  MINIMUM OF  MAXIMUM OF                      │
   └──────────────────────────────────────────────────────────────┘
```

In this example, select *AVERAGE OF* as the grouping calculation and, as shown in the next menu, the *SALARY* column as the column to be grouped:

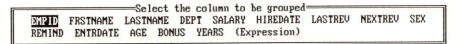

```
                     ══════Select the column to be grouped══════
   ┌──────────────────────────────────────────────────────────────┐
   │ EMPID  FRSTNAME  LASTNAME  DEPT  SALARY  HIREDATE  LASTREV  NEXTREV  SEX │
   │ REMIND  ENTRDATE  AGE  BONUS  YEARS  (Expression)                │
   └──────────────────────────────────────────────────────────────┘
```

Press ESC to return to the vertical data sets menu. Now select *vavesal* as the variable to plot on the vertical axis:

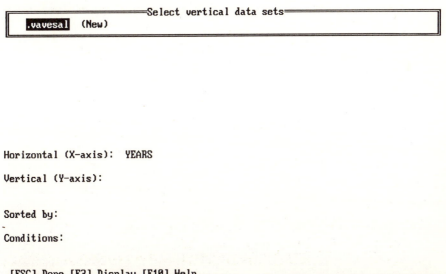

```
                     ══════Select vertical data sets══════
   ┌──────────────────────────────────────────────────────────────┐
   │ .vavesal  (New)                                                │
   └──────────────────────────────────────────────────────────────┘
```

```
   Horizontal (X-axis):  YEARS

   Vertical (Y-axis):


   Sorted by:

   Conditions:


   [ESC] Done [F3] Display [F10] Help
   GRAPH NAME: NEWTEST
```

Note that you can include as many as twenty columns or variables for plotting on the vertical axis. In other words, you can plot other columns (for example, the maximum salary) in addition to the average salary. To keep things simple, just plot the variable *vavesal*.

After you define the data type for the vertical axis, you are prompted to specify the columns to sort by and also the conditions that the data values must meet (if any). The *Sort* option determines the order in which the data is graphed. In most cases, you will sort the data values on the horizontal axis.

The *Conditions* option is equivalent to the *WHERE* clause in R:BASE. You use it to specify a range of data to be included in the graph. If you omit the *Conditions* option, all data in the database is included in the graph.

After you confirm the specified data characteristics, R:BASE Graphics computes the data to be graphed and then generates a line graph as shown in the following screen:

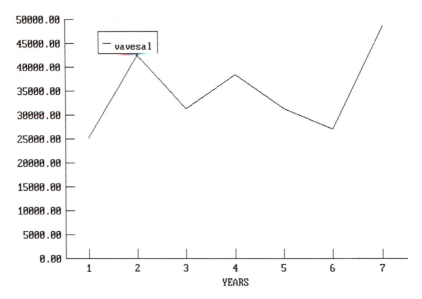

The computations may take several minutes.

Selecting other graph types and modifying the graph format: After R:BASE Graphics displays the graph, press any key to display the Graph Format menu. From this menu you can respecify the data for the graph (the horizontal and vertical axes), modify the graph format, or edit the actual data or format parameters used in the graph. (Editing data sets is discussed in the next section.)

The basic line graph shown in the above screen is a good starting point, but does not represent a finished graph. The legend *vavesal* probably will not mean much to the personnel manager or company president. Also, the line graph format is not the best way to present the data. Line graphs are appropriate for charting continuous functions, such as mathematical equations with an independent variable ($y = x^2$, for example) or for plotting data that varies continuously with time.

The relationship in our example, between average salary and years of employment, is not a continuous function represented by an equation. Although the data is correct for each integer value of years of employment, the data represented by the line between each integer value is meaningless, because YEARS is calculated only for integer values.

The best way to display this type of data is with a column or bar graph. With a column or bar graph, you see only the actual values for each unique number of years.

To change the graph type, select *Modify Format* from the Graph Format menu. At the Modify menu, select the *Change graph type* option. R:BASE Graphics then displays the available graph types:

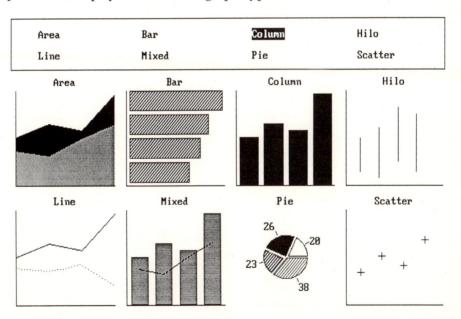

From this menu, select the appropriate graph type. In this example, select *Column* to redisplay the graph in the new format:

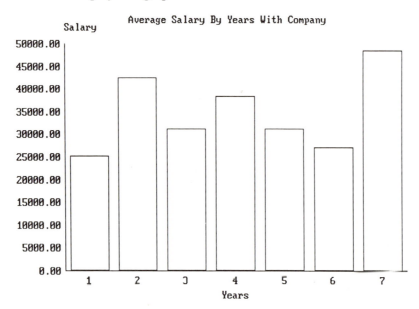

You also can change the text and style of the graph by using the *Edit graph format* option of the Modify menu. Selecting *Edit graph format* displays the Edit Format menu, which has two options: *Style* and *Text*. Use *Text* to edit, insert, or format text elements in the graph, such as titles, axis labels, legends, or descriptive text.

Use *Style* to customize the appearance of the graph. You can specify different graph backgrounds, such as a grid or a frame. You can relocate or remove the legend. You also can change the pattern of the graph columns, change the axes to logarithmic scale, highlight a baseline other than zero, or create a new graph with a smaller range.

To customize the colors or shading of the graph, select the *Data set colors* option or the *Foreground/background colors* option from the Modify menu. See the R:BASE Graphics User's Manual for further information on specifying colors.

Data sets: Although creating graphs with R:BASE Graphics is straightforward, you can use the package more effectively if you understand how R:BASE Graphics processes data.

The source of an R:BASE Graphics graph must be either a table in an R:BASE database or an ASCII data file. In either case, R:BASE Graphics does not graph the data directly from the source but first stores it in a file called a *data set*. The data set stores only the data necessary to create the graph. The size of the data set is limited to 100 rows by 20 columns. You must reduce any table containing more than 100 rows by using the data reduction techniques discussed earlier.

The following screen shows the data set for the example graph:

	1 YEARS	2 vavesal	3	4	5	6
	INTEGER	CURRENCY				
1	1	$25,142.86				
2	2	$42,500.00				
3	3	$31,285.71				
4	4	$38,437.50				
5	5	$31,222.22				
6	6	$27,000.00				
7	7	$48,500.00				
8						
9						
10						
11						
12						
13						
14						
15						

```
[ESC] Exit   [F1] Insert cell   [F2] Delete cell   [F6] Clear   [Shift-F10] More
Data Set Editor
```

This screen shows the data as it is displayed by the R:BASE Graphics Data Set Editor. To invoke the Data Set Editor, select *Edit file* from the Graph Format menu. Use the Data Set Editor to edit the data in the data set. Note, however, that only the data in the data set is modified, not the data in the database. You can also edit the graph format parameters from the Edit File menu by selecting the *Select* or *Format* option. See the table at the beginning of this entry for descriptions of the Data Set Editor key functions.

Graphs created from an R:BASE database are saved in a file with a *.GRF* extension. For example, the graph *AVESALRY* is stored in a file called *AVESALRY.GRF*. This file stores both the graph format and the data set. If you update the database after you display the graph, R:BASE Graphics normally re-computes the data set with the new data, although you can override this function.

ASCII data files: If you generate a graph from an ASCII data file, the data is stored in a file with a *.GRD* extension and the graph format is stored in a file with a *.GRF* extension.

ASCII data files must conform to a special format. Pressing F7 in the Data Set Editor saves a data set as an ASCII file. For example, the data for the sample graph looks like this in an ASCII file:

```
Data set header.
YEARS;INTEGER
vavesal;CURRENCY

1;$25,142.86
2;$42,500.00
3;$31,285.71
4;$38,437.50
5;$31,222.22
6;$27,000.00
7;$48,500.00
```

The first line must consist of the phrase, *Data set header*. The second line contains the label and data type for the X-axis. The third line contains the label and data type for the Y-axis. You can use as many as 20 lines to specify vertical axis data types. A blank line separates the data specification from the data itself. Note that a semi-colon (*;*) is used as the delimiter.

You can use the R:BASE Graphics Data Set Editor to enter data from the keyboard into an ASCII data file. In most cases, however, you will probably enter data into a database or edit an existing ASCII file.

Creating multiple graphs on a split screen: R:BASE Graphics includes a feature that lets you display multiple graphs on a single screen. A multiple-graph screen or page is useful for displaying the relationship between several graphs or for showing the same graph with different sets of data. You can display a maximum of 32 graphs in a split screen. Practically speaking, however, you can comfortably fit only about 6 graphs on a standard-sized monitor.

Use the *Split screen* option at the Output Utilities menu. You can include any graph in the current directory in a split screen. To create a split screen, select *Create* from the Split Screen menu and assign a filename to the split screen definition (split screen definitions are saved with a *.GRS* file extension). R:BASE Graphics then displays a screen containing a large blank box. Use the F1 key to split the box into separate areas (regions), each of which will contain one of your defined graphs. The F1 key splits the region in half vertically (with the down arrow key) or horizontally (with the right arrow key). Use the F2 key to expand or contract the region. You can split the screen to a maximum of 32 separate regions.

Place the graphs in each box by pressing the F4 key and then selecting one of the defined graphs from the menu of existing *.GRF* files. For example, we can create graphs of hyperbolic functions (see *Trigonometric functions*) in R:BASE Graphics and display them on a split screen. After you place the graphs on the split screen, the screen will look something like this:

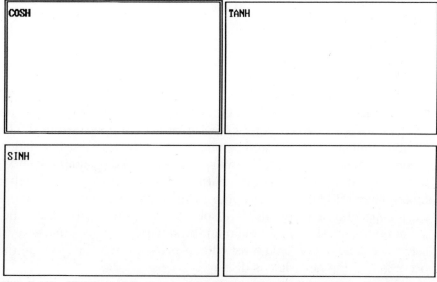

[F1] Split   [F2] Expand/Contract   [F3] Merge   [F4] Replace graph   [F10] Help

First divide the screen into regions. Then use the F4 key to place a graph in each region. If you don't place a graph in a region, the split screen display will leave the region blank. Press ESC when you finish, and choose *Display* from the Split Screen menu. The following screen shows the final result:

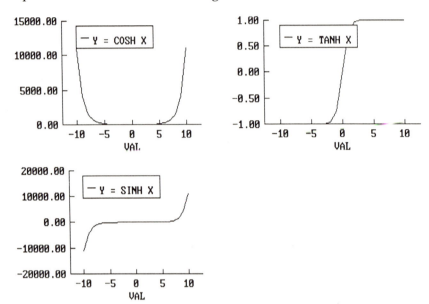

Slide shows: R:BASE Graphics provides a utility that lets you create graphics slide shows on your computer's display. Select *Slide Show* from the Output Utilities menu. To create a slide show, select *Create* from the Slide Show menu. Then select the graphs and split-screens to display in the slide show from the menu of graphs in the current directory. Select *(Done)* when you finish. Then select the *Display* option. The Display Mode menu then presents the *Manual* and *Auto* options. To display the slides manually, select the *Manual* option. Each slide will remain on the screen until you press a key. If you select the *Auto* option, you must enter a pause period (in seconds) that will occur before the next slide is displayed.

Printing or plotting your graphs: R:BASE Graphics supports many printers and plotters. For instructions on how to install the appropriate printer/plotter drivers, see the R:BASE Graphics Installation Guide. To print or plot a graph you have created or modified, press the F3 key to bring up the Display menu, then select the *Print graph* option. You also can select the appropriate output option from the Output Utilities menu.

Index

Symbols

#DATE variable 285
#PAGE variable 285
#PI variable 285
#TIME variable 285
$COMMAND 46
$MENU 47
$SCREEN 47
% variables 287
& variables 256, 287
. variables 108, 287
*(comment) 1, 186
+ (plus sign) 52

A

Abbreviations, command 53
ABS() 20
ACOS() 273
AINT() 57
ALL 2
Ampersand variables 256, 287
AND/OR operators 171
ANINT() 57
API file extension 15
APP file extension 15
APPEND 3, 206
Application EXPRESS 4–19
  adding command files in 18
  file names used by 15
  invoking from R> prompt 105
  nesting applications in 18
  reserved words in 18
  using in programming 187
Applications
  menu-driven 4–19
  modifying in Application EXPRESS 16
  multi-user 187 (*see also* Multi-user
    applications)
  nesting 18
  planning 5
  running Application EXPRESS 16
APX file extension 15
Arguments, function 139
Arithmetic functions 19–23
Arithmetic operators 168
ASCII
  characters 23
  files 23
    adding data from 159

ASCII files (*continued*)
  delimited 112–14
  fixed-field 115
  using in R:BASE Graphics 310
  format, backing up in 282
  values of characters 57
ASIN() 273
ASSIGN (R:BASE 5000) 35, 195
ATAN() 273
Attribute 24
AUTOSKIP, setting 241
AVE
  using with COMPUTE 54
  using with CROSSTAB 65
AVE() 20
Averages, calculating in reports 223 (*see
    also AVE*)

B

Backing up data 25, 281
BACKUP 25–28
Batch files 183
BEEP 29
BELL, setting 241
Binary files 45, 179
Blanks, setting *QUOTES* to 240
Boolean operators 168
BREAK 29
Breakpoints 216, 264
  printing reports with 178
BROWSE 30
Browse action (R:BASE 5000) 19
BUFFERS (MS-DOS) 56
BUILD KEY 32, 155

C

Capitalizing first letter 265
CASE, setting 241
Centering text 266. *See also* Text
CHANGE 33
  using expressions with 106
CHANGE COLUMN (R:BASE 5000) 195
CHAR() 57
Characters, ASCII 23, 57
CHDIR 35, 90
CHDRV 36, 90
CHECK 37
CHKDSK 38, 90
CHOOSE 38, 186, 286
CLEAR 42, 288
  setting 241

Nicholas M. Baran

Nicholas M. Baran is an Associate Technical Editor at *BYTE* magazine. He is co-author (with Jonathan Erickson) of *Using R:BASE 5000*, Osborne/McGraw-Hill, 1985. Baran has worked as a computer consultant and mechanical engineer. He holds Bachelor of Arts degrees in mechanical engineering and German studies from Stanford University.

The manuscript for this book was prepared and submitted to Microsoft Press in electronic form. Text files were processed and formatted using Microsoft Word.

Cover design by Steve Renick
Interior text design by Craig A. Berquist & Associates
Principal typographer: Jean Trenary
Principal production artist: Peggy Herman

The screen displays were created on the IBM PC-AT and printed on the Hewlett-Packard LaserJet Plus.

Text composition by Microsoft Press in Palatino, Palatino Italic, and Palatino Bold Italic with display in Helvetica Bold, using the Magna composition system and the Mergenthaler Linotron 202 digital phototypesetter.